DOSTOEVSKY

The Major Fiction

DOSTOEVSKY
The Major Fiction

EDWARD WASIOLEK

THE M.I.T. PRESS

Massachusetts Institute of Technology
Cambridge, Massachusetts

Second printing, first MIT Press paperback edition, August 1971
Third printing, May 1973

ISBN 0 262 23012 7 (hardcover)
ISBN 0 262 73026 X (paperback)

Library of Congress Catalog Card Number: 64-8089
Printed in the United States of America

For Emily

Even if it were proved to me that Christ was outside the truth, and it was really so that the truth were outside of Christ, then I would still prefer to stay with Christ rather than with truth.

Dostoevsky in a letter to N. A. Fonvizina, February 20, 1854

I have my own view of art, and that which the majority call fantastic and exceptional is for me the very essence of reality.

Dostoevsky in a letter to N. N. Strakhov, March 10, 1869

Preface

"Who has not written a book on Dostoevsky?"—so the wag has it, and yet who can find the book on Dostoevsky he needs? The biographies, source studies, editions of letters, and bibliographical aids come out year after year. Time has frayed away much that once seemed useful both in Russia and in the West. The works of Symons, Murry, de Vogüé, Pisarev, Mikhaylovsky, Volynsky, and Merezhkovsky are historical data today; they show us what Dostoevsky meant to their time, not what he means to us today. Who can read Gide's work on Dostoevsky today as an aid to understanding Dostoevsky? Where will you send the readers of Dostoevsky—and their number is legion—for help with specific points of interpretation? Which books will tell them why Nastasya Fillipovna deliberately puts herself forth as Totsky's concubine when she hates him and hates her "dishonor"; why Peter squeezes Stavrogin's hand in ecstatic worship; why Myshkin finds the essence of the religious spirit in the words of an atheist and in the acts of a murderer, a thief, and a peasant mother? You cannot send them for answers to the sociologizing of Mikhaylovsky, the metaphysics of Ivanov, the play psychology of Powys, or the theologizing of Berdyaev. Nor can you send them to those works that are supposed to deal with craft: to Grossman's studies of Dostoevsky's readings and his literary ancestors, or to Steiner's analogizings between drama and the novel, between gesture and the word. Mark Schorer has provided the slogan for a vicious tendency of recent American literary criticism in these words: "When we speak of technique, we speak of nearly everything." Technique is not everything, but there are historical reasons why technique in Dostoevsky criticism appears more and more tempting. Up to the twenties little attention was paid to Dostoevsky the craftsman. Murry and Berdyaev seemed proud to claim that Dostoevsky was not a novelist, and Rozanov said that Dostoevsky's ideas were great, but anyone could take a blue pencil and cross out unneeded passages in his work. Under the authority of newly published notebooks, Grossman argued for a change in attitude. But he felt he had to disprove Dostoevsky the thinker to make his case for Dostoevsky the writer. Critics like Bitsilli, Bakhtin, and Davidovich complemented Grossman's work by detailed studies of Dostoevsky's craft. Often the work was brilliant, but sometimes it was trivial. When M. G. Davidovich began to catalogue Dostoevsky's devices into "anticipation of action," "warnings of impending calamities," "multiple meanings," "mystery," "interruptions," "slowing and quickening of pace," and "preparations for the appearance of the hero," he was engaged in an idle and unilluminating exercise.[1]

The dichotomy between "technique" and "ideas" is always artificial, but in Dostoevsky's works it is disastrous. An exclusive concern with craft is as vicious as an exclusive concern with ideas. If craft and technique become ends in themselves, then we play at criticism and evade the work itself as surely as did the philosophical interpreters of the pre-twenties. We cannot neglect Dostoevsky's ideas, because Dostoevsky did not neglect them. When Grossman reminds

[1] M. G. Davidovich, "Problemy zanimatel'nosti v romanakh Dostoevskogo," *Tvorchesky put' Dostoevskogo*, ed. I. L. Brodsky (Leningrad, 1924), pp. 105–123.

us that Dostoevsky acknowledged the superiority of Solovyov, Strakhov, and Khomyakov in philosophy [2]—in an attempt to convince the reader that Dostoevsky would agree
with him that craft alone was important—he was playing on
the ambiguity of the word "philosophy," and he was forgetting that Solovyov had also acknowledged the superiority
of Dostoevsky over him as a "thinker." If we can find concern for, and even anguish over, the smallest technical details
in Dostoevsky's notebooks and letters, we can find even more
concern over his "ideas." Indeed, we seldom find him concerned about craft for its own sake, but almost always for its
power to express the living idea which he carries in his soul.
We want, of course, all the technique we can discern in
Dostoevsky's novels, but we want also all the ideas we can
understand, and we want neither as an end in itself. The
technique is there for the sake of the content, and the content is not Dostoevsky's unless it is seen through the technique. The wedding of both produces that unique logic that
characterizes the work of every great novelist. One of the
aims of the studies that follow is to work toward the defini-
tion of that logic.

Where does one begin? With Dostoevsky's paradoxical
heroes. They are satanic and holy, sacrificial and cynical,
proud and humble, compassionate and cruel. They murder
old women to prove an idea, throw away a 100,000 rubles to
satisfy the whim of the moment, and are ready to blow up
the world for a cup of tea. Nastasya Fillipovna in *The Idiot*,
for example, meets the slander of vicious tongues by deliberately acting so as to confirm the slander! Lise from *The
Brothers Karamazov* has Alyosha, whom she loves, carry a
note offering herself to his brother Ivan, whom she does not
love. The Underground Man has golden dreams of virtue
and love when he is sunk in the most vicious vice, and a
desire for debasing vice when he is dreaming of virtue and

[2] "Isskustvo romana u Dostoevskogo," *Poetika Dostoevskogo* (Moscow, 1925), pp. 163–181.

love. Raskolnikov murders an old pawnbroker for money to help his career and the careers of others, and then he throws the money away; he trembles with fright before the pursuit of authorities, but leaves clues everywhere to encourage the pursuit; Stavrogin reaches the highest levels of St. Petersburg society, and then he marries at the lowest level, an impoverished half-wit. Kirilov prepares to commit suicide, and then exercises every day to keep fit. Katerina Ivanovna tortures Ivan, whom she loves, and sacrifices herself for Dmitry, whom she hates.

Unless these paradoxes can be resolved and the contradictions serve some end, we will have mystery without clarity, horror without motive, and suspense without probability. These are the kinds of problems I have attempted to confront, and to answer, in the studies that follow.

This is a book about the "major fiction" of Dostoevsky, and by this I mean the *Notes from the Underground* and the great novels that follow. But what is major in Dostoevsky is his vision and his grasp of the human situation, and part of this is already in some of the early works. Consequently, I begin my study by a brief consideration of what is "major" in the works that precede the *Notes from the Underground*.

Note: I have used Constance Garnett's translations—corrected where necessary—for *Crime and Punishment, The Idiot, The Possessed,* and *The Brothers Karamazov.* Everything else has been translated by me.

In transliterating from the Russian, I have modified in the following way the system used by the Library of Congress: 1. Diacritical marks are not used. 2. I have used "y" for "ï" except after "i," when another "i" is used. In the combinations "yï" and "iï" (nominative), I have used "y." 3. I have changed "iu" and "ia" to "yu" and "ya."

EDWARD WASIOLEK

Chicago, Illinois
May 1964

Contents

CONTENTS

DOSTOEVSKY

The Major Fiction

I

The Early Works

THERE ARE NO MURDERERS, prostitutes, demonic wills, or child torturers in Dostoevsky's early works; no great dialogues on socialism, the rational organization of human happiness, free will, sin, suffering, or God. Everything we think of when we think of the great Dostoevsky seems to be missing. Yet much that was to become recurrent, insistent, and centrifugal in his later work is already in the early work. It may be hesitant, uncertain, and not always clear, but it is already there. A sponger and buffoon like Polzunkov will be reborn in Lyamshin, Lebedev, and Fyodor Karamazov; a drunkard with a golden heart with nowhere to go like Emelyan in *The Honest Thief* (1848) will be reconceived in Marmeladov; a husband who victimizes his wife out of moral superiority like Pavel Alexandrovich in *Netochka Nezvanova* (1849) will reappear as the victimizing husband in *The Gentle Spirit* (*Krotkaya*); the corruption of a child as in *The Christmas Tree and the Wedding* (1848) anticipates a frequent exploitation of the same theme, as in the seductions of a young girl by Svidrigaylov in *Crime and Punishment* and by Stavrogin in the suppressed chapter of *The Possessed;* the embryo of Raskolnikov is already in Ordynov of *The Landlady* (1847); the naïve dreamers who in impossible poverty and misfortune believe their wishes will remake the world in an instant, as Netochka Nezvanova's mother, will find expression in the naïve dreams of Katerina Marmeladova in *Crime and Punishment.* The "bulls" and the "mice" of *Notes from the Underground* are already in *Poor Folk* and in almost every other work of the forties. The bulls are at home in the world; they know what they want and they take it, and they usually take it from the mice. Bykov (the first part of the name means bull) takes the beloved Varenka from Makar Devushkin in *Poor Folk;* Yulian Mastakovich takes the young girl from the red-headed boy in *The Christmas Tree and the Wedding;* a practical suitor takes a practical girl from the dreaming hero of *White Nights.* The bulls are insensitive, successful, and secure. The mice are scattered with the stamp of the foot. They are Devushkin in *Poor Folk,* cowering in gratitude before his excellency's generosity; Vasya Shumkin in *The Faint Heart* (*Slaboe serdtse*), trembling in obligation before his protector; Prokharchin paralyzed by the fear of losing his job. They cannot handle life; they are cowardly, fearful, and beaten. Almost all of them go mad before the demands life puts on them. Devushkin is headed for madness by the end of *Poor Folk;* and Golyadkin, Prokharchin, Vasya Shumkin, and Efimov actually end up mad.

There is something else in the early works, too, and it is more basic and pervasive than either themes, character types, or situations. The psychology of Dostoevsky's mature works is already faintly present. God, crime, and the universal dialogues are missing, but the springs of human motivation that will bring to birth the great questions are unmistakably there in embryonic form.

The new psychology appears already in Dostoevsky's second published work, *The Double* (1846), and seems to his contemporaries to be willful obscurity. The sensitive barometer of contemporary taste, Belinsky, showed his dissatisfaction, and his judgment reflected his age to perfection. Belinsky was still warm with the adulation he had showered on Dostoevsky's first work, *Poor Folk,* and his criticism of *The Double* was tempered both by this consideration and the youth of the writer. But like the general reader he talks about in his review, Belinsky finds *The Double* long-winded, lacking in measure, unclear in point of view, and, most important, "fantastic":

But in *The Double* there is still another essential fault: this is its fantastic coloring. The fantastic in our time can have a place only in an insane asylum, and not in our literature; it has a place in the art of the doctor, but not in the art of a poet.[1]

In the same review, he added: "There should be nothing dark and unclear in art." [2] He was right. Art should always be clear, but what is clear to one age may not be clear to another. What Belinsky considered clear was not what Dostoevsky considered clear. Belinsky, for instance, cannot understand why Golyadkin acts as he does:

It is all the more amusing that neither by fortune, rank, intelligence, or talents can he in any way awaken envy in anyone. He is not intelligent or dumb, wealthy or poor; he is very good and gentle to the point of sweetness. He could very well live in the world comfortably, but a pathological suspiciousness and sensitivity to insult are the dark demons of his character, and these demons make a hell of his existence.[3]

There is no reason for Golyadkin to feel economically insecure, yet he feels insecure; his position is not high enough to inspire envy in anyone; yet he feels himself envied and intrigued against. Since he has no reasons (for Belinsky, social or economic reasons) to be frightened and to act like a madman, the novel is unclear in motive.

Another critic who held a view of art in some respects similar to Belinsky's will make the same criticism of *The Double* much later, but more explicitly and sharply. N. K. Mikhaylovsky, with more impatience, could not see what the fuss was all about; and what Belinsky saw as an artistic fault, Mikhaylovsky saw as a disagreeable motive on the part of the author. The only reason for the appearance of Golyadkin Jr. is to "construct a second level of suffering for Golyadkin." [4] Mikhaylovsky goes on to say:

Why did the second Golyadkin appear? There are no satisfactory reasons for his appearance in that corner of life which *The Double* represents. Golyadkin Jr. is dragged in by force and against living truth. [5]

In his comment on *Notes from the Underground* in the same essay, Mikhaylovsky sums up his objections to Dostoevsky's work by the word "causelessness" (*bezprichinnost'*). This word points to what Belinsky and the tradition of the social novel could not understand in *The Double*. Dostoevsky's "causelessness" was a new causality, a new logic and psychology of motivation that was already running against the grain of contemporary taste, and what Mikhaylovsky, an anachronism himself, could not understand almost a half century later. But the new logic is not yet in *Poor Folk*, Dostoevsky's first published work, and this explains in part why Belinsky hailed it with such enthusiasm.

The Double

The story of Belinsky's reception of *Poor Folk* is too well-known to bear repeating here. No writer was more suddenly and fully lifted from obscurity to fame with one quick stroke. For the Anglo-Saxon the effect of this recognition can be appreciated only by imagining a Dr. Johnson or a Matthew Arnold seizing upon the first created work of an unknown writer and spreading throughout London the news that a new Shakespeare had arisen. From the perspective we now enjoy, *Poor Folk* promises less than many other of Dostoevsky's works in the forties. It is unconscionably long, repetitious, and dull. Its main point, which Belinsky discerned and dwelled on lovingly, is made over and over again: in a creature poorly endowed by nature and crushed by an unjust economic and social system, there glimmers nevertheless a golden heart, which is the pledge of the brotherhood of all men.[6]

There is none of the "fantastic" element that irritates Belinsky in *The Double* or the "causelessness" that later irritated Mikhaylovsky in *The Double* and in *Notes from the Underground*. We know why Makar suffers: he has to endure the smells of the kitchen, listen to the screams and racket of the lodgers, bear the jokes of his fellow lodgers, and he doesn't have enough money to buy Varenka grapes, candies, and frills. We know why he feels humiliated: the sole of his shoe comes off, he has to go slopping in the mud begging for a loan, with a cur at his heels, and the button of his uniform flies off in the presence of his excellency. We know what he wants: to be the protector of Varenka. And we know why he is unable to keep her: Bykov has more money, more power, and more guts. Makar's needs are real, and his desire to play the protector is understandable. He gets desperate when he cannot borrow money, and when there is a villain trying to take Varenka away from him; and he feels rebellious when he sees fools favored by fortune and better men trampled by fortune. There is no "causelessness" in the fortunes of Makar Devushkin.

When Makar can peek through his window and catch a glimpse of Varenka and when he can send her sweets and books, all's right in the world for him. He waxes poetic and becomes as content as a bird under the summer sky. When he doesn't have a kopek to give to a child beggar and when he is helpless to aid Varenka, he feels humiliated, debased, and bitter. The springs of his emotions and actions are largely economic. But where are the springs of Golyadkin's feeling and action? Makar can say that he is content when he is well dressed, shod, and fed; Golyadkin cannot. He is well dressed, well shod, and well fed, but there are no happy moments, only desperately busy ones meeting a thickening atmosphere of plots, intrigues, and impending destruction. He sees plots about him when there are no plots; people envy him when there is nothing to envy, dangers threaten him when there are no dangers. Yet these "causeless" fears are real enough to send him flying to do battle with them, and strong enough to drive him mad.

The real Golyadkin is a titular counselor living on Shestilavochnaya street; he serves in an office copying official documents; and he is the butt of his fellow workers' jokes. There is reason to believe also that he is a toady, a coward, and a gossip; that he once basely offered his hand to a German lady in exchange for food and lodging, while he was engaged to a girl of high standing; and that he hypocritically tried to place the blame for his actions on others. Golyadkin hates gossips, toadies, and hypocrites because he knows he is one; he refuses to accept himself as he is. The distasteful Golyadkin, he thinks, is an invention of his enemies; the honorable, straight, courageous Golyadkin has been hidden, but will soon issue forth to chastise his enemies. Shortly after his visit to the doctor he meets two of his fellow workers, and while they snicker, he announces: "You all know me, gentlemen, but up to now you have only known one side of me."

What he tells his fellow workers is prophetic, because he has been acting all morning as if he expected another Golyadkin to appear. When he awakes, he checks to see whether he has changed; when he meets Anton Fillipovich, he tries to deny the "ordinary" Golyadkin; when he visits Dr. Rutenspitz, he talks about himself as if he were a "close friend"; and when he is thrown out of Klara's birthday party, he wishes to be annihilated. Scorned, shamed, humiliated, and physically ejected from Klara Olsufyevna's party, he can no longer face the old Golyadkin. When he can no longer face what he is, he "dies" and brings to birth another Golyadkin, who becomes the carrier of what he cannot face and has tried to annihilate. Hence, he purges himself by what Kenneth Burke would call a ritualistic giving of his distasteful traits to another. But it doesn't work. Though he may threaten, plead, and run away, everything Golyadkin Sr. does is frustrated by Golyadkin Jr. No "good" impulse is free of Golyadkin Jr.'s jeers; no decorous step in society is free of his scorn; no honorable intention is free of his smirking reminder of something dishonorable. What in his character prevented him from being "good" before he "gave" it to Golyadkin Jr. returns to torment him even more shamelessly and openly in the person of Golyadkin Jr. Golyadkin Jr. is a toady: he fawns servilely before his excellency. He is dishonorable: he deliberately lies to Golyadkin Sr. and steals his work so as to get credit for it. He constantly gossips behind Golyadkin Sr.'s back with the other office workers, and he reminds Golyadkin Sr. of certain embarrassing weaknesses he has. In particular he reminds him of his weakness for women and of a certain woman whom he took advantage of. He is in short everything Golyadkin Sr. hates in himself, given to Golyadkin Jr. and returned to persecute him. Golyadkin Sr. is, as he reminds himself, his own executioner.

Golyadkin's hatred of his wrong "self" has an important correlative: a desperate desire to be the right self. He has an overwhelming need to be a Golyadkin who is admired, respected, and envied. He will go to any lengths—even unto madness—to deny his bad self; he will go to any lengths to pursue his good self. It is his drive for *ambitsiya* (self-respect and dignity) that drives him to people his world with demons, enemies, and persecutors. He has to create the enemies so as to preserve for himself the image of a Golyadkin who is pure, well-intentioned, courageous, and straightforward.

What we get in Golyadkin—and admittedly it is not entirely successful—is the beginning of a new "logic" of human motivation. Belinsky looked for and could not find social and economic causes for Golyadkin's actions and feelings. But Dostoevsky was already sensing dramatically what he was to say explicitly later in his career: that man's tragedy and his deepest problems do not spring from social and economic causes, but from his own insecurities and his own unquenchable drive for self-worth and dignity. Dostoevsky portrays not how social and economic facts act on Golyadkin, but how Golyadkin acts on social and economic facts. Golyadkin distorts reality, reshapes it, and remakes it to fit the needs that drive him. There are no enemies, no intrigues, and no plots against him—not at least as Golyadkin imagines them—but the insecurity that drives Golyadkin to imagine them and believe in them is real. *Golyadkin "creates" himself.* He tries to create a world that will answer to how he wants to see himself; he succeeds only in creating a world that mirrors his inner conflict.

Golyadkin remakes the world in the way he wants it to be, but he is not strong enough to sustain it. Reality presses on him with more force than he can project his image on reality, and, finally, in a kind of ultimate protection, he withdraws from reality entirely. His madness anticipates those frequent crises of "brain fever" in Dostoevsky's later novels. In the later novels, this "brain fever" is often a harbinger of rebirth; but Dostoevsky has as yet no conception of "rebirth," and must leave Golyadkin trapped between the reality of himself and the reality of the world.

The "new logic" of human motivation Golyadkin represents is unclear, and this justifies to some extent the poor reception by its contemporaries and the negative criticism of Belinsky. Belinsky was looking for the wrong thing, but the right thing was not yet clear. Golyadkin is motivated by some impulse to self-worth—as he understands it—and this impulse is powerful enough for him to deny what he is (as an economic and social unity), and powerful enough for him to try to create a new image. But still, this is what madmen do, and if Golyadkin and the kind of logic he represents are to be more than a case of growing insanity, the causes that drive him to insanity have to be a sign of something more than derangement. If he is an aberration, then you might argue against him as proper subject matter for literature—as Belinsky did—or find him a fascinating pathological case history, as Grossman did. Aberrations may interest us, but they will not involve us. Dostoevsky's task was to make the "aberration" typical, the improbable probable, and the "fantastic" real. He was to succeed so well that he introduced a note of both terror and anxiety into the concept of realism. The rest of the forties is a search for grounds to make the dark psychology of Golyadkin probable.

With Golyadkin, Dostoevsky had at the very outset of his career touched on the springs of action that were to motivate—in different settings and in a different philosophical and religious framework—his later heroes. But Dostoevsky himself was not strong enough to resist the misunderstanding of his contemporaries. Always sensitive to criticism, always ready to believe the worst of himself, he backs away from Golyadkin and experiments less successfully with different character types, themes, and forms. It is not until *Netochka Nezvanova* and the brilliant conception of Efimov that he recaptures the enormous creative conception that he had embodied in Golyadkin.

The Landlady

There is a deceptive social and economic background to many of the tales that follow *The Double*. Many are about clerks, protectors, offices, jobs, lodgers. The settings are realistic and social as in *Poor Folk*, and they lead one to expect a social treatment. But something of the same psychology found in *The Double* continues to contradict the surface form. What we find in tales like *Mr. Prokharchin*, *The Faint Heart* (*Slaboe serdtse*), and *The Honest Thief* is a conflict between what appears to motivate the heroes and what really motivates them. Mr. Prokharchin, for instance, seems moved to madness by fears that he will have to pay more rent, that the lodging house will burn down, and that he will have to take an examination, and failing the examination, will lose his job. There is nothing to the fears. The examination is the invention of his fellow lodgers; the fire is something he imagines; and he has 2,500 rubles stacked away against economic contingencies. Though he has no reason (the causelessness again) to act as he does, the fears are real enough to move him—as other fears moved Golyadkin—to a comic revolt against his torturers, to panicky free thought against the established order, and, finally, to paralysis, madness, and death.

Vasya Shumkin invents his obligation in *The Faint Heart* as Golyadkin had invented his enemies, and Prokharchin, his impending starvation. The menacing consequences of his failure to meet the deadlines rages only in his head, as the fire Prokharchin feared had raged only in his head. Dostoevsky carefully eliminates the apparent causes for Prokharchin's and Shumkin's madness but does not give us "real" causes, leaving us with comic tragedies. Dostoevsky needs to liberate himself from the social setting: clerks, offices, jobs, protectors. All these lead the reader to expect economic and social motivation. He finds his liberation by turning to an entirely different form—the gothic tale.

The gothic tale was to permit Dostoevsky to give full rein to terror, mystery, powerful emotions, secret powers, and untouched and unfathomable recesses of the human soul. It was to give him new settings, a new vocabulary, and a new convention of causality. The terror and mystery of *The Landlady* are improbable and farfetched, but they are already an adumbration of the terror and mystery that Dostoevsky was to make probable and real. *The Landlady* (1847) is Dostoevsky's first mystery, his first crime (and in not being committed, but only intended, it anticipates Ivan's crime in *The Brothers Karamazov*), his first treatment of the opposition of reason and the whole living man, and his first treatment of beauty as a terrible and paradoxical mixture of something holy and sinful (anticipating Dmitry's similar conception of beauty as a place where all contradictions meet).

From the perspective of the later works we can see what Dostoevsky was trying to do. He was trying to catch with the devices of the gothic novel some of the mysterious and unfathomably complex threads of man's unconscious self that moves him far beyond the control and understanding of his rational processes. But Dostoevsky's attempt comes out as device, vagueness, manipulated mystery, and even foolishness. The novel is filled with pronominal indefinite endings: everything is "sometime" (*kogda-to*), "something" (*chto-to*), and "something or other" (*kakoe-to*). The emotions are generalized and artificially intensified.

Murin, for instance, is both judge and corrupter of Katerina. From the vantage point of Dostoevsky's later moral distinctions, we can see in him a presketch of the dark force of the will that underlies our moral judgments. But in the story itself, what we get is flashing fire in his eyes, mysterious bowings to the four corners of the church, incomprehensible mumblings, and readings from cabalistic books. Katerina is supposed to represent the terrible force of beauty, but she is really a hysterical and incomprehensible female who is alternately frightened and bold, crying and laughing, praying and seducing. Ordynov's change from abstract to sensuous life comes out in dizziness, tremblings, and fainting spells. He doesn't understand what's happening to him, and he doesn't want to understand. Dostoevsky was not able—as he was later—to impregnate the mystery and paradoxes with the reality of everyday life. Raskolnikov is great because what drives him to murder, and then to suffering and rebirth, is not "somehow-or-others," or faintings, tremblings, and hysterics, but motives that are real, clear, and close to all of us. The fatal attraction of Sonia will lie not in diabolic toasts and hysterical laughter and fright, but in a clearly defined and believable attitude toward life and one's fellow man. The mature Dostoevsky's paradoxes become fascinating because he shows them to be real; his terror becomes frightening because he shows it to lie at the marrow of our real experiences. It was in *Netochka Nezvanova* that he was to show, especially in the portrait of Efimov, how the gothic could become real.

Netochka Nezvanova

Belinsky could not understand why Golyadkin acted as he did when he was decently enough endowed by nature and circumstances. He would have been even more baffled by Efimov's actions. Efimov is richly endowed by nature, helped by friends, and favored by circumstances. But he willfully destroys his talent, alienates his friends, and assiduously pursues failure, poverty, dissolution, and self-destruction. Efimov does not want to be a good musician or even a great one; he wants to be the greatest musician. He wants to be—in Dostoevsky's own words—*aut Caesar, aut nihil*. As long as he can create the world about him so that it prevents him from showing his greatness, he can rest in the conviction that his talent is unmatched. To this end he needs to be without a job, to be penniless, and to live in an apartment where it is impossible to work. To this end he will sacrifice his own well-being and the well-being of those about him. He remakes the world so that it will answer to his wishes. But he can remake it only so long, for finally he meets a fact that he cannot remake. Even though he had successfully overcome the threat of every new composer that came to town—after long and intense struggles—he cannot finally deny the genius of composer S——. Once his dream of preeminence is shattered, he no longer has any desire to live. Once he is no longer Caesar, he must be nothing. The madness and death that follow are both a protection and an effect.

We get in Efimov our first sketch of a character choosing circumstances to remake the world for a purpose. There is a hint of this in Golyadkin, but in Efimov it is clear and powerful. We see in him what we will see so often in the later heroes of Dostoevsky: a hero who paradoxically hurts not only those about him, but himself also; a hero who pursues, welcomes, and needs failure, hurt, and destruction. And for the first time we are beginning to see why someone should do this. Efimov destroys his talent, those about him, and finally himself, because by such destruction he can keep the image of himself as great, unsurpassed, inviolate. He creates a world which prevents him from being Caesar, even if the price he must pay is his own destruction, so that he may continue to believe in himself as Caesar. We are glimpsing in this process the mature dialectic of Dostoevsky in which the self uses any weapon to satisfy and justify itself. *The terror and mystery of the Gothic tale become real for Dostoevsky in the terror and mystery of the human will.*

Dostoevsky's early work was not cohesive. It was experimental, uncertain in aim, and easily deflected by adverse criticism. Works like *A Novel in Nine Letters* and *A Strange Wife and a Husband Under the Bed* are good fun and have little to do with the serious later works. The second and third parts of *Netochka Nezvanova* (revised and published after returning from prison) show the experimental quality very well: in them we find Dostoevsky touching on child psychology as he had already done in *The Christmas Tree and the Wedding* and was to continue to do in *The Little Hero;* we find him reworking the gothic devices of secret letters, secret guilt, and the terror of the despotic will; we find him touching, too, on the confessional form which was to be used so effectively in *Notes from the Underground.* Some of the other works of the forties point to devices, types, and themes that Dostoevsky will take up again. In *Polzunkov,* Dostoevsky gives us an early portrait of the "suffering buffoon" which we meet so often in the later novels. Even in the excellent short novel *White Nights*, which in tone and atmosphere appears so remote from the "dark psychology" of *The Double*, we find elements that look forward to the later Dostoevsky. The narrator of *White Nights*, like Golyadkin, Prokharchin, Devushkin, and Efimov, is an ineffectual "mouse." Unlike them, however, he is not driven by self-destructive tendencies, but is delightfully at peace with the world, which he knows better through the romantic books he reads and the dreams he pursues than by actual experience. He is conceived in lyrical affection, but his bookish dreams are a sentimental analogy to the dark dreams (also often bookish) of most of Dostoevsky's heroes.

In the forties, there is none of the massive consistency that Dostoevsky's work will have beginning with *Notes from the Underground*. Dostoevsky experimented with different forms, themes, and character types in this decade, but what comes through most consistently is a growing awareness of the springs of motivation that will develop into his mature psychology and metaphysic.

2

The Petrashevsky Circle
and
The House of the Dead

DOSTOEVSKY'S LITERARY CAREER came to an abrupt end in 1849 with arrest and sentencing to four years of imprisonment and four years of Siberian army service. When he returned after a ten-year absence from St. Petersburg and virtual literary silence, he seemed vastly changed as man and writer. The works of the forties and the works after *Notes from the Underground* did not seem to be the work of the same man. Similarly, the publicist who wrote "Constantinople Must Be Ours," who defined war as morally uplifting, who came to despise everything un-Russian, and who became a staunch defender of the Czar and Orthodoxy did not seem to be the same person who had worshiped Europe, nourished himself on French socialism, and had been imprisoned for plotting against the Czarist government.

The change has often been formulated into opposites. What Dostoevsky was in the forties, he was not after returning from Siberia: atheist became believer; revolutionary, staunch defender of the status quo; enemy of the Czar, faithful follower of the Czar. The following from Mochul'sky's fine book is representative of this view: "Up to his imprisonment Dostoevsky was an idealist, utopist, socialist, humanist. All these *ist's* were based on the axiom of Rousseau: 'Man from nature is good.' After imprisonment his faith in natural good was destroyed." [1] Conventionally, too, since a decisive change is assumed, critics have busied themselves finding the point of this change. Most commonly the point of change has been found in his prison experience, where under the influence of the Bible and the good people he meets in prison, he changes from revolutionary to Christian. Others, like Leonid Grossman, have put the change as late as his first trip to Europe in 1862 and his consequent disillusionment with the fount of liberal ideas that he had worshiped as a youth.[2] Still others, like Shestov, have refused to see any change at all until the publication of *Notes from the Underground.*

The contrasts by which this change are often expressed are oversimplifications. Dostoevsky was a different man, after returning, in philosophic and religious outlook, but not entirely so; and he was a different kind of writer, but not in every respect. Dostoevsky's activities as a member of the Petrashevsky circle and his autobiographical *The House of the Dead* (1860) are often contrasted to show the extent of change. In one—the Petrashevsky circle— we have Dostoevsky the liberal, socialist, revolutionary, and in the other the penitent who discovers the Bible, Russia, and the golden heart of the Russian people.

What was the Petrashevsky circle? The Petrashevsky circle was an assorted group of liberal thinkers, united in enthusiasm for French socialist thought. At one time or another they had all been influenced by Fourier, and had read avidly and discussed with fervor the works of Saint-Simon, Cabet, Considérant, Proudhon, and Robert Owen. The group met on Fridays from 1845 to 1849, a little less than five years. Beginning on March 11, 1849, an informer from the third section, A. P. Antonelli, began to attend the meetings. Dostoevsky and other members of the circle were arrested on April 22, 1849.

The members read forbidden books, talked of freeing the peasants, and dreamed of remaking man, beautifying the earth, and ushering in a golden age. Petrashevsky honestly believed that he would end his days on a Fourier-type phalanstery. He even once tried to transfer his own peasants to a newly constructed, phalanstery-like communal hall, but the peasants burned down the hall the day before moving in. His admiration of Fourier was boundless: "When I read his works for the first time, I felt myself reborn." [3] Some of the rhetoric at the meetings was inflammatory. Montbelli said of the Czar in one speech: "The Emperor Nicholas is not a human being, but a monster, a beast; he is that anti-Christ of whom the apocalypse speaks." [4] And Petrashevsky in a speech at a dinner honoring Fourier on April 7, 1849, said of their aims: "To destroy cities and capitals and to use the remains for new buildings, and to transform all this life of suffering, misfortune, poverty, shame, and groans into a harmonious, happy, luxurious life, one of wealth and happiness; and to cover this lowly earth with fruit, palaces and flowers: that is our great aim, and there is no greater aim on earth." [5] But for the most part what went on in the circle was only talk, and except for some abortive plans for a printing press in the Durov subcircle (to which Dostoevsky belonged), there was little in the way of a practical political program.

We can fix Dostoevsky's participation in the group quite precisely. We know when he became a member, when he began to visit the Durov circle, and some of the things he said at some of the meetings; we even know some of the books he read while a member. In addition, we have the reminiscences of fellow members of the group, and Dostoevsky's own later estimates of the whole experience. Pleshchev introduced Dostoevsky to Petrashevsky in 1846. He began to attend meetings in 1847, but it was not until the winter of 1849 that he attended regularly. At different meetings he read aloud Belinsky's forbidden letter to Gogol, defended the superiority of Pushkin over Victor Hugo, and extolled Miliukov's translation of Lammenais' *Les paroles d'un croyant* over the original. The Petrashevsky circle ran a lending library and the library records are among the trial materials that have come down to us today. We know that Dostoevsky read Fourier, Cabet's *Le vrai Christianisme suivant Jésus Christ*, the French translation of Strauss's *Das Leben Jesu*, and probably other French socialists.

Despite all this, we cannot fix with the same accuracy Dostoevsky's attitudes toward the beliefs and programs of Russian utopian socialism. His own estimate has not been consistent. At the trial he was to play down the practical political character of the group and to play up its theoretical and harmless character. When he was asked at the trial to explain how his thoughts began to have a "socialist trend," he answered in this way:

In all sincerity, I repeat once again that my liberalism consisted only in wanting the best for my fatherland; I wanted only an uninterrupted progress toward perfection for my country. These desires began when I began to understand myself and with time they grew more and more intense, but they never passed beyond the possible and reasonable. I have always believed in our government and in the autocracy.[6]

He was explicit in what he considered socialism to be, and what he thought its future to be:

Socialism proposes thousands of ways of social structuring, and since books on socialism were written with intelligence, passion, and at times with genuine love of humanity, I read them with interest. I am not a socialist, but I have studied various social systems. Although my understanding is hardly complete, I see the errors of each system. I am certain that if socialist theories were put into practice, they would result in inevitable ruin even in France. I made this clear more than once. Finally, here is the conclusion on which I rest. Socialism is a science in embryo, it is chaos, alchemy before chemistry, astrology before astronomy. But it seems that from today's chaos, something harmonious, sensible, and beneficial for social good may arise, just as chemistry arose from alchemy, and astronomy from astrology.[7]

He also characterized the Petrashevsky circle as lacking in seriousness:

These evenings, speeches, and discussions were as serious as cards, chess etc., which also can carry men away and act on them irresistibly. Many members, in my opinion, deceived themselves and confused the game with reality and took what was amusement for a real occupation.[8]

Later in life (in the 1870's) he was to look back on the experience with a mixture of nostalgia and disgust. When he remembered the enthusiasm, spirit, and faith of the dreamers of a new Russia and a new man, he would look back with wistfulness, but only until he remembered how wrong the dreamers were. First, the wistful confession:

It was impossible for all of us to resist the conviction that Christian society, religion, the family, and property rights were immoral. We were convinced we had to destroy national distinctions and to feel contempt for the fatherland because it was an obstacle to progress etc. We couldn't resist all these ideas; they seized our hearts and minds with the power of something sublime.[9]

Then, the bitter condemnation:

Some of us came in contact with French socialism and accepted it without the smallest doubt as the final answer to humanity's unity, that is, as the answer to all the dreams that swept us at the time. In accepting its aims, we accepted what was the height of egoism, inhumanity, economic nonsense, insult to human nature, and destruction of human liberty—but none of this bothered us a bit.[10]

The impact of this experience was enormous; references to the socialists dot all his major novels, and he was to fight the deterministic rationalism implied in the program of the Russian utopian socialists and developed in the views of radical critics with massive weapons from *Notes from*

the Underground to "The Legend of the Grand Inquisitor."
He fought like a man who had been duped, like someone
who had failed to see his error, who should have seen it,
and who had to atone for his error by striking out again
and again at the monster he had been partly responsible
in bringing to birth. He was never to make real distinctions
between the generation of the forties and the bilious ones of
the sixties, even though, as *The Possessed* amply shows, he
was able to keep them separate. Qualitatively, they were
cause and effect, and everything that was terrible about
the generation of the sixties was already there in the forties
in its high-minded and blurred romanticism. In 1879 he
wrote to V. F. Putsykovich: "If you are going to write
about Russian nihilists, then for God's sake don't blame
them as much as the fathers. Develop this idea: the root
of nihilism was already in the fathers, and the fathers were
really worse than the sons." [11]

But the impact is curiously delayed. There is no reflection of his socialistic reading and his flirtation with utopian
socialism in the works he writes while attending the meetings. While he was reading Fourier, Cabet, and Straus,
listening to plans for establishing phalansteries and dreaming of the rebirth of man and the renovation of the earth,
he was writing comic burlesques like *Polzunkov* and *A
Strange Wife and a Husband Under the Bed*, gothic and
sentimental tales like *The Landlady* and *Netochka Nezvanova*. The man and his works at this point are different.
What attracted him as a man, what he read, and what he
discussed did not touch his creative nerve ends until much
later.

The experience of the utopian socialist was not to affect
his work until he had gone through the bitter years of
imprisonment, and until a new generation of socialists was
to make utopian socialism a platform for action. Dostoevsky
had to write *The House of the Dead* (1860) and to read
Chernyshevsky's *Anthropological Principle in Philosophy*
(1860) and *What Is to Be Done?* (1863). In Chernyshev-

sky's work he found the massive antagonist that was to call forth the tragic view of man he discovers in prison and writes about in *The House of the Dead*. Both were to raise the paradoxical insights of his works of the forties to a philosophical and universal level.

It is, then, the man, and not the writer, who changes drastically under the impact of arrest and imprisonment. The man changes from the naïve youth who believed uncritically in beautiful "ends" to the man who discovers that man is tragically fated to hurt others and himself, and that all his beautiful dreams are at best deceptions and at worse deadly weapons for duping others. But what he discovers as a man in "the house of the dead," he had already dramatized, at least in embryo, in *The Double, Netochka Nezvanova*, and in other works of the forties. The "fantastic" element of *The Double*, the gothic chiaroscuros of *The Landlady*, and the self-destructive "dignity" of Efimov in *Netochka Nezvanova* are confirmed by what he experiences in the house of the dead. Critics have persisted in having Dostoevsky discover the "golden heart" of the Russian people in prison, but what he really discovered was the soundless irrational depths of destruction.

The House of the Dead

Vladimir Solovyov in *Three Speeches* (1881–1883) says that "The bad people of *The House of the Dead* gave back to Dostoevsky what the 'best' of the intelligentsia had taken away from him," and that Dostoevsky's "religious faith was reborn and made whole again under the impression of the humble and devout faith of the prisoners." [12] Mochul'sky saw the birth of Dostoevsky the populist in prison; [13] and Ernest Simmons points to the good qualities Dostoevsky found among the prisoners: "Without obtruding the fact, Dostoevsky sustains the theme that many of these criminals possessed qualities of calm, courage, real goodness, and even a certain nobility of soul which he associated with the common people. In this interaction of the artist and his material one can deduce Dostoevsky's growing faith in the Russian masses." [14]

What courage, goodness, and nobility? What religious faith? Almost without exception Dostoevsky saw them as pitiless, cruel, and emptied of any suggestion of moral feeling. The narrator tells us: "Only in prison did I hear stories of the most frightful and most unnatural acts and of the most monstrous murders, all told with highly unrestrained and childlike laughter." And, "Most of them do not blame themselves for anything. I have already noted that I could not detect in them any remorse of conscience even in those cases when the crime was against one of their own kind. As for crimes against the masters, it goes without saying that there was no remorse."

What does Dostoevsky set against this sweeping impression of cruelty, hardness, bestiality, and amorality? A few mild types like the young Aley, the old believer, and Sushilov. They are few, and their goodness is qualified. Aley is young, and the young are always good for Dostoevsky; the old believer is good in a formalistic and somewhat senseless way; and Sushilov is "good" in a dependent, doglike fashion. There is no qualification of the evil characters. Gazin looks like a spider and finds his delights in the world in torturing and cutting up little children; a prisoner from Tobolsk has a face that expresses only wild hunger, voluptuousness, and fleshy monstrosity; Orlov looks with contempt at any mention of conscience; and A-B strikes the narrator as a "kind of piece of flesh, a monster with teeth and a stomach with an insatiable hunger for the most coarse and most animalistic bodily pleasures. For the satisfaction of the smallest and most capricious of his pleasures, he was capable of killing and butchering in the most coldblooded manner. He was capable of doing anything, as long as all traces were hidden."

In prison Dostoevsky found human nature capable of almost anything: Sushilov killed his commanding officer for no reason at all; Petrov became transformed from a calm, questioning, and humble man to a raging beast. The Major would storm through the barracks ordering men who slept on their left sides to sleep on their right sides. Zherebyatnikov devised ways of increasing the pleasure of punishing by first raising the hopes of the prisoners. He would lead them to believe that he would be merciful, so that he could then savor both their pain and their disappointment.

All the evidence of *The House of the Dead* suggests that Dostoevsky's abstract and simplified conception of human nature gives way to an astonished insight into the complexity of man and his tragically evil nature. *The House of the Dead* profoundly changed Dostoevsky, but not from atheism to faith in the golden heart of the masses, as many critics have led us to believe. Rather, he is brought to the terrifying perception of the moral abyss of human nature. *It is not the golden heart, but the executioner that he finds in each man.* The narrator tells us: "In almost every man today there may be found the executioner in embryo." (*Svoystva palacha v zarodyshe nakhodyatsya v pochti kazhdom sovremennom cheloveke.*)

In the face of the Gazins, Petrovs, Orlovs, and Zherebyatnikovs, Dostoevsky had to build his faith in man, for once having seen man in the "house of the dead," he knew that evil was part of man's nature, no matter how protected by the constraint of society, the apathy of individual temperament, or the restrictions of opportunity. No faith would be worth anything that built itself on less than reality, and reality was what he had seen in the "house of the dead." The beast and the executioner were part of human nature, and no program of social organization and no faith in man would be realistic without taking them into account. What he believed in in the forties—a vague, naïve faith in the essential goodness of man in the abstract; something he would later call "Schillerism"—had become untenable. He had to rebuild his faith in man, and in the face of man's tragic and ineradicable bent toward the hurt of others and in his capacity to twist the universe to his meanest desires. The hope of a new faith lay unexpectedly in the very core of this evil. If man's revolt against the limitations of society and the limitations of others was evil—and it was—these same destructive impulses were paradoxically impulses to freedom. *Dostoevsky was to build his new faith not only in the face of the abyss that had yawned before him in the house of the dead, but he was to build it in the abyss.*

3

Chernyshevsky
and
The Insulted and the Injured

WITH HIS CRY "THE WHOLE WORLD IS MINE," Valkovsky of
The Insulted and the Injured (1861) raises to philosophic
principle the destructive drive Dostoevsky had already per-
ceived in Efimov and Golyadkin and confirmed in *The
House of the Dead*. What is evil in Valkovsky's "destructive
will" becomes in the Underground Man "good," "free will."
What raises insight and experience to philosophical premise
is new antagonists.

These are a new generation of social thinkers: Chernyshevsky, Dobrolyubov, and Pisarev are the most important.
Lacking the aesthetic and moral sensitivity of the liberals
of the forties, they are smug in their oversimplification of
moral problems, overweening in their confidence in science and reason, and coarse in their dismissal of the views
of others as primitive and unscientific. Their principles are
in direct contradiction to Dostoevsky's, and the aggressive-
ness of their belief that man's happiness depends on a
rationally constructed society provokes Dostoevsky's refutation and consequently his own perception of his premises. Of the group, Chernyshevsky is by far the most
lucid and the most systematic in exposing the grounds of

his beliefs. Two works had a direct and lasting influence on Dostoevsky: *The Anthropological Principle in Philosophy* (1859) and the novel *What Is to Be Done?* The *Anthropological Principle* is one of the clearest expositions of the basic philosophical principles of the revolutionary democrats. It shows its immediate influence in *The Insulted and the Injured*, and its long-run influence in Dostoevsky's frequent attacks on shallow and vulgar liberals in his major novels. *What Is to Be Done?*, Chernyshevsky's phenomenally popular novel and one of the major influences on Dostoevsky's *Notes from the Underground*, is a dramatization of the philosophical principles of *The Anthropological Principle*.

The basic premise of Chernyshevsky's piece is "the unity of nature"; [1] his other conclusions follow on this premise: that man has no special nature, that free will is an illusion, [2] that moral science as accurate as the science of trees and stones is merely a matter of time, [3] that good is the same as the useful, and that if man has enough to eat most crimes will disappear. Chernyshevsky, like most revolutionary democrats, was not one to edge away from extreme statement. By the unity of nature, he meant simply that there was literally no qualitative difference between a rock and a tree, a tree and an animal, or an animal and a man. Or, in sum, there was no difference between a rock and man. There were quantitative differences or differences of degree only. Whatever quality you can find in one order of nature you can find incipiently in another. Motion may be the distinguishing trait of animals, but it is incipiently present in plants—in the movement of saps and the growth of branches. Furthermore, some animals, like polyps, do not move, but some plants do. If man is traditionally distinguished by his reasoning power and his moral qualities, Chernyshevsky is quick to show that dogs are capable of syllogisms, [4] that horses show more heart and courage, and dogs more fidelity than most men are capable of.

Since the unity of nature is a fact for him, special faculties and the special nature of man are an illusion. Man's special "moral" nature is a misunderstanding of a prescientific age; and man's special faculty of free choice is naïve and unreal. Moral actions are caused, as are all events in the universe, by a chain of causes in nature or simply by circumstances. These causes are much more complex than "events" concerning animals or plants, but in no way different either in fact or in the methods needed to explain them. Indeed, all moral questions are already solved, at least in a theoretical sense: "A theoretical explanation of almost all moral questions which are important for life is already available, but in many cases people do not have the means to put into practice what theory points to." [5] To attribute a special "first" cause to the will is the equivalent of saying that a plate broke because it wanted to break, or to say that the house burned because it burned.

Good and evil become the useful and the useless for Chernyshevsky presumably on the logical grounds that the natural law is one of self-preservation or self-interest. Hence, a man will always do what is to his interest or pleasure. This is neither good nor evil. He does "evil" when he must hurt others to satisfy his self-interest; he does "good" when he can satisfy his self-interest by helping others. Chernyshevsky believed that social organization can be so constructed that man will rationally satisfy his self-interest and will be so educated that he will see that by helping others he will help himself.

Everything that Dostoevsky held precious is smugly and coarsely written off as illusion and anachronism. Free will is an illusion, at best a tautology; good and evil are what is useful and useless; man is motivated only by self-interest; and it is only a matter of time until science demonstrates the essential sameness of man and polyp. In one important sense, Dostoevsky and Chernyshevsky seem to be in agreement: that man is motivated by self-interest. What is essentially pessimistic is raised to optimism by Chernyshevsky's conviction that man is capable of "rational self interest." Dostoevsky rejects this by insisting that reason itself is a prey to man's self-interest. For Chernyshevsky, man satisfies his self-interest by serving others; for Dostoevsky, man satisfies his self-interest by sacrificing others.

The influence of *The Anthropological Principle* on *The Insulted and the Injured*, despite no direct reference, is clear. Valkovsky says:

I know for sure that at the core of every virtuous act lies a deep self-interest. And the more virtuous the act, the more self-interested it is. Love yourself; this is the only principle I acknowledge.[6]

And Chernyshevsky says:

Generally, one need only look a little more closely at any act or feeling which seems selfless and one will see that at bottom all the same lies the thought of one's profit, one's own pleasure, one's own well-being—that at bottom of the selfless act lies self-interest.[7]

Valkovsky's view of life is summarized by the choice he gives Ivan Petrovich between "prussic acid" and Schillerism, that is, between the "hard facts of nature" and naïve idealism. Chernyshevsky uses the same term, "prussic acid" (*sinil'nyaya kislota*), as proof of the unity of nature; the acids are the building blocks in organic as well as inorganic nature. Valkovsky gives Ivan Petrovich a choice between foolish and unrealistic ideals and the real facts of nature, and Chernyshevsky gives the reader a choice between prescientific, metaphysical views about special natures and the real facts of nature symbolized in "prussic acid." Valkovsky acts on Chernyshevsky's principles in *The Anthropological Principle*. He acts on these premises as Dostoevsky sees them: brutally, cynically, predatorily.

The Insulted and the Injured

No one has been satisfied with *The Insulted and the Injured*. Dostoevsky was not satisfied with it when he sent it off to his publisher. He blamed the conditions he had to work under, but consoled himself that perhaps fifty pages were good. Dobrolyubov found it long, rambling, and incomprehensible.[8] It is a poor work. It is too long, rambling, poorly constructed, improbable, sentimental and confused, and trite in places. There are three plots and a narrator who runs from one to another doing his best to tie them together. One plot has to do with a long legal argument between Prince Valkovsky and Ikhmenev, his estate manager, which arises over mysterious trifles and ends in the ruin of Ikhmenev. We are never quite sure what the point of the argument was to begin with and why it had to end with Ikhmenev's ruin. The second plot concerns Ikhmenev's daughter Natasha, who falls suddenly and overwhelmingly in love with Alyosha, the good-natured, irresponsible, and semi-idiotic son of Valkovsky. The talks about Alyosha's innocent evil are endless without being clear, and Natasha's voluntary suffering of his love is similarly endless. The third plot has to do with Nelli, the little orphan. Nelli loses her mother from consumption and ends up begging on the streets for the old hag Bubnovaya, from whom she is rescued by Ivan Petrovich, the narrator. Prince Valkovsky ties together the plots superficially. He tries long and hard and at last succeeds in persuading his son to give up Natasha; he also turns out to be the callous father of Nelli, having at one point seduced her mother, robbed her grandfather, and left her to the fate of the streets and of strangers.

As a device for unifying these plots, Valkovsky is a failure, but as a character in his own right, he is almost great. He is the first of Dostoevsky's satanic heroes. His long talk with the narrator, Ivan Petrovich, in a restaurant (looking to Svidrigaylov's confession to Raskolnikov in an inn, and to Ivan Karamazov's confession to Alyosha), is a major advance in Dostoevsky's maturing psychology. He makes explicit and raises to philosophical principle what was implied in Efimov's behavior. "The whole world is mine," he cries, and nothing exists but one's own rapacious self-interest.

Below every expression of nobility, generosity, and love there lies the self, and indeed the greater the nobility, the greater the love of self. With this confession, we are at the threshold of *Notes from the Underground.* Indeed the likenesses between the two are many. Like the Underground Man, Valkovsky made a try once at believing in Schilleresque ideals. He had been a philanthropist and had even built a beautiful hospital, but while he was building the hospital, he was seducing a peasant's wife and conniving to send the husband off to the army. Like the Underground Man, Valkovsky (so it is rumored) loves to prowl the streets at night and enjoys haunting the dens of vice. As the Underground Man leaves Liza with an insult searing her soul—because the insult would be something to treasure—so, too, he refuses to send back the money he stole from Nelli's mother, because the suffering would be more precious and more enjoyable than repayment. As the Underground Man explains to Liza that wives like to hurt their husbands so that they can make it up with twice as many caresses, so, too, Valkovsky tells Ivan Petrovich that women hurt what they love so that they can love all the more. Finally, as the Underground Man finishes his confession with a nasty challenge to his readers (an insult, really), claiming that there is no difference between himself and others except that he has been more frank, so, too, Valkovsky tells the Schilleresque narrator the same thing.

Valkovsky is a towering figure of gratuitous evil, anticipating in his lascivious pleasures the figures of Svidrigaylov and Fyodor Karamazov, and in his amorality and will, Stavrogin. The problem that was to torture Dostoevsky and his heroes and which was to be at the center of the thematic conflict of *The Brothers Karamazov,* "All is permitted," is presented here in the actions and words of the Prince. Whereas the alternatives will later be "God or nothing," they are here "ideals or nothing," or "naïve Schillerism" or "prussic acid." A morality built on prussic acid is one of rapacious self-interest.

In Valkovsky we are given a glimpse into a soul that respects no good, no ideal, no other person; it is a glimpse of boundless evil. And yet it is hard to take him completely seriously. As in the forties, Dostoevsky has not yet learned to make the fantastic and the improbable the real and the probable. To be sure, Valkovsky has ruined Nelli's grandfather, has caused two fathers to curse their children, and has lived undisturbed though his wife had to stalk the streets with his hungry child, though she lies dying in a damp cellar, and though his child is victimized by a ruthless wench and forced to beg. This evil has all been done in the past and recalled in the narrative time of the story in a clutter of gothic paraphernalia of lost documents, curses, and damp cellars. It is all unbelievable, or rather believable only as convention. The point is important: the form of the *roman feuilleton* mitigates the reality of Valkovsky's evil. His evil too belongs to the machinery. The first scene, for instance, sets the tone of mystery, coincidence, and improbability. The novel begins with the narrator fascinated by a mysterious old man accompanied by a ghostly dog. The old man casts an evil eye on a German burgher, who then mysteriously dies—the dog too—uttering portentous words in his last breath. From the very beginning convention sets reality at a distance.

The novel is studded with coincidence, sudden climaxes, mysterious passions, and inexplicable motives. The narrator, for instance, decides to move into Schmidt's apartment (the old man who dies) without knowing why, where Schmidt's granddaughter Nelli comes looking for her grandfather, who happens to be the daughter of Valkovsky, who happens to be exploiting the narrator's friend, Ikhmenev, and his beloved, Natasha. Valkovsky's confession in such a context appears as part of the machinery: outlandish, improbable, fantastic. The same is true of Natasha's self-destructive love for Alyosha and its childish counterpart in Nelli's love for Ivan Petrovich. Every reader will recognize in Natasha's love for Alyosha an anticipatory sketch of those inexplicable, overwhelming, and fateful passions of Dostoevsky's later women. They love for no reason at all, and with total sacrifice. Natasha loves Alyosha hopelessly and inexplicably:

I am happy to be his slave, his willing slave; happy to bear everything, everything, just so he would be with me and I could look at him! Let him even, I think, love another, just so he would be near me, and I could remain near him. . . . Is it base to have such desires? What of it? I admit it's base. If he throws me over, I'll run after him to the end of the earth, even if he were to chase and shove me away. . . . He'll whistle, call me and I'll run to him like a dog. Suffering. I'm not afraid of any suffering from him. I'll know that *he* is making me suffer and I'll welcome it.

Alyosha makes a hell for Natasha by naïvely confessing his meetings with other women, his love for Katya; yet this hell ties her all the more closely to him. Dostoevsky calls this a *love from suffering* and the suffering seems to be the very essence of the love. Natasha looks for the suffering and deliberately puts "salt on her wounds." The same phrase is used for the childish love Nelli feels for the narrator Ivan Petrovich.

Nelli is saved from the beatings of Bubnovaya and the humiliations of begging in the street by her knight, Ivan Petrovich. She comes to love and worship her rescuer. Yet, paradoxically, she leaves the man she loves and rushes off to damn herself to the life she hates. Why does she seek her hurt? Dostoevsky calls it "self-interested suffering" (*egoizm stradaniya*), and he seems to suggest the same thing about Natasha's love for Alyosha. The two loves seem to confirm by their "self-interested suffering" Valkovsky's statement that at the core of every virtue lies a deep self-interest. But neither Valkovsky's nor the paradoxical actions of the women are believable. Later, much later indeed, Dostoevsky is to use the same kind of love to make the "self-interested suffering" real, probable, believable, and powerfully effective in women like Nastasya Fillipovna of *The Idiot* and Katerina of *The Brothers Karamazov*. It may be that he had Natasha in mind when he created Katerina, for they both say pretty much the same thing. Natasha says she will follow Alyosha wherever he goes, forgive whatever vile things he may do, and even accept the humiliation of his loving another woman. Katerina forgives Dmitry his insults to her, accepts his love of Grushenka, and declares herself ready to follow him wherever he may go and whatever he may do. Natasha's love is simply some kind of mysterious and inexplicable attraction, but Katerina's is clearly motivated and supported by Dostoevsky's mature psychology and a refined metaphysic.

We are at the threshold of the great novels: the psychology that had germinated in the forties and that experience had confirmed in prison is explicitly formulated in several brilliant conversations and new insights. Valkovsky's "deep self-interest at the heart of every virtuous action" and his own use of virtue to gain his evil ends in persuading Alyosha to abandon Natasha for Katerina, as well as Natasha's and Nelli's self-interested love from suffering, are the basic premises of Dostoevsky's psychology and moral dialectic. But something is needed to wrench all these premises out of the vagueness and improbability of the gothic machinery and to thrust them into the terrifying familiarity and reality of the world of the Underground Man. For the Underground Man will say very little that is different, and yet its effect will be completely different. To be sure, the setting becomes realistic. Dostoevsky returns to the setting of some of his stories of the forties; we are once again concerned with a civil clerk, with imagined insults, busy St. Petersburg streets. The coincidences, mysterious documents, flashing eyes, and strange powers that still clutter *The Insulted and the Injured* disappear. But something more than setting and convention will change. Even if we abstract Valkovsky's confession from its gothic setting, there is something very essential that wars against its believability. *It has no metaphysic.* His self-interest has no end to serve but his own selfish comfortable life. As such, the reader can explain it away as some personal aberration or as the author's exaggeration. But with *Notes from the Underground* the same voracious self-interest takes on a purpose and with that purpose it becomes in one sense precious and real, rather than repulsive and unbelievable. What brings this about is a shift in dialectical oppositions.

In *The Insulted and the Injured* the idealism of Nelli's mother, Ikhmenev, and Ivan Petrovich is pitted against Valkovsky's voracious self-interest. The Schillerism is no match for Valkovsky's prussic acid; the Schillerites dash out their lives on the cold pavements of St. Petersburg reality to the cynical laughs of Valkovsky. But with *Notes from the Underground* a new dream appears, the dream of the rational organization of human happiness. The dream of the rational organization of man's happiness is a threat to Valkovsky's voracious self-interest and an answer to the hopes of the Schillerites. The Schillerites, like Nelli's mother, believe that the world will somehow become miraculously beautiful and all men good; the dream of the rational organization of human happiness promises such a miracle.

The dialectical oppositions are sharply changed under the pressure of the new antagonist, and with their change is born the powerful appeal of Dostoevsky's mature metaphysic. Voracious self-interest (evil) versus Schilleristic idealism (good) becomes "the rational organization of human happiness" (evil) versus "voracious self-interest" (good). What has been cynicism and outrage becomes paradoxically good, precious, and indispensable, without, however, ceasing to be cynicism and outrage.

The principal works that come between *The Insulted and the Injured* and *Notes from the Underground* are

A Vile Tale (*Skverny anekdot*) (1862) and *Winter Notes and Summer Impressions* (1863). In both—one a work of fiction, the other the notes of his traveling—we see Dostoevsky preoccupied with the self-interest that lies at the core of "great ideas." Dostoevsky's worship of Europe is documented from his earliest letters to Ivan's confession of love for Europe in *The Brothers Karamazov,* and Grossman is undoubtedly correct in his assumption that the corruption Dostoevsky saw in the Europe he had loved was traumatic. But I believe that Dostoevsky was *confirming* rather than discovering corruption in Europe. The *Winter Notes* were another item illustrating his growing distrust of humanitarian abstractions.

In *A Vile Tale* we find Dostoevsky explicitly pursuing a contrast between the idea of humanity and the reality of human nature. Ivan Ilych believes that love of humanity (*chelovekolyubie*) is enough to effect reforms and to bring people, even of different social strata, to embrace "morally." He sets out to demonstrate this idea by visiting the wedding party of one of his subordinates. His experiment is disastrous: "When he came in, his arms were open to all of humanity and to all his subordinates; and an hour later, he realized, no matter how painfully, that he hated Pseldonimov and cursed him, his wife, and their wedding. What's more he could tell by his eyes and face that Pseldonimov hated him."

The contrast of a great humanitarian idea with ridiculous and corrupt nature will be taken up in *Notes from the Underground* and indeed is a presketch of the pretensions of the "rational organization of humanity" that Chernyshevsky was writing of in *What Is to Be Done?* (1863). It is, in a sense, Dostoevsky's first skirmish with the new antagonist, but as is so often characteristic of Dostoevsky, he destroys the antagonist easily and even a little crudely. As is also characteristic of Dostoevsky, he comes to grant more and more to his antagonists, until, as in *The Brothers Karamazov,* he grants so much that the antagonists are al-

most unanswerable. Ivan Ilych's defense of the laws of
nature is crude and comic. He tries to put it in the form of
a syllogism: "Take a syllogism. I am humane, consequently
I am loved. I am loved, so they trust me. They trust me,
therefore they believe in me. They believe in me, therefore
they love me . . . that is, I want to say, if they believe in
me, they will believe in my reforms." But in *Notes from
the Underground* Dostoevsky grants much more to those
who would argue that the laws of nature will unite everyone in harmony and happiness; he grants enough to make
the Underground Man foam in spite.

4

Notes from the Underground
and
Dostoevsky's Moral Dialectic

THE UNDERGROUND MAN IS VAIN, nasty, petty, tyrannical, vicious, cowardly, morbidly sensitive, and self-contradictory. He hates his fellow workers, never forgets an insult, tyrannizes over those who offer affection, and offers affection to those who tyrannize over him. He turns love into lust, friendship into tyranny, and principle into spite. He respects neither love, nor affection, nor friendship, nor principle, nor logic. He is a sick and spiteful man. And yet Dostoevsky approves of him. Even more, he makes him his hero. For in this vain, petty, nasty, vicious, spiteful creature, indeed in the very marrow of that cold and malignant spite is a principle that is precious for him and for Dostoevsky: freedom. The Underground Man is determined above all to follow his sweet, foolish, capricious will. Before the implacable laws of nature, which reason discerns and by which it destroys freedom and erects the universal social anthill, the Underground Man will stand up, with no weapon but his puny will, put his arms akimbo, stick out his tongue, and give the whole edifice one shattering kick.

The Underground Man is a man of "acute consciousness," and with his acute consciousness he sees what the laws of nature fully imply. The normal man of action believes at the same time in the laws of nature and in personal responsibility. The two are contradictory. When the normal man of action is wronged, for instance, he charges like an infuriated bull at the wrongdoer to get his revenge. In his innate stupidity, he believes that someone is responsible. But the man of acute consciousness knows that if there are laws of nature, then no one is to blame for the wrong. What seems to be a wrong committed by someone's will is really an act occurring according to the mechanically inevitable and logarithmic laws of human nature. We can no more take revenge on such a wrong than we can on a toothache, which also makes us suffer according to the laws of nature. All one can do is moan, to no end of course, retreat to one's hole with a disdainful wave of one's paw, and chew on one's malignant and inexpressible spite.

Why are personal responsibility (free will) and the laws of nature contradictory? If there exist "laws of nature" which man can discern and by which he can organize his life, then his choices will be necessarily in accordance with these laws. If his acts are necessarily in accordance with these laws, he will be able to act in no other way. And if he can act in no other way, then he cannot really choose how to act. If man persists in believing that he is free to act—when the laws of nature exist—he will be either ignorant or self-deceptive. The Underground Man refuses to accept the laws of nature. Against science, against the laws of reason, against the whole movement of man's systematic accumulation of knowledge, against the ideal of the Crystal Palace, which will envelop into one unified system not only inanimate nature but man himself—against all that man pursues and dreads—the Underground Man opposes his unique, capricious, subjective world of feeling: wish, dream, hope, and, yes, cruelty, suffering, pettiness, and viciousness. If the law of nature (defined by reason) really exists, then "free will" is a private dream, an illusion that will be dispelled by reason like a mist over humanity's dawn.

But if the Underground Man is right and man prefers sticking gold pins into others, or having them stuck into himself, to the Crystal Palace, and if his subjective revolt is really the pledge of a reality that is full, complex, and true —of which reason is only a small part and not the whole— then the laws of reason are an illusion, a dream that has arisen like a mist over the scientific infancy of man. Which is the dream and which the reality in this weird dialectic?

Do the laws of nature exist? Is man a function of some infinite calculus, or is he free to follow the sweet curve of his foolish will? When the Underground Man talks about the "bulls," the normal men of action, he talks as if he believed the laws exist, and when he talks of the helpless delight he tastes when he sins according to his nature, he reasons as if the laws exist. When he insists that man everywhere has always believed in his free will and that such a free will makes a mockery of the logarithm tables, he reasons as if the laws did not exist:

. . . man everywhere and at all times, whoever he may be, has preferred to act as he chose and not in the least as his reason and advantage dictated. And one may choose what is contrary to one's own interests, and sometimes one *positively ought* (that is my idea). One's own free unfettered choice, one's own caprice—however wild it may be, one's own fancy worked up at times to frenzy—is that very "most advantageous advantage" which we have overlooked, which comes under no classification and against which all systems and theories are continually being shattered to atoms. And how do these wiseacres know that man wants a normal, a virtuous choice? What has made them conceive that man must want a rationally advantageous choice? What man wants is simply *independent* choice, whatever that independence may cost and wherever it may lead. And choice, of course, the devil only knows what choice. . . .

Still what man has always believed in and what he wants to believe in may not be what is. Man has always acted as if he had free choice, but he may have always deceived himself. We cannot prove one way or the other whether the laws of nature exist, but what we can know is what follows a belief in the laws of nature and what follows their rejection. The Underground Man does not believe in the laws, and what follows from this disbelief is brilliantly explained and dramatized by Dostoevsky.

As a man of acute consciousness, the Underground Man comes to understand—but not to believe in—the implacable laws of reason and nature. The more he is conscious of the "wall" (the laws of nature), the more his resentment and spite is kindled against it. It is in the defiance and spite that he finds the will to oppose the wall. His free, foolish, unfettered caprice is his only weapon against the laws of nature, and his only gauge of freedom. He can know his freedom only by acting his freedom. Consequently, he must dramatize to others, but most of all to himself, that he is free. The *Notes* itself is such a dramatization. What characterizes his behavior more than anything else is self-contradiction. He despises his fellow men and thinks they are superior to him; he calls himself a coward and a slave and secretly believes he is more highly developed than others; he is a spiteful man, but if you were to bring him a doll or a cup of tea, he would be appeased; he is as sensitive as a hunchback or a dwarf and as quick to take offense, but there are moments when he is positively glad to have his face slapped. He pursues vice up the dark alleys of his soul, but dreams of the sublime and the beautiful; he is coldly indifferent and meekly sensitive to the good opinions of others; he is a tyrant but grateful for the tyranny of others; a humbler of others, but pleased to be humiliated. And he believes and does not believe what he says. At the end of Part I, he tells us: "I will tell you another thing that would be better, and that is if I myself believed in anything of what I have just written. I swear to you, gentlemen, there is not one thing, not one word of what I have written, that I really believe. That is, I believe it, perhaps, but at the same time I feel and suspect that I am lying like a cobbler."

The Underground Man does not want to be defined, and cannot be defined. At every moment he redefines himself by contradiction and denial. Why does he do this? Because such denial and contradiction and such constant and continual redefinition, are a pledge of his freedom. To the extent that he has a nature that is defined and knowable, to that extent his actions and his choices are a function of that nature. His nature must be the result of his choices, and not his choices the result of his nature. If he is to be free, he must make his nature, and he must make it with every choice. Like the French existentialists who were to follow three-quarters of a century later, he must be *"en marge"*; he must be in revolt not only against society, but against himself, not once, not only today or tomorrow, but in eternal revolt. He must maintain an unremitting struggle against a defined nature. Sometimes the Underground Man talks as if he wanted a definitive nature. He has a kind of mock-envy for someone he knew who had been a connoisseur of Lafitte, and he regrets that he could not have been a "sluggard," for "it would mean that I was positively defined; it would mean that there was something to say about me." But the impulse to be defined is but another contradiction to the impulse not to be defined: the Underground Man carries the principle of contradiction to every cranny of his consciousness, opposing every belief, action, thought, and attitude with their opposites in a ceaseless and unremitting struggle to assert his freedom by denying himself.

But this freedom implies an implacable and terrible truth about the actions of men and their treatment of others. If there are no laws to one's nature—and there cannot be if one is to be free—then man alone is his own law. And if he is his own end, he will make everything else serve that end, including other people. This conclusion is not only logically deducible from man's freedom, but is itself empirically observable in the actions of men. Between men, Dostoevsky reasons, there can exist only an unremitting duel in which each strives to subject the other to his "free" will. The metaphysic implies the psychology; the psychology—empirically observed—confirms the metaphysic. The second half of the novel is precisely that kind of empirical confirmation, for it dramatizes actions in which such a duel is expressed.

Liza

N. K. Mikhaylovsky said in 1882 what has been repeated often since: "As for the mental baggage of the Underground Man, you can find quite a variety of things, including certain philosophic reflections (for example, about free will) that have absolutely nothing to do with Dostoevski's cruel talent." [1] Since the cruel talent in the *Notes* shows itself primarily in the Underground Man's torturing of Liza, Mikhaylovsky is saying essentially that the second part of the novel has nothing to do with the first part. But as a matter of fact, the two parts are tightly connected, for the free will of the first part, which stands in contradiction to the logarithms of man's known nature, is dramatized in the second part. The second part takes place sixteen years earlier, and is a narration of a number of bizarre incidents that the Underground Man encountered. The Underground Man's irritation at the clanking sword of an officer, his desire to be thrown out of a billiard room window, and his ceaseless contradition of himself may appear quite remote from the abstract discussion of reason and free will, but they are all the very living matter from which the abstract discussion has been drawn. The second half of the novel contains the living psychology which implies the metaphysic of the first half.

One night, for example, after having bruised his body in filthy vice, the Underground Man sees someone thrown out of a window of a billiard room. He envies the gentle-

man who was thrown out and goes into the tavern to provoke a similar fate. The Lieutenant, who had done the
throwing, refuses to be provoked. The Underground Man
blocks the Lieutenant's way, but the Lieutenant merely
moves him from one spot to another without seeming to
notice him. The Underground Man had sought to be insulted by being thrown out of the window; he is also insulted when he is not thrown out of the window. What he
has not been able to find he tries to provoke, and what he
cannot provoke he creates. As far as we know, the officer
is not even aware of his existence, but the "imaginary" insult rankles in his breast, giving birth to real plans and actions of vengeance over a period of more than two years.

He makes inquiries about the officer, follows him to his
flat, learns about his personal life, and tortures himself
about ways of "paying him back." He writes a satire un-
masking the officer's villainy, but it is not printed; he
challenges him to a duel in a charming letter in which he
implores him to apologize, but he does not send the letter.
Finally, he hits upon the simplest way of avenging himself.
He decides to refuse to step aside when he meets the officer
head on while walking on Nevsky Prospect. These strolls
have been for him a regular exercise in the pursuit of humiliation:

Sometimes on holidays I used to stroll along the sunny side of
the Nevsky about four o'clock in the afternoon. Though it
was hardly a stroll so much as a series of innumerable miseries,
humiliations, and resentments; but no doubt that was just what
I wanted. I used to wriggle along in a most unseemly fashion,
like an eel, continually moving aside to make way for generals,
for officers of the Guards and the Hussars, or for ladies. At
such minutes there used to be a convulsive twinge at my heart,
and I used to feel hot all down my back at the mere thought
of the wretchedness of my attire, of the wretchedness and
abjectness of my little scurrying figure. This was a regular
martyrdom, a continual, intolerable humiliation at the thought,
which passed into an incessant and direct sensation, that I was

45

a mere fly in the eyes of all this world, a nasty, disgusting fly—more intelligent, more highly developed, more refined in feeling than any of them, of course, but a fly that was continually making way for everyone, insulted and injured by every one. Why I inflicted this torture upon myself, why I went to the Nevsky, I don't know.

On Nevsky Prospect his officer wriggles like an eel before people of high rank, but steps unswervingly over people like the Underground Man. The Underground Man decides to "conquer" the officer by making him swerve aside, and to this end prepares himself by getting a pair of black gloves, a decent hat, a good shirt with white bone studs, and, most of all, a new beaver collar for his coat. What follows is a comic opera of frustrations. The Underground Man loses his nerve time and time again and always moves aside for the officer at the last moment. Once, despite his prayers for God's help, his courage fails him when he is only six inches from the officer: he stumbles at the officer's feet and the officer steps over him. Finally, he closes his eyes and runs full tilt, shoulder to shoulder, into him. Although he gets the worst of it physically, and though the officer pretends not to notice anything, he is convinced that he has avenged his insult.

Dostoevsky obviously had a scene from Chernyshevsky's *What Is to Be Done?* (1863) in mind when he wrote this. Chernyshevsky's work, we know, was uppermost in Dostoevsky's mind while he was writing the *Notes*. The Crystal Palace is already in Vera's fourth dream, and the bubbles of bliss which the Underground Man sneers at are already in her description of the happy life under the steel and glass dome. Even the love affair of Liza and the Underground Man may be said to be an answer to the way love is handled in *What Is to be Done?*. Rakhmetov and Lopukhov handle the complex affairs of the heart and instincts with a few minutes of objective reasoning, whereas the Underground Man stews about his motives, doesn't entirely understand them, and acts against his own interests. Chernyshevsky's laws of reason and nature, in short, are answered by the Underground Man's lawless self and malignant spite. The Underground Man's encounter with the officer on the boulevard finds its prototype in Lopukhov's encounter with a dignified gentleman on the street. Lopukhov never turns aside for anyone except women; consequently, he refuses to turn aside for the dignified gentleman, and they bump. When the dignified gentleman calls him a pig, Lopukhov takes him by the scruff of the neck and dunks him in the gutter. Neither social considerations, nor dignity, nor self-worth poses any problem for Lopukhov or Chernyshevsky. It is all simple and straightforward. It is not so simple for the Underground Man. This is apparent in the incident: the Underground Man wants to be insulted and humiliated, looks for insult, and provokes it when he cannot find it. Why? Because there is pleasure in being hurt, because it increases the self's consciousness of itself, and, most of all, because it provides the motive for hurting others. Seeking out hurt is the mechanism that keeps the vicious and barren circle of hurt and being hurt moving. This duel, which the self provokes and in which it is trapped, is even more apparent at the farewell party given by Zverkov, which the Underground Man insists on attending.

If the Underground Man is right and man is free—and Dostoevsky believes him to be right—then not only an implacable duel of wills follows upon this freedom, but every general truth becomes an illusion. If general truths are not illusions, then the general truths will exist prior to our choice of them; and if they exist prior to our choice, then the choice is not free but determined by them. Truth as something absolute, timeless, and pre-existing to our choices is impossible in Dostoevsky's dialectic of freedom. Truth like everything else in his world depends on our wills. If we continue to believe in general truths, then we are believing in illusions. The consequences of this dialectic of freedom are terrifying: every action of principle, every act of unselfishness, every good, beautiful, virtuous, reasonable act is only appearance. No matter how much the naïve and tender romantic soul may want to believe in them, the man of acute consciousness knows that they are deceptions, for beneath them is the reality of man's free will and his deadly duel with other "free" wills. For some, the battle is waged not only beneath the appearance of general truths, it is waged *with* them. For the will in its freedom will subvert all to its uses: weakness as well as strength; virtue as well as vice; good as well as evil; the beautiful as well as the ugly. All this is implied in the philosophical chapter of the first part and in the incidents with Zverkov. The Underground Man comes to recognize, especially in his encounter with Liza, that the sublime and the beautiful are a lovely and unreal dream, a deception, and even more, a deadly weapon for the imposition of his will upon others.

As Valkovsky had once been a Schilleresque soul and had written poetry and philanthropically worked for virtue, so too the Underground Man had once believed in the sublime and the beautiful:

And what loving-kindness, oh Lord, what loving-kindness I felt at times in those dreams of mine! in those "flights into the sublime and the beautiful"; though it was fantastic love, though it was never applied to anything human in reality, yet there was so much of this love that one did not feel afterwards even the impulse to apply it in reality; that would have been superfluous. Everything, however, passed satisfactorily by a lazy and fascinating transition into the sphere of art, that is, into the beautiful forms of life, lying ready-made, largely stolen from the poets and novelists and adapted to all sorts of needs and uses. I, for instance, was triumphant over everyone; everyone, of course, was in dust and ashes, and was forced spontaneously to recognize my superiority, and I forgave them all. I was a poet and a grand gentleman, I fell in love; I came in for countless millions and immediately devoted them to humanity, and at the same time I confessed before all the people my shameful deeds, which, of course, were not merely shameful, but had in them much that was "sublime and beautiful," something in the Manfred style. Everyone would kiss me and weep (what idiots they would be if they did not), while I should go barefoot and hungry preaching new ideas and fighting a victorious Austerlitz against the obscurantists. Then the band would play a march, an amnesty would be declared, the Pope would agree to retire from Rome to Brazil; then there would be a ball for the whole of Italy at the Villa Borghese on the shores of Lake Como, Lake Como being for that purpose transferred to the neighborhood of Rome.

As he recalls the naïve faith he once had, he also expresses his present attitude toward it. He knows that his beautiful dreams of universal love serve him and not mankind: "I, for instance, was triumphant over everyone; everyone, of course, was in dust and ashes." He knows that his benefactions for the human race are planned so that "everyone would kiss me and weep (what idiots they would be if they did not)." The Underground Man does not believe in his dreams; he knows that the dream of the sublime and the beautiful is a truce between orgies, perhaps even a piquant sauce, and he cures himself of his universal love for mankind by sitting through a couple of hours of conversation with specific bores at the home of his department head.

At the dinner with his childhood friends, to which he has forced himself to be invited, his fantasy-making reaches ridiculous heights, and his recognition of the ridiculousness is the most explicit and sharp. He goes to the dinner dreaming of "getting the upper hand, of sweeping the floor with them, of forcing them to admire and like me—if only for my 'lofty thoughts and indisputable wit.' " After he has failed to wipe the floor with them, and they have rushed off to Olympia's, the Underground Man rushes in rage after them, confident that "either they'll implore me for my friendship on their knees or—or I'll slap Zverkov's face." But in a moment of honest perception he recognizes that "They won't go down on their knees to ask me to be their friend. That's an illusion, a cheap, romantic, fantastic, horrible illusion—just another ball on Lake Como. And that's why I *must* slap Zverkov's face! I simply must do it. Well, that's settled then. . . ." He must make them feel his presence, if not by respect for his admirable qualities, then by the hurt he can inflict on them and on himself. Recognizing that Zverkov and his companions will not go down on their knees to him, he immediately goes off on a more elaborate fantasy of ruin and degradation that they will inflict on him, below which, of course, lies the magnanimity of his forgiveness. He dreams of being sent off to prison for having bitten Zverkov and having spit in his face. After fifteen years of imprisonment, he sees himself in this way: "I shall set out in search of him, in rags, a beggar, and at last I shall find him in some provincial city. He will be married and happy. He will have a grown-up daughter. I shall say, 'Look, monster, look at my hollow cheeks and my rags! I've lost everything—my career, my happiness, art, science, *the woman I loved*—and all through you. Here are the pistols. I've come to discharge my pistol and—and I forgive you.' And then I shall fire into the air, and he won't hear of me again. . . ." But he cannot go on, for he knows that the whole thing has come from Pushkin's *Silvio* and Lermontov's *Masquerade*.

Because of his corrosive consciousness the Underground Man cannot believe in his dreams; he knows them to be improbable and unreal, and he knows that they are a kind of self-indulgence. All he can do is gnash his teeth and break into tears of frustration. But the incident with Liza intervenes, and in his duel with Liza comes a flash of insight: if he cannot believe in his dream, he can *use* it. After he has finished making love to the prostitute, the Underground Man sits silently in the darkness with the humiliation he has suffered at the hands of Zverkov and company burning in his heart. Liza sits silently and indifferently in her corner, and the Underground Man turns to move her from indifference. He tries to move her first by radiating sullen and silent hatred to her, and then by narrating a coarse and invented story about watery graves and the dropping of a coffin. She answers perfunctorily, neither frightened nor interested. Irritated by her attitude and convinced that he has been too gentle with her, he begins to paint a picture of the sweetness of life even in sorrow as a contrast to her deplorable state, when suddenly "something flamed up in me, a sort of aim had *appeared.*" What follows is a moral lecture on the joys of familial and conjugal love. The point of the beautiful picture is to express concern and sympathy for Liza's plight and a desire that she, too, might enjoy these delights. The effect of his sympathetic and compassionate concern is to leave Liza in convulsive despair before the condition she finds herself in and with a desperate desire to leave her present way of life.

But it is his success in moving her to a desire for a better life that irritates the Underground Man afresh, for he understands that something other than concern for her life had prompted his compassionate moral lecture. What he had really intended, although only dimly apparent to him while he had waxed eloquent, becomes clear shortly after he leaves her. On the way home, "The truth was already blazing through my bewilderment. The disgusting truth!" That Liza had taken his compassion and sympathy for true coin prompts him to say to himself: "Oh, the loathsomeness, oh, the stupidity, oh, the insensibility of these blessed sentimental souls! How should she fail to understand! Why, anyone would have seen through it." The truth that had appeared dimly to him when he began to move her indifference and that had blazed out at him disgustingly after he had been successful is this: that though he had by his compassion and his eloquent picturing of a different kind of life reduced her to convulsive despair and to the desperate decision to give up her old life, he had been laughing at her the whole time. He had extolled the sweet pains of conjugal love, had appealed to her imagination and her innate sense of self-worth, had shown sympathy, compassion, and even love to move her soul to forgo vice and accept virtue. But he had not believed in any of his beautiful pictures; he had used them because they were the subtler weapons to work with. A few days after this encounter with Liza, he thinks to himself: "How few idyllic descriptions were necessary (and those, too, affected, bookish, insincere) to shape a whole human life at once according to my will. There's innocence for you! Virgin soil!"

What the Underground Man discovers in his encounter with Liza is the effectiveness of "good" in exercising his will on another person. What he wants, as is clear from his fully developed psychology in the first and chronologically later part, is to feel the power of his will over other wills. When the Underground Man meets Liza, he is smarting from hurt and humiliation, and the agents of these indignities have turned their backs on him. Someone has to pay for the humiliation he had suffered, and circumstances provide him with Liza. If he cannot feel her in his power by direct insult and fear (the coffin-dropping story), he discovers that he can do it with the subtler weapons of sympathy, morality, compassion, and even love.

But Liza refuses at first to act as he has expected her to. She refuses to return insult with insult, hurt with hurt. At first she refuses because she takes his sympathy and concern to be sincere; and then, when he confesses that he has been laughing at her, she sees in a flash of insight his unhappiness, and through the warmth of true love she momentarily breaks through the vicious circle of hurt and being hurt. But it is not love but insult that the Underground Man wants, because by the return of insult, Liza will acknowledge and justify his "rules." Her love, however, is at once a "liberation" from the trap of hurting and being hurt and, because the Underground Man is a victim of his own psychology, a new motive for insult. In her embrace, his head sunk in a cheap leather cushion, he begins gradually to feel that when he raises his face, he will look like an ass; he begins to realize also that their parts have now been reversed: that she is now the heroine and he the humiliated creature. He can take her love and her compassion only as he has given them: as weapons for humiliating him. He can see them only as fresh insults and as provocation for the vengeance he takes in treating her as a prostitute. The Underground Man leaves Liza with an insult burning in her soul, convinced that "this highest form of consciousness" (consciousness of self) is better than the love he might offer her if he overtook her. And he leaves the pages of the novel with an insult to the reader, charging him with living only from books, afraid of life, and comfortable only as some stillborn, general man. "I have simply taken life to an extreme, whereas you have been afraid to carry it halfway, and on top of that you take your cowardice for good sense, and with that thought take comfort and deceive yourself."

The Moral Dialectic

Vyacheslav Ivanov, André Gide, and many others have stated that *Notes from the Underground* is the great prologue to the major novels that follow. This is true, but not for the reasons usually given. The *Notes* is not the great prologue because in it Dostoevsky first touches on the great themes of free will, the rational organization of human happiness, and the value of suffering. It is great because Dostoevsky's psychology, metaphysic, and craft first take mature form in it. The psychology which he uncertainly discerns in *The Double*, which he pursues erratically in the forties, which life confirms in prison, and which the threat of the radical critics raises to a philosophical level, finds its mature metaphysic in *Notes from the Underground*. This metaphysic—the core of which is a moral dialectic of choice of value—is as much in the Underground Man's comments on sluggards, on officers with clanking swords, or on the necessity of wiping the floor with Sitnikov as it is in his philosophical arguments about the laws of nature and the Crystal Palace.

What is the psychology that takes mature form in the *Notes* and that will lie at the core of the motivations of the great characters to follow? It begins with characters who—like the Underground Man—are as sensitive as hunchbacks, quick to take offense, terrible in their hurt, boundless in their vanity, unforgiving in their grudges, and delighted in their pettiness. And it begins and turns on the word *obida* (hurt).[2] Hurt always generates another hurt; every hurt person wants immediately to make someone else bear his hurt. Thus, our abnormally sensitive hero is always paying back someone for something. The Underground Man is humiliated by his friends and wants to wipe the floor with them; Raskolnikov wants to pay society back for his poverty and its neglect of his fine qualities; Ippolit wants to spite the universe because it has not given him enough time to show what a fine fellow he is. Nastasya Fillipovna wants to pay Totsky back for the hurt and humiliation he had visited on her as a young girl; Ganya will pay her back for humiliation he is suffering at the hands of General Epanchin by marrying her and wiping the floor with her; Rogozhin pays Nastasya back for humiliations by killing her. *The circle of hurt-and-be-hurt is the basic psychological law of Dostoevsky's world.*[3] A few refuse to pay back: the Idiot, Sonia, Alyosha. They are of another world.

But there is something more. The Dostoevskian hero not only pays back for the hurt he suffers, but he looks for hurt to suffer. He likes being hurt. When he cannot find it, he imagines it, so that it will sting in his blood with the pungency of real hurt. He has a stake in being hurt: he seeks it, pursues it, and needs it. The vicious circle of "hurt-and-be-hurt" is something of his own making. He is at once provoker and sufferer, persecutor and victim.

But why does he do this? We can explain why the Dostoevskian hero hurts others by the law of self-preservation, but the desire to be hurt contradicts the same law. The answer lies in Dostoevsky's conception of the *will* as an unqualified first premise of existence. It finds satisfaction in hurting others and in hurting itself. In hurting others, it is conscious of its power over others; in hurting itself it is conscious of itself. What the will wants more than anything else is awareness of itself, and it will subvert every motive to gain this satisfaction. The will or the self for Dostoevsky is limited by nothing; it is boundless in appetite; and it is universal in presence.[4] It makes of social relations a relentless duel, and of the individual a monster who will set the world on fire to satisfy a whim. The terror and freedom of the will are indissolubly linked. A freedom that is qualified is not freedom, and an unqualified freedom is a monstrous force unleashed on the world. Dostoevsky accepts the freedom, and he accepts the horror. The great novels that follow are in part a long search for something that will limit the horror and preserve the freedom.

Reason, despite conventional critical opinion, is not such a force. For Dostoevsky, reason can neither limit the horror nor preserve the freedom. In its pretensions—but they remain pretensions—it would destroy the freedom of the will. The Underground Man argues—and Dostoevsky agrees with him—that if rationally defined laws of nature exist, then the freedom of the will is impossible. The Underground Man's logic is impeccable; if the laws of human nature exist, then by their very comprehensiveness—like the laws of physical nature—they will be predictive of every human action.

But the laws of nature do not exist, because reason itself, as an objective entity, does not exist. There is no "reason" in Dostoevsky's world, only reasoners. Behind every rational formula, there is a formulator, and behind every generalization, there is a generalizer. There are no "ideas" in Dostoevsky's world apart from the men who carry them. An idea for Dostoevsky is always someone's idea, and reason is always someone's reasoning. *Every act of reason for Dostoevsky is a covert act of will.*

Reason cannot control the terror of the will's freedom, but something else can, and this something else brings us to the core of Dostoevsky's moral dialectic and consequently to the core of what motivates his characters. The will is the primary fact of man's nature, but man can, for Dostoevsky, create a "new" nature in Christ. *Dostoevsky's moral world is dialectical: man is poised with every choice he makes between the self and God.* These two poles are absolute and unqualified, and man *makes* his nature by choosing his acts to serve one or the other. The values his acts have are born with the choices he makes. Love, sacrifice, and other "good" acts are not good in themselves; for Dostoevsky, they are, like all acts, without value until their value is chosen. Man in Dostoevsky's world does not choose what is already determined, but determines what he chooses. Self-sacrifice abstractly considered or as conventionally classified is "good," but it may be, in Dostoevsky's world, "bad." Conversely, something like murder, which abstractly considered is always "evil," may in Dostoevsky's world be "good." Raskolnikov's "murder" is, as Dostoevsky himself reminds us in his notebooks, the first step toward his salvation.

Man freely chooses the value his act shall have, and the value his act shall have comes from the choice—the most basic in Dostoevsky's moral world—of the act for *self* or for *God*. What serves God is good; what serves the self is evil. What we ordinarily understand as "evil" may be, because it serves God, "good." Without God, man triumphs over evil only to meet in a kind of ascending scale of transformed evils—usually apparent goods—always equal to his weakness or his strength. Without God, the Dostoevskian hero is condemned to meet only himself, no matter how beautiful his intention, no matter how "good" his act.

Nor does Dostoevsky's moral dialectic introduce by the back door abstract moral distinctions in the form of acts that can be neatly and determinately classified as "for self" and "for God." No division of "for self" and "for God" can be made beforehand, because the moment of choice can suborn any "good" for its own use. Nothing astonished Dostoevsky more, in his own world and in the world of his created characters, than the endless transformations the self could undergo, using for its own purposes any impulse, no matter how good, the infinite refinement of the mind in rationalizing any act, no matter how evil. For the hero who does not understand the full implications—Raskolnikov, Ippolit, Katerina—the good act without God is self-deception, at times subtle and at times coarsely obvious. For the hero who knows what he is doing—a Svidrigaylov and Stavrogin—the good act without God is but the more exquisite weapon for manifesting one's will over others.

Dostoevsky saw the world through the prism of a highly conscious metaphysic: man striving to express his will upon man and seeking confirmation of self in injuring and being injured; man meeting at every victory over himself a transmuted image and temptation of his self; man pursuing evil up the ladder of good, using the highest goods for the deepest injuries; and man, with God, occasionally wrenching himself out of these traps into selflessness. The Devil truly finds his most secure footing in Dostoevsky's world, as in traditional Christianity, in the most sublime virtues. For Dostoevsky's drama of the injured and the injuring, in its highest reaches, is translated into the drama of the forgiven and the forgiving. In his world, the highest virtues can be suborned to the work of the deepest vice, and the deepest vice may be transformed into the highest virtue. No wonder that Dostoevsky's dark angels carry with them the afterglow of a heavenly light; they battle close to God's citadel.

The world view that takes mature form in *Notes from the Underground* and that will be refined in dramatic form in the great novels that follow is neither confused, nor contradictory, nor paradoxical. At its base lies the dialectic in which good may be chosen to be evil and evil chosen to be good. Not every character who does "good" in Dostoevsky's world is good, and not every character who does "evil" is evil. Unless we are ready to recognize the dialectical nature of this world, we shall continue to take love as love, when it may be hate as in *The Gambler;* sacrifice as sacrifice, when it may be insult as with Katerina in *The Brothers Karamazov;* and suffering as suffering, when it may be willfulness and self-love as with the Underground Man.

The dialectic of man poised between nihilistic freedom and God, which Dostoevsky takes up in *Crime and Punishment,* has its roots in the aberrations of the forties. The process by which the aberrations of the forties become the pledges of man's freedom in the *Notes from the Underground* and the great novels to follow has been itself dialectical. The Crystal Palace makes the wild dreams and actions of the crushed and humiliated clerks of the forties superfluous. In the Crystal Palace the Golyadkins and the Prokharchins will drown in bubbles of bliss, and the Schilleristic dreams these heroes have in an unjust social system will be fulfilled by a universal happiness more beautiful than they dreamed of. But the universal happiness poses a universal threat: the bliss is bought at the price of the freedom of the individual. To meet this new threat, the very aberrational traits for which the Crystal Palace is a solution become elevated into traits of universal value. What was individual, exceptional, and aberrational in the forties becomes in *Notes from the Underground* and in *Crime and Punishment* the universal pledge of freedom. But the oppositions that emerge in *Notes from the Underground* are not final. The individual freedom that contradicts the laws of universal rational harmony is in turn contradicted by what the freedom implies: a destructive will. The problem that Dostoevsky faces after writing the *Notes* is how to preserve the freedom and restrain its destructive implications. In the next novel, *Crime and Punishment,* he attempts to dramatize a way out of this, for *Crime and Punishment* is a trying-out of the consequences of a "free will" unleashed on society, and, at the same time, an attempt to find a force to restrain the free will, God. But God in turn poses a contradiction. As the Crystal Palace met the destructive aspects of the existing social structure by destroying free will, so God threatens to restrain the destructive aspects of free will by destroying the freedom. What begins with *Crime and Punishment* is the drama of the terrible consequences that follow on an unleashed will, and the groping for the psychological and metaphysical roots of God in reality.

5

Crime and Punishment

THERE IS IN *Crime and Punishment* a little of everything
that Dostoevsky had experimented with in the forties and
the early sixties: character types, Gothic elements, sentimental situations, social elements. Luzhin, for instance, is not
much different from Yulian Mastakovich of *The Christmas
Tree and the Wedding*, or from Mme. M's husband of *The
Little Hero*. He calculates his marriage to Dunia in the
same cold-blooded way that Yulian had calculated the little
girl's dowry on his fingers. Sonia resembles the prostitute
Liza in *Notes from the Underground;* Marmeladov resembles the self-dramatizing buffoon *Polzunkov*, and the
suffering drunk Emelyan of *The Honest Thief;* Katerina
Marmeladov looks back to naïve dreamers like Nelli's
mother in *The Insulted and the Injured;* and even Porfiry
is anticipated in the sleuthing of Ivan Petrovich in *The
Insulted and the Injured* and of Yaroslav Ilych of *The
Landlady*. But under the pressure of the dialectic that is
brought to maturity in the *Notes,* many of the elements are
transformed.

The gothic elements that had appeared in *The Landlady*, *Netochka Nezvanova,* and *The Insulted and the*

Injured are a case in point: Svidrigaylov and Alyona Ivanovna are not far removed from the conventional villains of
the gothic novel, yet both are raised to profound moral
significance. Svidrigaylov has flaxen hair, pale blue eyes, red
lips, and a masklike face; he carouses in the dens of the city,
seduces young girls, and mysterious crimes are reported
about him. He embodies all the artifice and melodrama of
the gothic villain, but he is also something more. As Raskolnikov's double and as the bronze man who can commit
crimes without feeling any pangs of conscience, the terror
and mystery which was artifice and melodrama become,
at least in part, the terror and mystery of the will and the
moral nature of man.

Alyona Ivanovna has sharp evil eyes, a pointed nose,
hair smoothed with grease, a flannel rag wrapped around
a neck that looks like a chicken leg. She is not just a victim,
but the kind of victim Raskolnikov needs. For him, she
represents the heart of the corrupt society against which
he revolts.[1] Her image is almost mythic: a kind of female
Minotaur devouring the prey of society until a white knight
is able to destroy her. She is "gothic," yet she is real, and
she is real because she answers to one of the deceptive
motivations Raskolnikov gives himself: the killing of evil
to do good. For this purpose Raskolnikov needs a useless
evil; in her active hurting of good lives and her exploitation of her sister, Raskolnikov finds the useless arbitrary
evil he needs. Alyona exploits so that praises to her soul
may be sung after she is dead.

The Marmeladov subplot is almost a paradigm of the
sentimental situation, which had already influenced many
of Dostoevsky's early works, especially *The Insulted and
the Injured*. A civil clerk because of misfortunes goes from
bad to worse; he ends up destitute in the capital; his daughter is forced into prostitution; his wife, who had come from
a good family, becomes consumptive, and the children go
hungry. The plot reminds us of the Gorshkov family and
Varvara's plight in *Poor Folk*, and of Nelli's misfortunes in

The Insulted and the Injured. But in *Crime and Punishment* the sentimental situation takes on a new significance; it becomes a tool of moral perception.

Consider the scene in which Marmeladov and Raskolnikov return to Marmeladov's apartment: Katerina, her arms clutching her breast, is walking back and forth, consumptively coughing; she is breathing unevenly, her eyes are flashing unnaturally as if from fever; her lips are parched, and the reflection of a dying candle flickers on her consumptive, pale, sickly face. In the corner a seven-year-old boy is trembling and crying from a recent beating, and his nine-year-old sister with a torn shirt and arms as thin as matchsticks tries to comfort him. Her eyes follow with fear the nervous walking of her mother. A third child, a six-year-old, is asleep on the floor. And on the threshold, kneeling down and ready to accept his punishment, is Marmeladov. The scene is classically sentimental and repeats situations Dostoevsky has used before: weeping children, a sick wife, joblessness, a daughter in prostitution, a husband who from weakness has been reduced to stealing money from his family and to drinking from the gains of his daughter's prostitution. But something has changed! Katerina, for instance, refuses to close the door of the adjoining apartment from which billows tobacco smoke; she insists on leaving the door open to the staircase from which the smells pour in; and she refuses to open windows, even though the room is very stuffy. She *wants* to irritate her coughing and feels satisfaction in coughing up her blood. She has apparently just beaten the little boy, whose misery has driven her to desperation. It is clear that she is intentionally irritating her misery, and seeking to exaggerate it. The same is even more true of Marmeladov. At the tavern where we first meet him, he is described as a drunk with a bloated greenish face, puffed eyelids, hysterical eyes, and ruffled hair. He holds his head with his hand, the table is sticky with liquor, his clothes are awry, the buttons barely hanging on and wisps of hay sticking to them after five nights on a hay barge. He has been, in his own words, reduced to destitution by drink and misfortune. Before a circle of jeering bar bums, Marmeladov narrates, as if on stage, all the intimate details of his misery. He seems almost to caress the vile things he has done: he has lost his job, driven his daughter to prostitution, and stolen the last kopeks from his family. He repeatedly calls himself a pig. Like Katerina, he takes pleasure in lacerating his wounds; this is what Dostoevsky had called "self-interested suffering" in *The Insulted and the Injured*.

The conventional sentimental scene in which circumstances *bring* an unfortunate individual to misery and destitution is transformed into one in which the individual *looks* for his misery and destitution, and derives some strange satisfaction from displaying it and even exaggerating it. *Marmeladov has, clearly, chosen his destitution.* Five days before his confession to Raskolnikov, when the solution to all his difficulties was entirely in his hands, he was at the peak of happiness; his wife, delighted with his job, was calling him darling and protector; suddenly he throws it all over, steals the last kopeks from his children's mouths, spends it all on drink, sells his uniform, and ends up taking kopeks earned by his daughter from her prostitution. Why does he do this? Marmeladov himself gives us a hint when he says: "I am a dirty swine; but she is a lady! I may be a beast, but my dear wife, Katerina Ivanovna, is a highly educated lady and an officer's daughter. Granted, I am a scoundrel; but she, sir, is an educated lady of noble heart and sentiments. And yet—oh, if only she'd take pity on me!" She is a lady, and he is a beast—he insists on it—but it is because he is a beast and she is a lady that he cannot help dragging both her and himself down. He cannot live up to her high feelings and sublime pride. He calls her "pitiless" (*bezzhalostnaya*). He had married her when she was destitute, and she had gone to her wedding with him weeping and wringing her hands. She never let him forget that she had been a captain's daughter and had onced danced

63

at the governor's ball. When he realizes that he will never match the dream of her past life, he begins to drink and to pursue the opposite. "And for a whole year I did my duty by her conscientiously and well, and never touched a drop of this (he pointed to the half-pint), for I have my feelings. But I'm afraid even that did not please her." If he cannot participate in her life, he will make her participate in his life. It is no accident, I think, that he destroys all the reminders of her past life: he sells her green shawl and her stockings (he has apparently long ago sold her gold medal) for drink. What he wants is to be accepted as a person, not as someone who couldn't live up to her former husband. And it is by his lowness that he attempts, and succeeds, to turn her attention to him.

Marmeladov is Raskolnikov's double. Like Raskolnikov, he has been swept out of society; he has nowhere to go and is, or feels, persecuted by society. This is obviously one of the reasons Raskolnikov feels sympathy for him and is interested in him. More important, Marmeladov repeats the basic psychology of Raskolnikov. In his desire for self-worth he hurts himself and those he loves. Unable to command the respect and admiration of his wife through good acts (hard work, position, sobriety), he forces her attention through bad acts (theft, drunkenness, and destitution). The pleasure he gets out of having his hair pulled is analogous to the pleasure Raskolnikov gets in having society punish him for his wrongdoing.

If much of Dostoevsky's old material is welded into new tools of perception and interpretation, the most important theme of *Crime and Punishment* is new. This is the sudden emergence of "crime" as the dominant theme of the novel and of almost all the works that follow.

Crime and Freedom

The dialectic that Dostoevsky brings to maturity in *Notes from the Underground* had outrun the drama of the work. The Underground Man's spiteful forays against his school friends, against Liza, against the reader, together with his ceaseless contradiction is "thin" drama for the implications of the dialectic. The dialectic implies a dreadful freedom that is contained by no values, because it is before values; and it implies a hero that is in perpetual revolt against society, himself, and God. Dostoevsky needs a theme that will do justice to his dialectic, and it is in the theme of crime that he finds the right proportions.

Crime becomes Dostoevsky's great theme, not because he had a dark, secret sympathy for crime, but because it expresses and dramatizes so beautifully the metaphysic of freedom that had taken form in the *Notes*. Crime becomes precisely the theme that permits him to wed drama and metaphysic so masterfully. Why? What is the criminal for Dostoevsky? He is someone who has broken a law and thus put himself outside of society. Every society draws a narrow circle of what is permitted, and every human being carries within him the impulses and dreams of acts that pass the pale of the permitted. Crime is this "might be" which the forces of law, convention, and tradition hold at bay. It lies in the undefined regions beyond the clear line that society has drawn about us. In those regions man's nature is unrealized, undefined, and undared. Society, like individual man, is for Dostoevsky an arbitrary power, constructed by arbitrary wills for purposes of self-protection. What is "lawful" is arbitrary; and what is unlawful, *crime,* is arbitrary. The criminal merely opposes his arbitrary will against the arbitrary will of society. He transgresses no sacred canon; he merely dares what the timid and unfree dare not do. It is only when one is free of the domination of society's will that one is free to exercise one's will. A free act is necessarily a "criminal" act, in the special sense of being beyond what is permitted by law and custom. It is in this sense that all of Dostoevsky's great heroes are criminals; all of them step outside the circle of the permitted into the undefined region of the unpermitted.

Where did the theme of crime come from? The suddenness with which it bursts upon Dostoevsky's world, as well as the completeness with which crime dominates his themes, is puzzling. Dostoevsky is interested in crime before writing *Crime and Punishment*—after all he spent four years in prison—but there is almost no exploitation of the theme in his previous works. Except for the autobiographical *The House of the Dead*, there is almost nothing. In *The Landlady*, we have the rumored crimes of Katya and Murin, and the symbolic crime of Ordynov against Murin. In *The Insulted and the Injured*, we have the unofficial crimes of exploitation by Valkovsky of Nelli's mother; and there is finally the column on criminal news of Paris life that Dostoevsky writes for *Time* early in the sixties.[2] This is pretty meager preparation for the sudden emergence of this major theme.

It is too little. But if we take crime less legalistically and if we see it, as Dostoevsky understands it, as a protest against what is fixed and defined, then the impulse to crime is everywhere in his early works. Crime is already in the Underground Man's hurt of Liza, and it is in the impulses of Golyadkin. The anticipatory resemblances of Golyadkin to Raskolnikov are striking. Golyadkin is convinced that he is a victim of the plots and intrigues of his fellow workers; Raskolnikov is convinced that he is a victim of the unjust and arbitrary power of society. Golyadkin dreams of a beautiful Golyadkin who will be born if he can outwit his enemies; Raskolnikov dreams of a superior Raskolnikov who will be born when he defies and outwits society. The frantic desire of Golyadkin to be someone else becomes the methodical plan and act of Raskolnikov to be someone else (a superior Raskolnikov). Golyadkin reduces his enemies to ashes in thought; Raskolnikov kills his enemy in cold blood. The "aberration" that Golyadkin carries off to the madhouse is in Raskolnikov turned loose on society. Protest against one's place in society becomes the supreme protest of crime against the idea of society itself. Crime does not appear until Dostoevsky's dialectic requires it: when freedom in its protest against everything fixed in society and the universe makes its appearance in the *Notes,* crime and sin burst on Dostoevsky's world as the most dramatic embodiment of the theme. Raskolnikov's crime is his free act. In the *Notes* the Underground Man had reasoned out the terrifying consequences of being unfree; in *Crime and Punishment* Raskolnikov acts out the terrifying consequences of being free.

Raskolnikov

From the first lines Raskolnikov is moving toward the crime. We meet him on the staircase: he slinks past the open kitchen where his landlady is with her humiliating demands for payment, goes out onto the hot, smelly summer streets, and then on to the rehearsal for the crime. For more than a month he has lain for whole days in his closet-like room, crushed by poverty, badgered by his landlady, eaten up by an idea that hovers like a tempting nightmare about the fringes of his belief. From the first lines we have a sense of "something having to give," and Dostoevsky plays upon this tension unabashedly. What has to be done has been incubating in his mind for more than a month, first only as a tempting flicker, then as a half possibility, and finally as a half-believed rehearsal. On the way to rehearse the crime, he has already measured off the steps to Alyona Ivanovna's house, studied the staircase, traced out the habits of the caretakers, and taken note of the layout. Dostoevsky uses the popular technique of giving the reader the criminal's intention and preparations so that he can, for suspense, play off what the criminal does against what he has prepared. He frankly exploits a "will-it-happen-and-will-he-get-away-with-it-if-it-happens" situation. Almost every detail contributes to the suspense: the lucky break of overhearing that Lizaveta will not be home at seven the next day, the unlucky break of oversleeping and of finding

Nastasya in the kitchen, the lucky break of the caretaker being absent and of the haywagon shielding his entrance into Alyona Ivanovna's building; after the murder the unlucky break of Koch's and Pestryakov's arrival when he is ready to leave, the unlucky break of their returning when he has started down the stairs, and the lucky break of the second-floor apartment being vacant. Throughout, Dostoevsky plays upon the most elemental springs of suspense: alarm and relief. The murder scene itself is a classic in technique from beginning to end. Raskolnikov has to ring three times, and for him and the reader there is acute tension between each ring. Before the third ring, Raskolnikov puts his ear to the door and has the sensation of Alyona putting her ear to the door also: murderer and victim sense each other's presence through the partition. When Alyona Ivanovna opens the door a crack, only her eyes are seen; and there is the suspense of not knowing whether she will let him in or not. Then there is the excruciating moment when she turns to the light to untie the string of the pledge, and Raskolnikov realizes—as he slips the hatchet out of its loop—that it would have to be then or never. Perhaps more than anything, the tension and drama of Raskolnikov's half-conscious rummagings during the murder come from Dostoevsky's use of sound, or rather from the lack of it. The windows are closed, and nothing is heard from the landing. There is only the dull sound of the axe falling on Alyona Ivanovna's head and her weak cry, the faint cry of Lizaveta, the sound of the keys, and the sound of Raskolnikov's heavy breathing. The murder takes place in a ghastly pantomime that throws into relief both the sound of the murder weapon and the sound of the keys. The scene ends with Saturday matinee thriller gestures: Koch and Pestryakov pull at the door; Raskolnikov, with two murdered women and a pool of blood behind him, watches the hook of the door bob up and down.

But no matter how skillfully done, such techniques touch only the superficial layers of our minds and feelings. If there were only this level, *Crime and Punishment* might be an interesting, surely an entertaining book, but it would not be a great book. However, *Crime and Punishment* is a great novel, and part of its greatness comes from a technique that assaults the reader's intellectual complacency and challenges him to continual refinement of understanding. Whenever the reader begins to relax into what he thinks he understands and can accept, Dostoevsky introduces some fact, some scene that contradicts what the reader expects and forces him to rethink the novel. The reader is constantly being challenged by Dostoevsky to reappraise what he has already concluded.

The reader quickly sees, for instance, that there is more to the crime than the murder, and thus more than the suspense of "Will he do it?" and "Will he get away with it?" He sees that the crime has a social significance. Our sympathy is drawn toward Raskolnikov: he is poor and unable to continue his studies; his mother is ruining herself for him; his sister is being forced into voluntary prostitution by marrying Luzhin for his sake; he is young and talented, but for lack of money, his talent is wasted. And as he reminds us, there are thousands like him in St. Petersburg. On the other hand, the old hag Alyona Ivanovna, useless to everyone, lies in her lair like some spider, sucking out the blood of the best of Russian youth so as to erect some lasting monument to herself and to her soul after death. It is only a step from these considerations to the explicit justification of the crime as the "humanitarian" exchange of one worthless life for a thousand useful lives. The motive of economic necessity (no job, the economic plight of his family) suddenly becomes not *necessity* but a bold claim, *a right*. Crime is put forth as virtue, evil as good. What a moment before made a claim on our sympathy makes a claim on our judgment. It is an attack on our values, and for a moment the justification almost sounds believable; and although we are not taken in, the powerful argument provokes our attention. The other important motive Raskolnikov puts forth, the superman theory, makes the same kind of appeal-attack on us, but it is not radically different in kind. Mochul'sky and many before him have reasoned these into very different and even contradictory motives, but both justify crime for humanitarian reasons.[3] The superman theory simply gives to exceptional people only the prescience to know what crimes are beneficial to humanity. After we have made our peace with both motives, we settle down to watch what is a misguided act run its course. According to our moral and aesthetic dispositions, the criminal must be pursued, caught, and punished in order to satisfy our legal sense, and he must be brought to see the error of his ways in order to satisfy our moral sense. And this seems to be precisely what happens: Raskolnikov runs, Porfiry pursues, Raskolnikov gradually sees that he was wrong, and he is caught, converted, and punished.

But Dostoevsky has a way of introducing a contradiction at a point where we feel we understand what is going on, and thus challenging us to think through our conclusions. As readers we are always sinking back into an aesthetic and moral sloth which Dostoevsky continually assaults. We classify certain situations and expect them to confirm our judgments and interpretations. His technique is to trap the reader into more and more refined explanations of Raskolnikov's motives, constantly to challenge our understanding, and to attack our moral predispositions. According to conventional moral explanations, Raskolnikov should be running from the crime, and he should begin with the wrong moral idea and be converted to the right one. But Raskolnikov, we shortly see, is not running *away* from the crime but *toward* it.

Raskolnikov wants to be caught. He commits two murders and leaves the door open; back in his room with his clothes stained with blood and his pockets bulging with stolen articles, he promptly falls asleep and sleeps until two o'clock the next day—with the door unlatched! When he is summoned to the police station the following day, he faints at precisely the moment when suspicion may fall on him. He had come fearing that the summons had to do with the crime and learns that it has to do with his failure to pay a promissory note. When he is relieved to learn that there is not the slightest suspicion of him, he faints so as to provoke suspicion. Later he again provokes suspicion upon himself by almost confessing to Zamyotov in a tavern, by returning to the scene of the crime and deliberately baiting the workman there (Porfiry later acknowledges that his return to the scene of the crime first aroused his suspicion), and by intentionally putting out clues to encourage Porfiry's suspicion and pursuit. In fact, the more we examine the elaborate pursuit of Porfiry, the more apparent it is that Raskolnikov has a stake in keeping the pursuit alive. It is almost comic, the way he breathes life into the pursuit, providing it with clues, offering himself as bait, and supporting it when it falters. When the scent fades into nothing but Porfiry's double-edged psychology, and when Porfiry himself admits in the last conversation he has with Raskolnikov that he has no clues, Dostoevsky tells us that "Raskolnikov felt a rush of a new kind of terror. The thought that Porfiry thought him innocent began to frighten him suddenly." After this, only Svidrigaylov is left to incriminate him, and yet when he learns that Svidrigaylov is dead, "Raskolnikov felt as if something had fallen on him and was suffocating him." Why? Raskolnikov is terrified and crushed by the thought of not being pursued; and when the last person who can incriminate him dies (Svidrigaylov), he incriminates himself by confessing his crime.

But need this trouble us? Dostoevsky had told us in his famous letter to Katkov, in which he outlined the plot of *Crime and Punishment*, that the criminal would want to be punished, presumably from guilt. Can we not see Raskolnikov's punishment as a sign of his guilt and his desire to atone for his crime? He has killed, recognizes his error, and seeks his punishment. It is not our moral anticipations that are violated by Raskolnikov's elaborate pursuit of punishment, but only our dramatic anticipations.

Raskolnikov does not believe he is wrong. He believes he has a right to kill when he lies in his attic room, when he kills the moneylender, when he "seeks his punishment," and indeed when he gives himself up. Raskolnikov seeks punishment, but acts as if he feels no repentance. It is here that the dialectic can help us, for the desire for punishment in Dostoevsky's metaphysic need not be redemptive. The meetings between Raskolnikov and Sonia in the second half of the novel illustrate brilliantly the dialectical nature of Dostoevsky's world.

Raskolnikov visits Sonia twice, first to rehearse his "confession" and then to confess. The first visit is weirdly beautiful: the harlot and the murderer gathered over the reading of the Holy Book; the pale flickering of candlelight over the feverish gaze of Raskolnikov and the terrified look of Sonia. Sonia is wretched and shamed and pleased (*ey bylo i toshno i stydno i sladko*) by his visit. She feels herself defenseless before him. She is shamed at having him where she receives her guests, and timid in the defense of her beliefs and hopes. After Sonia has finished reading the Lazarus passage, Raskolnikov gets up, and with trembling lips and flashing eyes he falls down before her and says, "I did not bow down to you, I bowed down to all suffering humanity." This phrase has been underlined by critics since de Vogüé as a key to the novel because, presumably, it shows a repentant Raskolnikov, one who after killing a human being now recognizes his debt to human beings. *In fact, it is but another expression of the self-willed and rationalizing Raskolnikov.* It is a bookish reassertion of his first self-flattering and self-deceptive humanitarian motive. He bows down to those who have suffered out of pride and not out of humility. We are quick to accept Raskolnikov's bowing to suffering humanity as a sign of repentance because we expect the criminal to have a change of heart, and especially because we expect such a change

of heart to take place under the influence of the Bible. But
if we read carefully, we see how the dramatic situation contradicts our conventional expectations.

Raskolnikov does his best in this visit to provoke in Sonia
the kind of revolt against society that he himself has carried
on. He starts out—before the reading of the Lazarus passage—by cruelly insisting on the desperate and hopeless
fate that awaits Katerina, Sonia, and especially the children. Katerina will die, and the children will have to share
Sonia's terrible life, or at best Sonia will get sick, and
Katerina will have to go begging in the street, bang her
head against stone and die. The children will have nowhere
to go, and Polya will end up a prostitute like Sonia. Without
mercy he tears one illusion after another from Sonia, attacking even her most precious protection, her belief in God.
He does this by suggesting with malicious joy that God
does not exist. It is at this point that he inconsequently
asks her to read Lazarus. He listens to the reading of Lazarus, not because he has changed or is changing, but because he is fascinated that someone in such a hopeless position should be buoyed up by something so odd. After the
reading, he calls upon her to follow him, because both of
them are "damned." But the road he calls her to follow is
his, and not hers. He repeats what he said at the beginning: it is folly to cry like children that God will not permit terrible things to happen. In answer to Sonia's agonized
cry as to what is to be done, he answers: "What's to be
done? We have to break what must be broken once and
for all—that's what must be done; and we must take the
suffering upon ourselves. What? You don't understand?
You'll understand later. Freedom and power—power above
all. Power over all trembling creatures and over the anthill. That's our goal." It is his suffering, and not hers, he
offers. And his suffering is a suffering of pride and will;
it is a suffering of "power over all trembling creatures and
over the anthill."

In his second visit to her, he confesses; but before he confesses he makes explicit what he had done in the first visit. In his first visit he had asked her to follow his path by proving to her how hopeless her own path (faith in God) was. In his second visit he puts the choice of his way of life to her openly. He asks her, hypothetically, to "kill" to do "good." Both have come from the funeral dinner, where Luzhin had, from petty revenge, tried to ruin Sonia and the Marmeladov family. Raskolnikov asks Sonia: "Suppose this were suddenly left up to you—I mean, whether he or they should go on living, whether, that is, Luzhin should live and go on doing wicked things or Mrs. Marmeladov should die. How would you decide which of the two should die? I ask you." Sonia answers as only she can—that it is not up to her to decide who is to live. Once again, as in the first visit, he changes suddenly from torturer to supplicant. He asks her to forgive him and then confesses. But the confession is no more than the "bowing down to suffering humanity" a sign of repentance. After he has finished, Sonia cries out in terrified compassion that they will go to prison together, and he replies, a hateful and arrogant smile playing on his lips, "I, Sonia, may not want to go to prison." And after Sonia calls upon him to "take suffering upon him and by suffering redeem himself," he answers: "How am I guilty before them? Why should I go? What will I say to them? Why, the whole thing's an illusion. They themselves are destroying people by the million and look on it as a virtue. They're knaves and scoundrels, Sonia. I won't go." Later, he will say the same thing on the eve of confessing to the authorities when he comes to take leave of Dunia and when she reminds him that he has shed blood. He answers with impatience: "Which all men shed . . . which flows and has always flowed in cataracts, which men pour out like champagne, and for which men are crowned in the Capital and afterwards called the benefactors of mankind." And he adds a few minutes later, "Never, never have I understood why what I did was a crime. Never, never have I been stronger and more convinced than now."

To be sure, he had committed a crime; he had stepped over the line of the permitted, but that line had been traced arbitrarily by those who had power. The criminal breaks only arbitrary laws, and with daring and strength enough he can make his own laws. He is consequently violating nothing but the wills of others, doing only what society itself has always done. His crime was, therefore, according to the rules of society; liberated from fear and habit, he had a perfect right to commit a crime. With clear logic, he acknowledges that those in power have a perfect right, even an obligation, to assert their restraint of his freedom. He had a right to commit his crime, and they had a right to pursue and punish him for it, and victory lay waiting for the stronger and cleverer. What is clear, then, is that Raskolnikov needs the duel with Porfiry, needs the pursuit, and when this flags, he needs the punishment that society inflicts on him. And he needs all this without having changed his mind about the "rightness" of his crime. Why should he pursue punishment when he is convinced that he has a right to kill? *So that he can prove his strength by bearing the punishment.* If he hasn't been strong enough to carry off the idea of his superman indifference to moral feelings, then he will be strong enough to bear society's punishment. It is not guilt or atonement that drives him to pursue his pursuers, but pride and self-will. He had committed the crime to prove his superiority; he pursues punishment and suffering to protect this superiority. Even more, he committed the crime in order to fail. At the end of Part Three, he summarizes all the reasons why he has failed, and concludes: "And, finally, I am utterly a louse . . . because I am perhaps viler and more loathsome than the louse I killed, and I felt *beforehand* that I would say that to myself *after* killing her!"

His strength in failure is not an alternative to strength in success, because he expected from the beginning to fail. He had not committed the crime to be reborn, but to fail. We have something of the same kind of process already at work in *The Double*. Golyadkin creates his "enemies" as Rashkolnikov provokes his pursuers; Golyadkin knows beforehand (the same word *predchustvovat'*, literally "to prefeel," is used by Golyadkin and Raskolnikov) that he will be thrown out of Klara's party, that the "Double" will appear, and that he will be taken away to a madhouse; he knows he will fail, but he pursues failure anyway. Raskolnikov does the same thing for an analogous purpose. Golyadkin can keep alive the image of himself as "good," as long as he can keep alive the image of those who are preventing him from being good. Raskolnikov can keep alive the conception of himself as "superior," as long as he can keep alive an image of society that prevents him from being superior. He provokes pursuit so as to show his strength in bearing the punishment, but he also provokes it —and this is perhaps more important—so that they will be the pursuers and he, the pursued; they, the victimizers and he, the victimized; they, the oppressors, and he, the oppressed. By its pursuit of him society confirms what Raskolnikov has made of it. If he can sustain the image of society against which he has revolted, he can sustain his belief in the rightness of his crime. By failing, he makes the kind of world and the kind of Raskolnikov he wants.

We are here at the core of Raskolnikov's motives. In his confession to Sonia, he is explicit about false motives. He is not a victim of economic conditions, nor of hunger, nor of lack of money. He admits to Sonia that he stayed in his room on purpose and went hungry out of spite. He knows that he might have supported himself as had Razumikhin, if he had wanted to. "Ah, how I hated that garret! And yet I wouldn't go out of it. I wouldn't on purpose! I didn't go out for days together, and I wouldn't work, I wouldn't even eat, I just lay there doing nothing. If Nastasya brought me anything, I ate it, if she didn't, I went all day without;

I wouldn't ask, on purpose, out of spite." And he is explicit about his real motives:

I wanted to murder, Sonia, without casuistry, to murder for my own sake, for myself alone! I didn't want to lie about it even to myself. It wasn't to help my mother I did the murder—that's nonsense—I didn't do the murder to gain wealth and power and to become a benefactor of mankind. Nonsense! I simply did it. I did the murder for myself, for myself alone, and whether I became a benefactor to others, or spent my life like a spider catching men in my web and sucking the life out of men, I couldn't have cared at that moment. And it was not the money I wanted, Sonia, when I did it. It was not so much the money, I wanted, but something else. I know it all now. Understand me! Perhaps I should never have committed a murder again, if I followed the same road. It was something else I wanted to find out, it was something else that led me on: I had to find out then, and as quickly as possible, whether I was a louse like the rest or a man. Whether I can step over or not. . . . Whether I am some trembling creature or whether I have the *right*. . . .

To kill, of course, as Sonia cries out. Raskolnikov killed the moneylender for himself, and for himself alone. This has apparently been too bare and simple a motive for critics who have busied themselves looking for Raskolnikov's motives in incest, homosexuality, and earth mothers. In the context of Dostoevsky's metaphysic "for himself alone" is a profound statement, pointing to the self's capacity to exercise its freedom and power without limit. He killed to see whether or not he had the right to step across: step across what? Obviously, the conventional (and to him arbitrary) line of right and wrong, where he can make his own right and wrong. Raskolnikov kills to prove that he is free, and if anything—including the taking of another's life—is interdicted, then he is not free. Raskolnikov fails because he did not have the courage to kill, with indifference, because he chose the most "useless" member of society when he should need no reasons to kill; and because

77

he suspected beforehand that he would not be able to kill indifferently. He does the act anyway so as to confirm his weakness and turn it into strength by giving the reason for his failure to society and thus keeping inviolate his superiority.

But it is all a mad drama of the self making its own reality to fit its dream of itself, and in the face of failure, remaking reality with the failure. In Dostoevsky's metaphysic this remaking of reality illustrates the self's capacity for endless self-justification, its ability to seize with endless refinement upon anything to impose its own image on the world and to support its own belief of itself. Raskolnikov kills the old pawnbroker, visits pain and punishment upon himself, and finally confesses so that he can justify his own rightness and destroy any suggestion of his wrongness. This explains his vicious reaction, even in prison, to any suggestion of another kind of Raskolnikov. According to his theory he should be insensitive to what he does, indifferent to the fate of others, and sublimely content to be proud and independent. But he is not: he takes the drunken Marmeladov home, leaves money out of pity for Mrs. Marmeladov, feels compassion for the young girl on the boulevard who had just been raped and anger at the rake who follows her. He asks Polya to love him, listens sentimentally to the organ grinder, and talks nostalgically about the beauty of falling snow. He desires unaccountably to be with other people, feels disgust for the very act of murder that is supposed to prove that there is no reason to be disgusted with anything, and falls unaccountably in love with Sonia.

But he hates this "other" Raskolnikov that erupts from some suppressed layer of his consciousness to contradict the image of himself as sublimely independent of life he does not control. When these feelings of love, compassion, and beauty erupt, he dismisses them contemptuously, as in the boulevard scene concerning the raped girl: "Anyway to hell with it! Let them! That's how it should be, they say. It's essential, they say, that such a percentage should go every year—that way—to the devil." Frequently he misinterprets these eruptions of another Raskolnikov. After caring for Marmeladov and giving sympathy and love to the dying man and his family, he feels a great sense of rebirth and exhilaration: "The sensation might be compared to that of a man condemned to death who has quite unexpectedly been pardoned." Clearly, the upsurge of life within him— a short time before he had looked upon a dead universe— is caused by the sympathy and love that had welled up within him for another person. But he misinterprets it as a pledge of the rebirth into will and power:

"Enough!" he said solemnly and resolutely. "I'm through with delusions, imaginary terrors, and phantom visions! Life is real! Haven't I lived just now? My life hasn't come to an end with the death of the old woman! May she rest in peace—enough, time you leave me in peace, madam. Now begins the reign of reason and light and—and of will and strength—and we'll see now! We'll try our strength now," he added arrogantly, as though challenging some dark power.

Again and again he is moved to actions he does not understand but cannot help. His visits to Sonia, both in rehearsal and in confession, show this double character. He has, as has been shown, challenged Sonia to join him in revolt, blasphemed against her faith, confirmed himself in his rightness, and yet, though his "suffering" is a suffering of pride, he is still drawn mysteriously to her. He invites her to join him, but he is happy she doesn't; and if she had, he would have hated her.

It may appear that the compassion, love, and suffering Raskolnikov feels contradicts the elaborate explanation by which these positive motivations are corrupted by his will. Not at all. The fact that both poles exist in him at once dramatizes the most refined point of Dostoevsky's moral dialectic. Raskolnikov shows how the will attempts—and in part succeeds—in corrupting every virtue to its own uses. He feels compassion for the raped girl on the boulevard, and yet leaves her indifferently to her fate; he loves Sonia, but tries to corrupt that love by inviting her to share his self-willed revolt; he pursues punishment from some deep-seated unconscious urge to "reunite" himself with his fellow men, but he attempts and succeeds in corrupting it—at least on a conscious level—into a weapon of self-justification. But even while he is attempting and succeeding in part to corrupt every sign of another nature, these other impulses move him relentlessly—by a logic beyond his intentions and his will—toward another kind of issue. The battle is intense, and he tries with fury to kill every sign of weakness within him, or to use the weakness as a weapon of self-justification. It is not a simple matter of attempting to corrupt his good impulses and failing. In part, he attempts and succeeds. When he bows down to "suffering humanity," he is not repentant; and when he confesses to Sonia and indeed later to the authorities, he is not confessing from a chastened heart or from changed convictions. Dostoevsky knows that the will has almost infinite resources in justifying itself, but the will is not his entire nature. The will, for Raskolnikov, apparently cannot prevail against what is the most deep-seated and essential part of his character.

The pledge of another kind of logic, and of the existence of God, is made to lie upon the evidence of these impulses of compassion, love, and communion with one's fellow men. They properly prepare for the redemptive scene in the epilogue. Dostoevsky sees the opposed impulses in Raskolnikov's nature as the signs of two kinds of "logic" that are basic to the human condition. They correspond to the two poles of his moral dialectic. There is God, and there is the self. Each has roots in the real impulses of men. There is no bridge between these two natures, and man is poised in fearful anxiety with every choice between them. Raskolnikov carries these twin impulses throughout the novel; and in the second half of the novel, he confronts them objectified in the persons of Sonia and Svidrigaylov. His choice between these impulses is dramatized as a choice between Sonia and Svidrigaylov. The skill with which Dostoevsky expresses this choice in structure, incident, and detail is commensurate with the refinement of his dialectic. Sonia and Svidrigaylov are doubles of Raskolnikov in that they embody in a fully developed manner the two impulses he carries within him. The first half of the novel is structured by Raskolnikov's visits to Alyona Ivanovna; the second half of the novel by his visits to Sonia and Svidrigaylov. Sonia, the symbol of true rebirth in faith, balances antithetically the image of the murdered Alyona Ivanovna, the symbol of false rebirth. Raskolnikov now visits Sonia instead of Alyona, and instead of death, there is birth in the reading of the story of Lazarus. If the murder is the central point of the testing of the rational principle, the confession becomes the central point of the testing of Raskolnikov's rebirth. Appropriately, since these two scenes balance each other, there is a rehearsal for the confession as there was for the murder scene. To be sure, Raskolnikov attempts to corrupt Sonia, and his listening to her reading of Lazarus and his confession do not come from compassion and repentance. But Sonia remains uncorrupted, and the mysterious attraction Raskolnikov feels for her is already a sign of Raskolnikov's acceptance of what she represents.

In going to see Svidrigaylov, Raskolnikov goes toward the destructive idea that had ruled his life in the first half; he goes to meet the ultimate consequences of the idea. Everything about this line of action is characterized by limitation and futile circularity. Raskolnikov and Svidrigaylov hunt each other out to learn from the other "something new," but when they meet—significantly near Haymarket Square, where Raskolnikov's idea grew into decision to act —they are like mirrors reflecting each other's dead idea. Sonia had offered Raskolnikov a new word; Svidrigaylov, the old word, only in grimmer, more naked terms than he had known it. Between the two Raskolnikov wavers, coming to a decision only with the death of one part of himself, only after Svidrigaylov—the objective correlative of the part—has acted out his play of self-destruction.

All of Svidrigaylov's actions, after Raskolnikov visits him in the inn near Haymarket Square, are a preparation for death, culminating in the grim ritual in the small hotel on the eve of his suicide. The hotel and its small empty room, cold veal, mice, and the Charon-like lackey are like a foretaste of the dismal hell that Svidrigaylov's fancy had accurately divined for itself. It is at this point, while Svidrigaylov prepares for death and Raskolnikov struggles with his dilemma, that Dostoevsky shows most vividly the ties and differences between the two men. Svidrigaylov's room looked like an attic: it was so small and low "that Svidrigaylov could scarcely stand up in it"; and the wallpaper was torn and yellowish. In a room that is, in fact, a replica of the small attic room where Raskolnikov's monstrous idea had come to birth, Svidrigaylov prepares to bring it to an end. End touches beginning, and, in his attempt to show the relationship between Svidrigaylov and Raskolnikov, Dostoevsky seems to bring the dreams Svidrigaylov has on his last night into correspondence—not wholly exact—with those Raskolnikov had earlier. Svidrigaylov's first dream is of a spring day on which he looks at the dead body of a girl who had apparently killed herself because of the atrocity he had committed on her body. Raskolnikov's first dream is of the mare beating, which, in the final furious shout of a frenzied peasant—"Why don't you strike her with an axe?"—is linked with his killing of the moneylender. Svidrigaylov looks with apathetic curiosity at the body of his victim; Raskolnikov reacts with furious aversion to the image of the victim-to-be. Svidrigaylov's second dream is of a little girl in whose eyes, even as he tries to protect her, he sees a reflection of his rapacious lust; Raskolnikov's, of his futile attempt to kill again Alyona Ivanovna. Raskolnikov is unable to act in his dream as he had in his conscious state; Svidrigaylov is able to act in no other way. At the point at which the ties between the two are about to be severed, the dreams, pointing perhaps to the essential nature of both men, show the unbridgeable gulf between them.

Now as Svidrigaylov prepares to meet the end to which the self-willed principle had brought him, the circumstances of the beginning of the crime are recreated. As on the night when he committed the atrocity which had led to the girl's death, the wind howls, it rains, and he goes, as before, to find a bush under which he can crawl and douse himself with the water he hates so much. At the precise moment, at dawn, when Svidrigaylov kills himself, Raskolnikov—who had been wandering around St. Petersburg all night —is peering into the muddy waters of the Neva contemplating suicide. With Svidrigaylov's death, Raskolnikov turns to confess. One part of himself, the self-willed principle, dies; the life-giving principle, objectified in Sonia, remains.

Raskolnikov carries within him the antithetic poles of Dostoevsky's dialectic: human logic and divine logic. There can be no compromise between them. The English word "crime" is exclusively legalistic in connotation and corresponds to the "human logic"; but the Russian word for crime, *prestuplenie*, carries meanings which point both to human and divine logic. *Prestuplenie* means literally "overstepping," and is in form parallel to the English word "transgression," although this word no more than "crime" is adequate to translate *prestuplenie* because of its Biblical connotations. But *prestuplenie* contains both poles of Dostoevsky's dialectic, for the line of the permitted which one "oversteps" may be drawn both by human or by divine logic.

Because the two impulses of self and God battle within him to the very end, Raskolnikov's confession is at once a sign of his self-will and his acceptance of God. He confesses because he will no longer be pursued, and it is only by his confession that he can provoke the punishment and hence the image of society he wants; yet he is simultaneously being moved toward the kind of punishment that Sonia wants him to accept. The battle between the two principles continues to the very end. Dostoevsky resolves the conflict by legislating Raskolnikov's conversion. The conversion is motivated, as indeed suicide or a new crime is motivated, in Raskolnikov's character. Dostoevsky does not really have grounds for ending the conflict, and it would have been much better, I believe, to have ended the novel with Raskolnikov's confession. The confession itself is at once, as I have explained, a self-interested and a selfless act. This is to say that the confession would have dramatized at the very end of the novel the fury of the conflict, and the effort of the will to penetrate and corrupt even the holiest of gestures.

But Dostoevsky was not yet ready to grant so much to his antagonists. He had dramatized masterfully the strength and power of the self, and his very skill had increased the probability of the self's domination of Raskolnikov. But he had also discerned the springs of another "nature" in Raskolnikov's compassion, and he had set this against the powerful and cunning self-interest of Raskolnikov's nature. For the moment Dostoevsky settles the issue by nudging Raskolnikov into God's camp. But Dostoevsky will not be satisfied with his own solution, and again and again he will grant more and more to his antagonists, so as to test his belief that man can be reborn into selflessness.

6

The Idiot

Lebedev, a comic and improbable character, gives us what can be the epigraph to *The Idiot*. He has been interpreting the apocalypse with Nastasya Fillipovna and both have agreed that contemporary reality has arrived "at the time of the third horse, the black one, and of the rider who has a measure in his hand, for everything in our age is measured and settled by agreement, and all people are merely seeking their rights: 'a measure of wheat for a penny, and three measures of barley for a penny.' And on top of it, they still want to preserve a free spirit and a pure heart and a sound body and all the gifts of the Lord. But they won't preserve them by seeking their rights alone, and there will therefore follow the pale horse and he whose name is Death, and after whom Hell follows. . . ." The nihilists who come with Burdovsky clamor for their "rights" from the Prince and from the times. Ganya has sworn to stop at nothing in self-abasement to amass a fortune. General Epanchin and Totsky seek their rights with the quiet certitude that their position and the social structure will give them what they want. Ippolit lashes out in spite against a world that has not given him a chance to show what a superior person he is: "I wanted to be famous —I had a right to." Lebedev, the court jester of this society, seeks his rights blatantly, without scruple or shame: he fawns on Rogozhin and his millions when we first meet him on the train; he begs Nastasya Fillipovna for the chance to put his gray head into the fire for a few thousand rubles; and he betrays the Prince shamelessly throughout the novel.

Everyone in this society is seeking his rights, and the common measure of these rights is money, as the market imagery of the money-burning scene makes clear. Everyone makes his bid for Nastasya Fillipovna, and she hysterically encourages higher and higher bids. Totsky offers 70,000 rubles as payment for her "imaginary hurt"; Ganya is willing to buy her for that sum; General Epanchin has put down a necklace as the first installment for the purchase of her favors; Rogozhin bids 18,000 rubles, then 40,000, and finally 100,000, which he brings wrapped in *The Stock Exchange News*. Even the Prince makes his bid, and it is the highest bid. After offering marriage, he announces to the startled guests that he has just learned that he has been named the heir to Pavlishchev's fortunes.

But Nastasya Fillipovna will not be bought. She refuses Totsky's offer of 70,000, the Prince's offer of Pavlishchev's million, and throws Rogozhin's 100,000 into the fire. The tongues of flame that eat at the 100,000 rubles wrapped in *The Stock Exchange News* hold in common mesmerism the spectators from the clown Ferdyshchenko to the pompous Epanchin. Everyone watches the burning money except Nastasya, Rogozhin, and Myshkin. Nastasya watches the dead white of Ganya's expression, and both Rogozhin and Myshkin watch her. Nastasya Fillipovna has provoked almost an obscene spectacle of the power and importance of money to that society, and she has provoked this spectacle of the common measure of society's conscience so as to defy society. Rogozhin has thrown the money at the feet of Nastasya, and Nastasya has thrown it defiantly at the society. Rogozhin and Nastasya are seeking their rights, too, but they are not of the common measure. What is Nastasya seeking? She sweeps like a storm through the lives of almost all the characters in the novel. She is a dominating force in almost everyone's consciousness: Rogozhin sends his life swirling into unknown destruction for her; Epanchin tries to make her his mistress; Totsky bows in fear and trembling before her caprices; and the Prince is mysteriously and fatefully attracted to her. There is no quietness about her: she does everything quickly—laughs inconsequently, cries out suddenly, shouts, and her eyes sparkle and flame. When she first appears at Ganya's apartment, she rushes in, throws her coat to the Prince, walks into the living room, shoves the Prince, laughs, talks, and offers her hand to every person. At her apartment, she goes from hysterical and purposeless laughter to gloomy reflection; she moves nervously about, laughs feverishly and hysterically, her dark eyes glisten, and red spots appear on her cheeks. She is conscious of her effect on others. She knows that her visit to Ganya's has sent his craven soul sinking in humiliation, for almost the first thing she asks about is the boarders. At her gathering, she has almost every soul present strung like a tense wire awaiting her pleasure, her "decision."

What does Nastasya Fillipovna want? She does not want respectability: she flaunts her "looseness" about by living in appearance as Totsky's concubine; she does not want vice: she lives chastely and is not tempted by Totsky or the young men he sends her; she does not want luxury and security: she lives quite simply and rejects Totsky's attempts to give her security through money or through an arranged marriage. Yet, it is clear that she wants some kind of payment, and that this payment has something to do with the hurt and humiliation she had suffered as a young girl in the country. Orphaned at seven, she is brought up in Totsky's charge, and from the age of sixteen, she is systematically violated by him. She comes to St.

Petersburg to avenge this hurt. She capriciously blocks his marriage to a lady of high standing and effectively keeps him in fear of her possible recklessness. But Totsky's fear, and even the offer of his hand, which he would have made had he not known it would have been refused, do not satisfy her. It is clear, too, that as the novel opens she has mixed feelings of resignation (hence her reasonableness in agreeing with Totsky for a change in their relations) and outrage (her defiance of society in the money-burning scene) because of her inability to get payment from Totsky. When she throws the 100,000 rubles into the fire with contempt, Nastasya Fillipovna condemns seven years of frustrated and fruitless waiting for the payment. Totsky does not know what she wants. In the parlor game of confessions, he sees his worst sin as some silly joke he once played on the lover of a provincial matron, and not the outrage he had perpetrated on Nastasya Fillipovna. Nor does anyone else understand what payment she wants. The novel begins as a metaphysical mystery, for Dostoevsky invites the reader to discover why Nastasya Fillipovna acts as she does.

What does Nastasya Fillipovna want? *As payment for her hurt, she wants to be hurt again.* This is clear in the way she permits the public to take her as Totsky's concubine, in the way she flaunts her "fallen state when she visits Ganya's apartment, in the way she provokes the bidding for her body, and in the way she makes her decision to go off with Rogozhin. She repeatedly calls herself shameless, seemingly enjoying her misery: "I have been shameless! I was Totsky's concubine." And when the Prince makes his offer, she says: "Look, Prince, your fiancée has taken the money because she's corrupt, and you wanted to marry her."

When she flings the 100,000 rubles into the fire and goes off with Rogozhin, she knows she is going off as "Rogozhin's slut," and it is as Rogozhin's slut that she wants to go off. After Totsky had defiled her innocence, she wished "a thousand times to throw myself in the pond, but I was a corrupt creature; I didn't have the courage to do it." The punishment by water she had wanted but feared she now pursues as punishment by Rogozhin's knife. The feeling of guilt is a hurt she inflicts on herself for the first hurt, and the death she pursues and finally provokes is the final hurt she inflicts upon herself for her guilt. By going off with Rogozhin she confirms her guilt.

At the beginning of Part Two, the Prince in his simplicity expresses this explicitly:

A little while ago I said that I couldn't understand why she should have consented to marry you. But though I can't make it out, there must be a clear and adequate reason for it. She's convinced of your love, so she must also be convinced of some of your good qualities. It doesn't make sense otherwise! What you told me just now supports this. You say yourself that she has learned to speak to you in a different way from the way she spoke and behaved to you before. You're suspicious and jealous, and that's why you exaggerate everything bad you noticed. I'm sure she doesn't think as poorly of you as you say. Otherwise, it could only mean that she's consciously courting death by drowning or the knife by marrying you. Can that be? Who would consciously ask for death by drowning or the knife?

And Parfyon answers, "By drowning or the knife! . . . Ha! Why, she's marrying me just because she knows for sure that I shall kill her. Can it be, Prince, that you haven't yet understood what it's all about?"

If Rogozhin is the confirmation of her guilt and the punishment for that guilt, the Prince is the kind, honest, silly creature who would come along and say, "You are not at fault Nastasya Fillipovna, and I love you." The Prince is her "innocence." As she dreamed him, he is. He sees her as unspoiled, uncorrupted, pure, and innocent—as she wanted to be. Rogozhin sees her as she believes she is, and the Prince sees her as she would like to be, and fears she can never be. He offers her a Nastasya who is washed clean of hurt, insult, and guilt. But the Prince in his faith can only offer forgiveness, and Nastasya in her faith must accept it. She cannot. Lebedev tells the Prince: "She's more afraid of you than she is of him, Prince, and there's something very subtle here!" She wants and fears both Myshkin and Rogozhin, flies from one to the other, and is unable to accept either. We can understand why she fears Rogozhin, but why does she fear the Prince, since he offers her what she yearns for? She tells herself that she would only corrupt him by her fallen nature, and offers him Aglaya, whom she sees as the embodiment of the innocence from which she has fallen. But this is not the whole answer. It lies elsewhere. It lies in the exultant cry Lebedev reports she had made when she ran from Rogozhin to Myshkin. "I'm still free," she says. "And you know, Prince, she strongly insists on that. I'm still completely free," she says. It also lies in the bitter analysis that Aglaya makes in that frightful and spiteful meeting between two women. Aglaya says, "You were able to love only your disgrace and the constant thought that you had been disgraced and humiliated. If your disgrace were less, or if it had not existed at all, you'd be even more unhappy." Nastasya loves her disgrace (*pozor*) more than she loves the innocence that the Prince embodies and offers her. Her living hurt is the flame in which her self burns and glows. Her "hurt" justifies her contempt for Totsky and society, and her guilt justifies her contempt for herself. And both shame and guilt are precious to her. The innocence Myshkin offers her would rob her of both. As the Underground Man could see only his subservience in Liza's love, Nastasya can see only the loss of her "freedom" in accepting the Prince's forgiveness. She is attracted to Rogozhin because she believes she is as he sees her; but she hates him because she hopes she is different. She is attracted to Myshkin because she hopes she is as he sees her. But she is afraid of him because he threatens to rob her of her shame and her guilt. She cannot accept either Myshkin or Rogozhin, and throughout the novel she burns in the service of the will, between guilt and innocence, turning both to the service of her pride and her "freedom."

The Prince compares her suffering to being trapped in a cage and whipped by a keeper. Nastasya is both in the cage and the keeper of the cage. Nastasya may fear the final confirmation of herself in Rogozhin's eyes and may run off to pursue the dream that Myshkin offers her, but in the final analysis it is only the shame and the guilt she can love, even while hating them. Freely, she chooses Rogozhin as the instrument of her punishment and, finally, of her death. She does everything she can to provoke him to violence: she has flirted with other men, received him coldly, thrown him out of her apartment, given his gifts to her maid, and kept him in fear and trembling. She has even provoked him into beating her black and blue, so that she could enjoy his humiliation and begging for two days. All the while she knows that in humiliating him she is fanning the hate that will be turned on her. She makes him beg for forgiveness and compares his begging to a king who had incurred the Pope's displeasure and who had spent three days on his knees without eating and drinking and, while begging for the forgiveness, making vows of vengeance for that begging. Nastasya is seeking Rogozhin's knife as a final justification of her contempt for others and for herself. Yet, while this drama is playing itself out, she is painfully conscious of her love for the Prince and of another Nastasya. If Nastasya accepts the forgiveness of the Prince, she accepts a Nastasya who is pure, innocent, good. But in accepting that Nastasya, she must accept those who have hurt her as innocent and good. She must in effect give up the Nastasya whose soul has burned on pain and vengeance. And she cannot.

The Prince himself, unconsciously, throws light on Nastasya's plight and perhaps on what could have healed her soul. Early in the first part of the novel, he recounts to Mrs. Epanchin the story of his four-year stay at Schneider's sanitorium and tells his listeners of the story of the unfortunate peasant Mary. The story is an analogue to Nastasya's history, and to her relations with the Prince. Like Nastasya, Mary is seduced; like her, too, she suffers the punishment of society; like her, Mary accepts her guilt. When Mary comes back after being abandoned by the traveling salesman, the villagers, with the approval of her mother, look at Mary as some kind of loathsome insect. The men cease to treat her as a woman, use foul language in her presence, and even cease to feed her. She roams the fields alone, sleeps in the open air, and finally earns crusts of bread by looking after cattle. When the mother dies, the Pastor joins in the condemnation and points his finger at her as the cause of her mother's death.

But there are differences. Although Mary accepts her guilt, she does not accept it as justification for revolt against others and herself. And unlike Nastasya, Mary accepts the compassionate love of Myshkin and the "angel wings" of the children's love. And by accepting their love, Mary comes to accept herself as they see her. "Because of them [*cherez nikh*] she forgot her hard misery. It was as though she had received forgiveness from them, for to the very end she considered herself a great sinner."

But Mary is a half-idiot; the incident happened in a foreign land, in a mountain village, and it has the air of a fable. Mary is, after all, not Nastasya, and perhaps the angel wings of the children's love would have been scattered to the winds before the breath of Nastasya's will.

Ippolit

If one were to define the central intrigue of the novel as Nastasya's choice between Rogozhin and Myshkin, Ippolit would be there to deny it. He dominates the middle of the novel, and he has almost nothing to do with the choice Nastasya must make between the Prince and Rogozhin. He arranges the meeting between Aglaya and Nastasya, but there seems to be no special reason why he should do so. But Ippolit, too, is seeking his rights, and the measure of his rights are similar to Nastasya Fillipovna's. He, too, has been "hurt," and only the agent of hurt has been different. He has been offended by a universe that is deaf to his excellence, to his beautiful soul, and to the great service he might have shown to mankind.

When we first meet him, as part of the Burdovsky company, he is a lad of eighteen, suffering from consumption and condemned to death in the flower of his youth. Under the pressure of death, he is struggling between belief in nothingness and belief in beauty and goodness of life. This struggle is caught in contrasting images: the image of Meyer's wall and the Pavlovsky trees. Meyer's wall, outside the window where he lies in sickness, is an image of the blank and meaningless universe. The Pavlovsky trees, which he has come to see for the last time, are an image of a universe with beauty and purpose. It is the wall he finally believes in, and not the trees: "That damned wall! And yet it is dearer to me than all the Pavlovsky trees, that is, it would be dearer if it did not matter to me now!"

Because of his sickness and the conviction that he has only a few weeks—a month at the most—to live, and because of the "wall" he believes in, he makes the decision to kill himself. His suicide will be an act of defiance against the dumb, indifferent laws of nature. This is his final decision, and he has written it all down in a thick testament of faith. Nastasya's final decision had been a gesture of defiance before the society that had hurt her; Ippolit's, a gesture of defiance before the universe that has hurt him. At the Prince's birthday party, amid the sound of champagne bottles and the clamor of debate between Lebedev and others about the railroads and the poisoning of the waters of life by progress, Ippolit rises to explain why he has come to his "final decision." The sources of his decision go back to the beginning of his illness six months before.

At that time he had closed himself in his room, and had

contemplated death and the nothingness of the wall, the wasted hopes, aspirations, and dreams of his eighteen years. During this period he does his last good deed by helping a provincial doctor, who is near exhaustion and poverty, to regain his position and reestablish himself. It is also a humanitarian impulse that brings him out to defend Burdovsky's "rights" against the Prince, and it is after this melee that he makes his first confession. He explains later that his intention at that time was to unite himself in a final farewell with the people there. And it is there also that he is first filled with the idea of his "final decision," to take his life into his own hands, and in that way pay nature back by destroying quickly what it was indifferently destroying. But the specific act that moves him from reverie to action is his meeting with Rogozhin and the sight of Holbein's picture of Christ's descent from the cross, which hangs in Rogozhin's apartment. Christ's body in Holbein's pictures is a human body, one that has been indifferently mangled by the dumb laws of nature: it has been beaten; the face is swollen with bruises; the body is still warm; the whites of the eyes still glisten, not with a spiritual light, but with the glassy lusterless and depthless sheen of the dead. In looking at such a body Ippolit cannot understand how the apostles and others who were witnesses could have believed that Christ was eternal.

A short time after seeing the picture Ippolit dreams that someone leads him with a lighted candle to look at a huge and horrible tarantula, who is the deaf and dumb infinite power that rules the universe. Ippolit remembers that after this dream Rogozhin entered his half-dream, half-waking consciousness—although he knew that Rogozhin could not have entered because his doors were locked—and laughed at his indignation at a universe ruled by a dumb beast. It is after seeing Holbein's picture and having his dream of the tarantula that Ippolit makes his last decision: to destroy himself as a last free act against the dumb power of the universe. He tells us: "That apparition humiliated me. I cannot humble myself before a dark power which takes the form of a tarantula."

Ippolit anticipates the arguments of Kirilov and Ivan in his revolt against the forces of the universe. Like Ivan, he admits that there may be an eternal life and some kind of eternal force; like him, he needs a force against which to revolt. Like Ivan, he refuses to accept a universe beyond his comprehension as a pledge—in some ultimate logarithmic calculation—of some kind of eternal harmony. Like Ivan—placing all his evidence on his "I am" and his personal indignation—he refuses to accept the universe as his mind understands it. If he had had the power of choosing not to be born, he would have so chosen. All he has left is the power not to live. It is with this suicide that he will show his freedom (anticipating Kirilov), doing the only free act he has left.

All of this raises Ippolit to a heroic level, for he is expressing some of Dostoevsky's most powerful arguments against Christ, faith, humility, and the acceptance of God. Indeed, he even expresses some of Dostoevsky's own cherished convictions. When he says that Columbus was most happy when he was discovering America, and not when he discovered it, that "it is life that matters, life alone— the continuous and eternal process of discovering it—and not the discovery itself!" he is saying what the Underground Man said, and what Dostoevsky said many times in his nonfictional writings. And yet despite the sympathy we feel for Ippolit's illness, his wasted youth, his sensitivity and suffering, and despite his heroic stand against the dumb laws of nature, we progressively see Ippolit also as something other than a sensitive, suffering youth, living for truth, beauty, and the happiness of all men. We know that the Ippolit who survives his attempted suicide and who appears in the last part of the novel is a very different Ippolit. He is petty, bickering, cruel, envious, spiteful. He tyrannizes over his mother, venomously attacks Ganya, spreads gossip, and is heartless and cruel to the pathetic weaknesses of General Ivolgin.

The two faces of Ippolit are one. If we go back to the sympathetic portrait we get in his two confessions, the roots of the petty, selfish, spiteful, sadistic coward of the last pages of the novel are already in the first sympathetic portrait. When he fell sick, he was a tyrant at home: he would not permit anyone to come into his room except to bring food; his mother trembled before him and went around the house whipping the children so that they wouldn't disturb him. He tortured Kolya, and especially Surikov, a fellow lodger. Surikov had been pursued by a series of misfortunes. Poor, ragged, and abased in character, he had watched his wife and baby die and his daughter forced into prostitution, helpless to prevent any of it. Ippolit feels no pity: "Oh, I've never, never had any pity for these fools, not now and not before—I say this with pride! Why isn't he a Rothschild? Whose fault is it that he hasn't millions, like Rothschild, that he doesn't have mountains of gold sovereigns, mountains as high as a carnival show? He's alive, so everything's in his power!" When Surikov was unable to buy medicine to save his baby, Ippolit made a special trip to him to tell him it was all his fault.

Ippolit is cruel and pitiless before the misfortunes of others and egoistical and self-glorifying in his dreams of helping humanity. When we look at his "humanitarian dreams" and his frustration over a wasted life, we find that they are shot through with impulses of self-glorification. After he reaches out touchingly to those present at his first confession, he then buries his head in shame because he has reached out. When he lifts his head—wheezing and foaming at the mouth—he turns with venom upon the Prince, whose compassion he takes for humiliating pity. He blames the Prince for bringing him to a shameful display of feeling. He looks upon his confession as cowardice, and upon the pity and compassion of those around him as contempt. Even his confession is rife with self-glorification: he wanted to be a man of action because "he had a right to," and he compares himself to Christ in his frustrating impotence before nature. His image of frustrated heroism is naïve and taken from sentimental novels. His fondest wish was to be chased out on the street as an eighteen-year-old, with only his clothes on his back, alone, in a large city, without lodging, work, friends, relatives, and a scrap of bread. Then he would show them.

If there were any doubts about the core of self-interest that corrupts his nature, his final explanation would remove it. The final explanation is blatantly egoistical, naïvely posed, and pathetically self-loving. He comes to the Prince's party prepared with a thick manuscript that takes more than an hour to read. The manuscript has a red seal to provoke mystery, and an epigraph from Louis XIV—"*Après moi le déluge*"—to show its importance. He consistently compares himself to great people like Louis, Napoleon, Columbus, and Christ; and he plays shamelessly on the suspense of what he is going to reveal. Although he has decided to kill himself at sunrise in the park so as not to disturb anyone, he leaps up on a chair as if on a stage, prefaces his reading with a quotation from the angel of the Apocalypse, "There will no longer be time," and advises the Prince to take notes on what he is to say. He orates his decision in the accents of the stage. Most important of all, he has no real intention of killing himself, but only of astounding into admiration all those about him.

It is not a question of hypocrisy. There is no reason to doubt Ippolit's sincerity: he has wanted to work for the benefit of humanity, to do some great deed or proclaim some great truth for its sake. The suffering he undergoes over what he believes is impending death is also genuine, as are his indignation and revulsion at a universe empty of beauty, love, or purpose. Nor is there any doubt that he *wishes* to kill himself in a gesture of heroic defiance. Yet it all turns out differently.

Ippolit is a humanist who, no matter how sincere his

desires, cannot do anything good for humanity; a hero who can only assume the gesture of heroism. *Ippolit embodies one of Dostoevsky's most important ideas: a corrupted nature (and a corrupted nature is one that believes in itself, and not in God) corrupts everything it touches, no matter how noble, good, sympathetic, and grand it may appear.* To stress this point Dostoevsky includes Ippolit's long anecdote about his last good deed.

Ippolit accomplishes a last good deed: an impoverished and desperate provincial doctor regains his position and means of livelihood; a family close to starvation is helped by his intervention. And Ippolit is sincere in wanting to do a last good deed before sickness takes him from the earth. Yet the good deed, despite Ippolit's sincere intention and the fact that the doctor is helped, is a self-interested act, a deed in which the movement of Ippolit's heart is not one of sacrifice for the doctor's family, but of the sacrifice of the family for him. Throughout the incident Ippolit is conscious of how he can use the act. When he returns the wallet to the doctor, he is not moved by compassion for the doctor's plight but by the pleasure he feels in impressing the doctor, and by the power he feels in changing the course of the doctor's life. Thus, he consciously (*tak vprochem sledovalo*) adopts a tone of quiet dryness and calm, which sets off the doctor's fright and gratitude all the better. By refusing to react to the doctor's irritation at having entered the room, and by minimizing his influence, he reduces the doctor to remorse and shame for his conduct. Everything is manipulated as if it were in a novel: "Everything came about and was settled, as though it had been purposely arranged, exactly as in a novel."

There is nothing to indicate that Ippolit does not believe that the universe is dumb and senseless, that immortality is a sham, and that the dumb force of the universe did not even spare Christ, the most perfect of creatures. But having turned from God, he can turn only to himself, and every good quality—according to the inexorable workings of Dostoevsky's moral dialectic—is corrupted because it must serve him. What he wants is not so much to express his convictions about the universe and suicide, but to *use* these convictions to force those about him to admire him for his daring and to force them to beg him to change his intention. Dostoevsky denies to Ippolit both "goodness" and "courage"; the first is a logical consequence of his moral dialectic; a man without faith cannot be good, no matter how sincere his intention. The other does not follow logically, but is a gratuitous debasing of Ippolit. Later Dostoevsky will give to Kirilov almost the same motivations and the same train of reasoning, but will also grant him the courage to be wrong.

There are those in the audience who are not taken in by Ippolit's theatrical and hysterical self-love and who insist from the very beginning that he is shamming. Ganya, Ptitsyn, Radomsky, and Rogozhin see exactly what Ippolit is up to; Myshkin, Vera, Kolya, and Mme. Epanchin do not. They are taken in, for they react with alarm, anxiety, and compassion for Ippolit when he attempts to kill himself. Yet, though Myshkin, Vera, and Mme. Epanchin are incorrect intellectually, they are correct morally; and although Ganya, Ptitsyn, Radomsky, and Rogozhin are right intellectually, they are wrong morally. When Ippolit cries out dramatically that the sun has risen (the time he has appointed for killing himself), Ferdyshchenko says sarcastically: "Did you think that it would not rise?" Ganya remarks with perfunctory irritation and in obvious deflation of Ippolit's heroic inflation: "Again a sizzler for the whole day." When it seems that Ippolit is reaching for his gun and is grabbed by four persons, Rogozhin observes rightly: "That is what he was leading up to; he wanted them to hold his hands; that is why he read his essay." They see correctly the falseness of Ippolit, and yet they are wrong. They are wrong because they judge that falseness; the Prince and Mme. Epanchin fail to see Ippolit's falseness, and yet they are right because they feel compassion for him. Dostoevsky's right and wrong are not determined by the facts in some objective sense. People are right when their hearts are right, no matter what the facts, and they are wrong when their hearts are wrong.

Lebedev

Nastasya and Ippolit express the paradox of the self's tragedy. Nastasya pursues its bitter pleasure unto death, and Ippolit shows how subtle and infinite are the deceptions the self draws over its motives. Nastasya is conscious of her motives. She chooses death and the bitter pleasure of the self without deception; Ippolit deceptively and almost comically believes he is living for the glory of mankind, and he chooses a death of heroic sacrifice (a suicide he really doesn't intend). The other characters show how the self seeks its rights in the grooves of society: mechanically and tiredly with Totsky, raucously and crudely with Lebedev's nephew and the Burdovsky crowd; viciously and meanly in Ganya's dream of becoming a Rothschild. Everyone is seeking his rights, and some attain the narrowness of their vision by money and social rank. One of the dramatic functions of the "lower" elements in the novel is to bring out clearly and even vulgarly the values that rule in the upper classes. Nowhere is this made clearer than in the parallelism Dostoevsky pursues between the Ivolgin family and the Epanchin family. The Ivolgins are the unsuccessful Epanchins. When we first meet Ganya and General Epanchin, we find them both struggling for advantage over the same woman, but because of their unequal social positions, Ganya is forced to accept the humiliation of being a lackey and pimp to General Epanchin. He is to be forced to marry a woman, while General Epanchin waits in the antechamber to possess her. He is the keeper of the General's pleasure. Ganya is General Epanchin in the making; General Ivolgin is an Epanchin who has failed. He had enjoyed the same society as Epanchin, but had been recently excluded from that society. Like Golyadkin, the exclusion had been more than he could bear, and he has retreated to a fantasy world where he gives advice to Napoleon and holds council with the great men of his era. During the siege of Sevastopol, for example, a truce is called to permit a famous physician to come to him in the name of science and to examine the thirteen bullets that are lodged in his chest. General Ivolgin's moments of high honor and sophisticated decorum are a caricaturing parallel to the same values by which General Epanchin lives. The parallel is pursued in the other members of the family. The daughter Vera is proud and quick-tempered as is Aglaya; she is forced to sell herself to Ptitsyn, the grubby financier, as the Epanchin daughters are offered for sale, but in a more decorous manner. The society is corrupt, and the mirror of that corruption is Lebedev.

It is a paradox that Lebedev, the most corrupt of the society's members, should pronounce the judgment on this society. He is a drunkard and lecher; he is faithless, covetous, and incorrigibly self-seeking. He is shamelessly hypocritical: he helps Keller write a defamatory letter against the Prince and then condemns the letter; he is corrupt and self-seeking: he does not defend the old woman who has been victimized by a usurer, but defends the usurer; he is unsympathetic and cruel: he taunts the helpless General Ivolgin and caricatures his pathetic sense of honor. And he is a betrayer of trust: he betrays the Prince repeatedly, and near the end of the novel he is busy trying to commit him to a mental institution.

Lebedev is nothing, as he himself exclaims on several occasions, and yet Lebedev is the living truth, because he embodies with almost caricaturing frankness all the corruptions of the society he lives in. He is the mirror of their souls, acting out without decorum, or measure, or concealment the codes by which they live. He is the society's conscience, taking its sins into his body and pronouncing words of judgment. Significantly, he often refers to himself in the third person, repeats the words of others, as if he were a verbal mirror, and pantomimes the gestures of others about him. He is Dostoevsky's great clown, a rival of Shakespeare's clown in *King Lear*. There is not a corruption of the society that he does not act out and which he does not embody: he is a sycophant like Ganya before Epanchin, and Epanchin before Mme. Obolonskaya; he is a lecher like Totsky, a drunkard like Ivolgin, and a hypocrite and self-seeker like almost everyone in the novel. And whatever atonement this society feels—like the self-congratulatory confessions of Totsky and Epanchin at Nastasya Fillipovna's gathering—Lebedev captures in the smirking and self-pleased gesture of beating his breast and exclaiming *"mea culpa, mea culpa."*

It is to Lebedev that Dostoevsky grants the judgment of this society, and it is to him that he entrusts a defense of his own convictions. At Prince Myshkin's birthday party, Lebedev attacks with passion the ideas and convictions of most of those present, and particularly the ideas and convictions of Ganya, Radomsky, and Ptitsyn. Dostoevsky would agree with what Lebedev says. Lebedev and Dostoevsky do not believe in bread without a moral basis. They believe that "a friend of humanity with shaky moral principles is a devourer of humanity, to say nothing of his vanity: hurt the vanity of any one of these innumerable friends of humanity, and he is ready at once to set fire to the world out of petty revenge, exactly like any one of us, and, to be fair, like myself, the vilest of all, for I will perhaps be the first to carry the fuel and run away myself." To be sure, he tells all this to a smiling and unbelieving audience. Sure of their enlightened beliefs, they look upon the views of Lebedev as equally grotesque as his actions generally are. To entertain his listeners further, Lebedev tells them a grotesque story about a medieval man who during a famine turned to cannibalism and ate sixty monks and six small boys. Finally, and in full knowledge of the medieval tortures, he gave himself up to the ecclesiastical authorities. Lebedev's moral is obvious: if a man with a conscience can, because of circumstances, be driven to cannibalism, then what may be expected of an age with no conscience?

Prince Myshkin

Into this society, where the fire of conscience has become the reflection in everyone's eyes of the burning 100,-000 rubles, and among those who would set the world on fire to satisfy a bruised ego, the Prince—like a knight with only his innocence as his armor—comes. He comes without friends, family, and almost without country. Russia to him, because of his long stay abroad, is like a foreign land. Even the language from lack of use is a little strange to him. He is of her, but he sees her afresh. Prince Myshkin is Dostoevsky's great love; he is his attempt to conquer that seemingly impossible task of creating a good man who is dramatically interesting and believable. But if he is meant to be the dramatic center of interest, he is a failure, since he is more often only a listening post, a sensitive recorder of the passions that explode about him. He holds far less dramatic interest than do Nastasya Fillipovna, Ippolit, and perhaps even Lebedev. Yet he is one of the great limited successes of literature.

In this large and rambling novel, he brings together all its varied richness. He is of ambiguous social status and without social pretension; hence he moves easily in the varied social classes of the novel. He has no self-interested motives; and he has thus the time and patience to listen to others. People often forget that he is present and talk freely to him or in his presence. His arrival is often a kind of descent of quietness into a storm. His most salient trait is that he refuses to be hurt or insulted. When we first meet him on the train with Rogozhin and Lebedev, he refuses to feel ashamed that he has no clothes and no place to sleep. The doorman at Epanchin's tries to insult him, but

the Prince good-naturedly does not take the insult. Epanchin is rude without provocation, treating Myshkin like a
beggar. Myshkin good-naturedly suffers the insults, and
by suffering them changes Epanchin's attitude. When
Ganya slaps the Prince for restraining him from slapping
his sister, the Prince not only receives the slap that was
meant for Varya, but he suffers the frustration and shame
that had led Ganya to slap him. By suffering the slap, by
"absorbing" the hurt, the Prince brings Ganya to remorse
and even to love. *The Prince pays for the hurt that is
visited on him by accepting it and suffering it, and by
suffering it he breaks the vicious circle of hurting and
being hurt, and by breaking the circle, he effects changes
in others.* To be sure, the changes are not permanent. The
repentance and affection he moves Ganya to will only later
doubly anger Ganya, because his repentance becomes his
humiliation. But this is only to say that the realism of
psychology prevails.

There is another characteristic of the Prince that is just
as important and to some extent allied. This is his refusal
to accept the corruptions of a person as the person himself:
the desire to make of Rogozhin a brother, of Nastasya
Fillipovna a wife and paragon of virtue, of the corrupt
self-seeking noblemen gathered to pass judgment on his
marriage to Aglaya, exemplary and disinterested servants
of the Russian people. He sees the corruptions of the people
about him, but he refuses to believe in the corruptions.
He refuses to accept Nastasya Fillipovna as she fears she
is, Rogozhin as the humiliated lover nourishing hate and
revenge for what he loves, Ippolit as the naïve, self-loving
egoist. To be sure, by some objective standard of judgment, they are that. But in Dostoevsky's world there is no
"objective" standard, no "objective" reason; there are only
people, and they create what they believe in. Ippolit is
what the Prince carries in his heart and his soul, and Nastasya
is what he believes her to be; but Ippolit is also what he
believes himself to be, and Nastasya is what she believes

herself to be. One's faith in oneself can change one's life, and one's faith in others can change them, at least in part. Dostoevsky illustrates this by showing how by a lack of faith Myshkin "creates" or "incites" Rogozhin to attempt to murder him.

The Prince's moral crisis comes in the second part of the novel. After Nastasya's birthday party, the Prince does not return to St. Petersburg for six months. When he returns, he seeks out Rogozhin and assures him that he has not returned as a competitor, and specifically denies that he intends to see Nastasya again. After leaving Rogozhin, the Prince fails to find General Epanchin or Kolya, and in a half-dreamlike state wanders about St. Petersburg, followed by the "eyes" which he had been conscious of in getting off the train that morning. He buys a ticket for Pavlovsk, sits down on the train, and then, disturbed by a thought that had been pursuing him, rises and goes off again. He remembers, or thinks he remembers, standing in front of a store window looking at an item. He goes off to check whether the store exists, and whether he had really been standing in front of it. The item is a silver knife, and it is tied in the Prince's consciousness to the knife that Rogozhin had recently bought, and which he had handled that morning in the Prince's presence. And the knife is tied in the Prince's mind to his fears of Rogozhin's intentions regarding Nastasya; and it is in pursuit of his "fears" or, as he exclaims to himself later, those "eyes" that he goes off to see whether or not Nastasya is at home. The sudden dark thought of temptation that floods his mind and weakens his will prompts him to see whether it is Rogozhin who has been following him. He knows that Rogozhin is jealous of him and suspects his motives, and the Prince acts to confirm Rogozhin's suspicions. He knows what he is doing is base: that in looking for the eyes, in tracing back his steps to that store and that item, and especially in going to see Nastasya Fillipovna, he is "imagining" what Rogozhin will do. And in imagining what another will do, he is anticipating it, and in anticipating it, creating it. The Prince creates, or at least helps to create, the attack upon himself that takes place on the landing in his hotel.

This is the Prince's fall; it anticipates Alyosha's fall from faith when the Elder dies, but in many respects it is subtler and more refined. The Prince fails, if only for a while, to live up to his own conception of the "essence" of religion and right action. Shortly before Rogozhin's attack on him, he had explained what the essence of religion was for him. He illustrates his understanding by telling Rogozhin of four experiences that he had early after his return to Russia. The first is a conversation he had with an educated, well-bred atheist who, in talking about religion, talked about something else without knowing it. The second was an incident that had occurred at a provincial hotel where he had stopped. On the previous night a peasant had murdered his friend for a silver watch, and as he cut open his friend's throat like that of a sheep, begged forgiveness of God. The third incident had to do with a drunken soldier who had duped him into buying a tin cross under the pretense that it was silver. The fourth concerned the words of a peasant woman who compared the delight a mother feels when her child smiles at her with the delight the heavenly father must experience when a sinner turns to him. "The essence of religious feeling," the Prince tells Rogozhin, "has nothing to do with any reasoning, or any crimes, misdemeanors, or atheism; there is something else here, and it will always be so; there is something here our atheists will always overlook, and they will never talk about *that*. But the important thing is that you will see it most clearly and readily in a Russian heart. That is what I've decided."

The Prince's conception of the essence of religion is paradoxically contained in the gesture of a murderer, the words of an ignorant peasant woman, and in his own attitude toward a thief. The peasant is weak and cannot resist temptation, but he knows that he is doing wrong. In knowing he is sinning, he acknowledges God. It is not the act as such, but the movement of the heart toward God that defines the religious value of a man. Similarly, the first movement of the Prince's heart had been toward judgment of the soldier, but he refrains from doing so. How can the Prince—or any man, Dostoevsky implies—know what lies behind the motive to deceive? How can anyone, except God, know the infinity of each man's soul? Prince Myshkin refrains from an act of judgment, for an act of judgment is an act of will and an arrogation of God's right. To judge is to lose one's faith in God. The essence of religion lies not in the act—not in the crime or the statement of atheism, or in the act of deception—but in the movement of the heart and soul toward God or in the free act of faith in which the soul turns its face from the self toward God. This is why Myshkin is so delighted by the words of the peasant woman. She sees correctly the essence of religion in man's face turned to God, as the baby's is turned to its parent.

The Prince's effect is limited. Indeed, sometimes he seems only to incite a more vicious hatred in a person by his refusal to be hurt. Ippolit repays the Prince's sympathy more than once by hating him more. This is inevitable, because the self-willed person will mistake every kindness as an act of the will. One can argue that the Prince is a complete failure, because he leaves the world as he had found it, perhaps even worse. The Epanchins and Totskys and Ptitsyns go on. Ippolit, before his death, is more vicious and petty than ever. Ganya is still trying to be a Rothschild. Aglaya, humiliated by his rejection of her, emigrates, marries a Pole, and becomes a Catholic (a fate Dostoevsky reserved only for the worst). Nastasya is murdered, Rogozhin loses his mind, and the Prince himself is taken back to the world of idiocy from which he emerged. The love and sympathy he brings to the world seem only to have blown more hotly on the conflagration of human hate and self-will.

Never is the Prince's helplessness more pathetic and more appealing than in the scene in which he stands between the hot tongues of Nastasya and Aglaya, and never is it more beautiful than in the final scene when he lies by the body of Nastasya and consoles the broken spirit of Rogozhin.

In the meeting between Aglaya and Nastasya, the veil of politeness is torn with the first words, and Aglaya pours forth venom and humiliation upon the white-faced Nastasya. Her criticism degenerates quickly into open abuse of Nastasya's virtue. She gleefully ends up pointing out that an honest woman would have become a washerwoman rather than choose Nastasya's path. Aglaya uses every weapon she can to hurt, even the truth. Her perception is sharp: she sees that Nastasya likes her hurt, needs it, that there was much that was theatrical in the way she gave up Totsky, that in working for the union of Myshkin and Aglaya she was flattering herself with her "virtuous" deed, and that in going off with Rogozhin she was playing the part of a fallen angel. Nastasya pays back in kind. She points out what Aglaya will not admit to herself: that she had come to see Nastasya out of fear. She was afraid that the Prince might love Nastasya more than her, and she had come to crush what she feared.

The Prince is not only helpless before the living hate, but is himself used by it. Each of the women uses the Prince to hurt the other: The Prince is finally forced to choose between them, and he succeeds in his fumbling way in choosing neither and humiliating both. The moment of hesitation on his part sends Aglaya rushing out of the room; the gesture of pursuit after her sends Nastasya into a faint of despair. When she awakens, she sees that the Prince has remained with her, and she is hysterically exultant. The Prince strokes her hair and cheeks as he will do with the hysterical and raving Rogozhin in the beautiful last scene.

The final scene is one of Dostoevsky's greatest. Throughout the novel we see Nastasya Fillipovna only in action: her body, eyes, gestures, and lips are in constant movement. When she is still, her eyes are flashing and her lips trembling; her dresses rustle, and her breath is hysterically heavy. But in the final scene she lies in motionless sleep, and only the beating of the Prince's heart is heard in the room as he peers into her bed. The white sheet annihilates the color and movement of her body and outlines only the vague contour of someone sleeping a motionless sleep. There is something frighteningly final and horrible in Dostoevsky's insistence on the neuter and indefinite reference to what is sleeping on the couch. The Prince sees only "someone" (*kto-to*), or "the sleeping one" (*spavshy*), and upon closer examination only limbs and the tip of a foot.

All night the Prince and Rogozhin lie by the side of the white figure, and in the morning when Rogozhin begins to scream and laugh, the Prince smoothes his hair and cheeks, as a final gesture in his attempt to soothe the hurt and to take it upon himself. The Prince is a failure as Christ was a failure, helpless to check the hurt that we do to each other, but ready to take it upon himself and by his own faith to give to all an image of the best of themselves. When critics charge him with being a failure, they seek what is dramatically unbelievable and morally impossible. The Prince cannot change the universe, but a universe of Myshkins might. The Prince is a success because for a moment he is able to kindle the faith in others of a truer image of themselves; for a few minutes he is able to quiet, by his own suffering, the rage of insult upon insult. His faith, or the faith of anyone, can change another person only if the person accepts the faith, or accepts the forgiveness, or, what is the same thing, forgives himself—all the most difficult things in Dostoevsky's world.

7

The Possessed

LATE IN THE NOVEL an extraordinary scene takes place between Peter Verkhovensky and Stavrogin. Stavrogin has just left a disorderly meeting of revolutionaries assembled by Peter at Virginsky's when he is overtaken by a breathless Peter at Kirilov's. There Peter delivers a startling confession, the high point of which is the following:

"Stavrogin, you're beautiful!" Verkhovensky cried out almost in ecstasy. "Do you know that you are beautiful? . . . You are my idol! You're just the sort of man that's needed. I—I especially need a man like you. I don't know anyone but you. You're the leader, the sun, and I am your worm."
He suddenly kissed his hand. A shiver ran down Stavrogin's spine, and he switched his hand away in dismay.

Upon this follows Peter's vision of the new world that will rise on the ashes of the old one. By the ministrations of monstrous vice, people will be reduced to the condition of happy slaves and fearful gratitude before the supreme autocratic will, which will give unity and cohesion to the new society.
There are two centers of gravity in the novel, and the

magnetic force that binds them is felt in the trembling adoration Peter expresses for Stavrogin and in his mad vision of a new world. There is the political pamphlet and the metaphysical drama, and they have only the weakest of structural ties. Peter is the center of the political drama, and Stavrogin the center of the metaphysical drama; and most of the characters belong to one or the other. The socialists belong clearly to Peter's plot, and just as clearly Shatov and Kirilov belong to Stavrogin's plot. The two dramas mix only tangentially. Peter may need Kirilov to take the blame for Shatov's death, and Shatov's death to bind his group in fear of blood, but he does not need Kirilov's monstrous dialectic or Shatov's messianic Christianity.

Dostoevsky himself had trouble connecting the two dramas. He began with a political pamphlet, but the metaphysical drama progressively took over. In a letter to Katkov, Dostoevsky, speaking first of Peter, says: "To my own great surprise this character comes out half comic for me. And despite the fact that he and the murder are of the utmost importance in the novel, they are nevertheless only accessory and a kind of background for another figure, whom one might really call the chief character of the novel. This other character (Nikolay Stavrogin) is a dark and criminal figure, but he seems to be a tragic figure." [1]

Peter and Stavrogin bring together the metaphysical and political dramas, but the beginning of both lies in Stepan Trofimovich, the father of Peter and the tutor of Stavrogin. He begins and ends the novel, giving birth to the events and also bringing them to a prophetic conclusion. What ends in chaos, fire, murder, and crime begins with him. Dostoevsky says almost the same thing in a letter to Maykov: "Stepan Trofimovich is a secondary personage, and my novel is decidedly not about him; but his story is tightly tied with the other events (the most important) of the novel, and I have therefore taken him as the cornerstone of everything." [2]

When the novel opens, Stepan Trofimovich has been

safely ensconced for a decade in a small provincial town; he lives comfortably under the protection of Varvara Petrovna, the mother of Stavrogin, and is the intellectual leader of the town. About him grows a small circle of the town's "free thinkers"; the townspeople look upon the circle as a hotbed of radicalism. Its members include Liputin, a scandalmonger, family tyrant, and miser; he locks up the scraps of food and the candle ends each night, but dreams nevertheless of Fourieristic phalansteries; Virginsky, who with his wife gets all his ideas from books and who always speaks in a whisper and with deep feeling about the "bright hopes" which he will never abandon; Lyamshin, the post-office clerk who does imitations on the piano of the squeals of pigs, thunderstorms, and the first cry of a baby. Later, Shatov becomes a member of the circle.

At these meetings Stepan Trofimovich orates about love, art, country, and religion to the applause of the members, whose eyes and wits have been dimmed by champagne. And there—as improbable as it may seem—the holocaust that descends upon the small town—the madness of the fête, the murders, the fires, and the moral degeneration of the town—are all prepared. But so, too, Dostoevsky tells us, our "Belinskys and Granovskys would not believe it if you told them that they were the direct fathers of the Nechaevs. It is precisely the close development of this thought, going from fathers to children that I want to express in my work." [3] The harmless talk of Stepan Trofimovich includes ideas on three topics dear to Dostoevsky's heart: the peasants, Russian nationalism, and God. According to Stepan Trofimovich, Rachel is worth more than all the peasants of Russia, who for the past hundred years had given Russia only the Kamarinsky dance; Russian nationalism is an outdated opinion and the consequence of sloth and idleness; and the God of the people is something to snicker at. This is the substance of his high liberalism—liberalism without an aim—and of his love for humanity and the fuel for Virginsky's bright hopes. The people are a joke, Russian nationalism is an opinion—and an old and unmerited one at that—and God is a function of the liberal mind. True, it is all innocent chatter, the bloated rhetoric of a comfortable and good-natured buffoon, orated to the approval of the champagne-soaked voices of the circle and the thumpings of Lyamshin on the piano. *The circle is both ideologically and structurally the source of the public events that follow.* These events culminate in the murder of Shatov, the suicide of Kirilov, the murders of Liza and the Lebyadkins, the madness of the fête, with its aftermath of fire, murder, and disintegration. What brews in Stepan Trofimovich's circle is brought into being in Julia von Lembke's circle and Peter Verkhovensky's circle. *Dostoevsky uses three circles as structure points of reference in tracing the growth of intellectual and moral degeneration.*

Julia von Lembke, the newly arrived governor's wife, is possessed by ambition. She dreams foolishly and romantically of conquering all the radicals of the province by her wit and kindness and of bringing upon herself the adoration of the radicals and the beneficence of a grateful government. "She dreamed of *giving happiness* and reconciling the irreconcilable, or, rather, of uniting everything and everybody in the adoration of her own person." With her circle a revolution in the town's hierarchy takes place. There is a shift in the intellectual leadership from Stepan Trofimovich to his son, who is the real power behind Julia von Lembke's circle, and in social leadership from Varvara Petrovna, the patroness of Stepan Trofimovich, to Julia von Lembke, the patroness of Peter Verkhovensky. The continuity of the change is signaled by the continuing presence of some of the same members, like Lyamshin and Liputin. With the shift in intellectual and social leadership comes a change in the intellectual and social temper. The good-natured, abstract, vague, and harmless "talk" of Stepan Trofimovich's circle becomes cynical, willful, and destructive action in the new circle. Stepan Trofimovich's liberal laughter at God, country, and the people is converted into pranks of an ugly sort. The sacrilege which was only an idea is translated into the blasphemies of putting a mouse behind an ikon and of hiding dirty pictures in the sack of the Bible seller. Stepan Trofimovich's criticism of Christianity for not appreciating women is translated into the liberal raillery of marriage and the kidnaping of a young lieutenant's wife, who is "unliberally" afraid of being punished by her husband for losing money at gambling. In going from Stepan Trofimovich's circle to Julia von Lembke's circle, we move from Stepan Trofimovich's abstract sacrileges to the ugly deeds the talk had implied. Ideas become acts. The change is symbolized by the replaying of the "Marseillaise" by Lyamshin at Julia von Lembke's circle. It was played at Stepan Trofimovich's circle at the end of an evening of high excitement and much champagne drinking. Whether it came off well or not, the narrator does not remember. When Lyamshin plays a duel between "O Du Lieber Augustin" and the "Marseillaise," "O Du Lieber Augustin" vulgarly triumphs over the high-minded rhetoric of the "Marseillaise," just as the vulgar elements of Julia von Lembke's circle have triumphed over the high liberalism of Stepan Trofimovich.

Despite the fact that the control over the forces she has gathered about her moves quickly out of her hands, Julia von Lembke is persuaded that the radicals are only boys who will finally be conquered by her high ideals. Her triumph in reconciling everybody to everything will be celebrated at the fête and the ball, which she has ostensibly organized for aid to needy governesses. Despite her plans, the fête unfolds by a logic of its own, devolving quickly into stupidity, crassness, and violence. Instead of a triumphal entrance, Julia is greeted by the wrong music and a drunken Lebyadkin reading a scandalous poem. Then follow the long and self-loving speech of Karmazinov, the impassioned plea of Stepan for the superiority of Pushkin over shoes—this is taken as an insult to liberal thought—and the hysterical approval for the curses that the fist-flailing professor from St. Petersburg hurls at Russia. The structural significance of the fête is made clear by Stepan Trofimovich and the narrator, both of whom recall Stepan Trofimovich's disastrous trip to St. Petersburg ten years before. Stepan makes his appeal to the superiority of art over shoes as he did then, and he is hooted off the stage in the same manner and by an audience just as liberal and just as crass and stupid. It is as if what had boiled and churned in St. Petersburg ten years previously had reached the provinces. The narrator tells us, in fact, that on the eve of the fête a small army of rabble, itinerants, poets with theses, seminarists, and liberals aggressively concerned with the "woman question" had invaded the small provincial town. The same crude, shrill, and aggressive clamor for human rights and the same hatred for everything Russian that had met and crushed Stepan's "high liberalism" ten years before in St. Petersburg seem to have poured into town. The mad professor from St. Petersburg, who follows Stepan, is an appropriate finale of a revolution in values and temper that had taken place from the high liberalism of Stepan Trofimovich's circle to the radical and vulgar liberalism of Julia von Lembke's circle. What is trampled on now—God, country, and the people—are the same things that Stepan Trofimovich, though more aesthetically, had laughed at. The stupidness, crassness, and destructive elements that lie just beneath the surface of Julia von Lembke's naïveté and self-deception are all openly and liberally nurtured in Peter Verkhovensky's circle.

Peter Verkhovensky's circle of secret revolutionaries is the conspiracy that Julia von Lembke had hoped to uncover and, in uncovering it, to reconcile everyone to everything. In Peter's circle the self-deception of the members is more explicit, the vulgarity more crude, and the hatred of Russia more intense. Our introduction to the members as an organized group is at the Virginsky name day party, where they have been gathered to hear explicitly the instructions Peter has brought from the European centers of revolution. He has convinced them that they are part of a vast network of "committees of five." The meeting is a bitter burlesque of the pretensions of socialists. They have gathered to organize the world, but they cannot even organize a meeting. They have gathered to preach the gospel of social harmony and the universal love of man, and they hate each other intensely and fall into chaotic disharmony over trifles. They are the flower of the town's liberalism, and never has Dostoevsky exposed more ruthlessly the contradiction between the abstract love of humanity men carry in their heads and the reality of their petty wills and vicious actions. The meeting is a chaos of conflicting, mean-minded people, who are filled with hate and contempt for each other. The spirit of the meeting is caught best in the personality and actions of Virginsky's sister, a young nihilist who has just arrived from St. Petersburg. Like a jack-in-the-box with eyes popping out, she keeps leaping to her feet to make some impassioned plea for support for suffering students and for help to arouse them to protest. Dedicated to humanity, she cannot stand the schoolboy who is present, turning on his every remark viciously, meanly, and with undisguised contempt. She calls the uncle she has not seen since childhood a fool and a spiteful person, and the schoolboy a case of arrested development.

The high point of the meeting is the calm, unhurried speech that Shigalyov makes on the necessary nature of the future society. His conclusion—in direct contradiction to the idea he started with—is that nine-tenths of the future state would be composed of happy slaves and one-tenth of masters. His scheme is an affront to those present, for Shigalyov has, with his logic, exposed the deception that lies at the core of the bright hopes of the socialists. As he himself says at the beginning of his speech—and what he says could be said of all those present—"I have come to the conclusion that all the makers of social systems, from the ancient times to our present year, have been dreamers, storytellers, fools, who contradicted themselves and who understood nothing of natural science or that strange animal called man." The meeting itself is a corroboration of this thesis, for those present have demonstrated the contradiction between the fictions men carry in their heads and the natural science of man's nature.

And just as the meeting itself provides an example of the deception that Shigalyov says has plagued all social thinkers, so too it shows us what the cohesive force of society must be. When the meeting is a babble of voices, a chaos of conflicting wills and egos, Peter Verkhovensky yawns, asks for cards, pares his fingernails, and otherwise takes no interest in the efforts of the flower of radicalism to organize itself. But at a certain point, he does bring unity and cohesion to this rabble, and he does it with the only weapon this group or any group of nihilists, socialists, or social planners can have at their command. Peter does it not with an idea, or a bright image, but with *force. For Dostoevsky only force, that is, the human will, remains when one has given up God.* Specifically, Peter asks if the members would inform on a comrade who had performed a political murder, that is, a murder that was necessary for the "cause." They are asked, in other words, to choose between loyalty to socialism and the existing moral order. Collective fear forces them to choose the murder. Later, Peter will attempt to enforce this bond of fear by an actual murder.

Peter provides with his question the hint as to why Shigalyov started with unlimited freedom and ended with unlimited despotism, and he also provides us with the hint as to what is wrong with Shigalyov's system. For despite agreement among critics that Shigalyov's system represents the extremity of Dostoevsky's dire forebodings about socialism,[4] Shigalyov himself has his "bright hope," and only Peter Verkhovensky sees it. As he tells Stavrogin shortly after the meeting, "Shigalyov is an aesthete and a fool like every philanthropist." Shigalyov's bright hope is the 10 per cent of the new order who would live in harmony of unrestricted power and absolute freedom. Peter knows that the dialectic of human psychology is such that the law which results in 10 per cent subjugating 90 per cent must necessarily operate in the 10 per cent until there remains only one will.

Peter is supremely without self-deception. Peter knows that 10 per cent free men is just as unreal as 100 per cent free; he knows that 10 per cent free men is a bright hope, and he is a man without bright hopes. Socialists have bright hopes, and he is not a socialist. As he himself says, he is a scoundrel. But this does not mean as the Soviets have bravely tried to interpret his statement, that the socialists are not scoundrels or, as Philip Rahv has tried to interpret it, that they must be something other than scoundrels. Rahv's interpretation is not even logical.[5] According to Peter, all men are scoundrels, and there are scoundrels who know they are scoundrels and those who believe they are something else. In other words, there are wise scoundrels and scoundrels who are fools. Socialists are scoundrels—like everybody—and they have bright hopes, but their bright hopes do not make them any less scoundrels. They make them fools as well as scoundrels. Peter is not a socialist because he is not a fool. He knows that the future state will have to be built on the real psychology of men, and not on the fictions of Virginsky, Liputin, or Shigalyov. He knows that reality is the human will, and that historic reality is a deadly and unremitting duel of wills. He sees what Dostoevsky saw and what the Underground Man saw and what all of Dostoevsky's great undeceived heroes were to see. Peter understands that only force will bind the conflicting egos of men into some kind of unity. Will is force, and only a greater force can resolve two conflicting forces. If there is to be harmony, it will have to be a harmony of force and will. And that will must be superior to all others, Godlike in its power to inspire submission and obedience. That will, for Peter, is Stavrogin's.

Does not Peter Verkhovensky's frantic obeisance to Stavrogin become clear now? He recognizes his spirit's father; and he recognizes the farthest reach of the strong will he is looking for. He knows that the truth of socialism is not the shining ideas of Virginsky or the Fourieristic phalansteries of Liputin's babblings, and he knows that even Shigalyov's stark discussion about the inevitable course of socialism harbors a self-deception. He knows that the future unity of society can be only a unity of force, and he sees in Stavrogin the supreme self-will that can compel society's unity.

Kirilov and Shatov

Peter is not alone in clutching Stavrogin's hand and in pleading with him to raise his banner. Shatov and Kirilov do the same with almost the same words. Liza ruins herself for one night with him, and expiates her act with a death indirectly caused by him. Dasha is ready to give up everything for him; Maria Shatov bears his son while cursing him; and Maria Timofyevna, the crippled half-wit, is his wife. Everyone needs him, and Stavrogin needs no one. He is detached, calm, quiet. He is like a dead sun about which the planets he has created continue to move with borrowed light and heat. We learn of him by these fragments of himself, which he has thrown off and which continue to live in the persons of others. Of these, Kirilov and Shatov are the most important.

They are twin creations of Stavrogin. They make a pilgrimage to America—the mecca of liberal ideas—endure its unspeakable humiliations, fall in worship before the ideas of Stavrogin, return to the same town, live together in the same house, and each in a sense causes the other's death. As each reminds him, Stavrogin has given to each the idea that consumes him, and although the ideas are contradictory, given them at about the same time. Kirilov is consumed with the passion to kill God and liberate man, Shatov with the passion of finding God and realizing man. At the core of each is a self-deception, and Stavrogin's liberation from each was a liberation from the self-deception of each. Shatov and Kirilov remind us what Stavrogin was and what he has overcome in himself.

Everything Shatov believes in, Stavrogin himself had declared more than two years before and had since given up. And everything Shatov confesses and Stavrogin had once believed in is what Dostoevsky holds most closely and dearly. According to Shatov, nations are moved by a force other than reason and science. Reason and science have never been able to give ends and indeed have never even been able to define the difference between good and evil. Man is moved rather by an unquenchable and irrational desire to go to the end and to deny the existence of an end. That is, to deny death and affirm life. God is the force that denies death, and he who affirms life carries in him the concrete attribute of God. Try to define that force, and the faith is destroyed. It is a force that is lived, and an unconditional acceptance of it is the condition of its existence. Shatov sees this force as carried in the being of the Russian people, but this is not to reduce God to an attribute of nationality, as Stavrogin cynically suggests and as critics of Dostoevsky have uniformly concluded.[6] It is an attribute of nationality only when the force is *thought* and no longer lived. If it is lived, it will and can be only your force; when it is yours and someone else's, it is no one's. Or, as Shatov puts it, when nations begin to believe in a general God, they no longer believe in God, but the idea of God. Faith in God, in the living affirmation of life, without conditions and particularly without the condition of reason's approval, sanctifies everything Shatov says about God and the Russian people. But Shatov does not have such a faith, as the remorseless questions of Stavrogin reveal. He hopes somehow that faith in the people will lead him to God, but only a faith in God will consecrate his faith in the people. As long as he poses this condition—and hence *thinks* his faith—he cannot *live* his faith in God. Stavrogin had at one point seen clearly his inability to accept God without conditions and had refused to live in the deception of believing in God and refusing to accept him.[7]

Kirilov is one of Dostoevsky's immense creations. All his life he has thought of one thing only—God. "God has tortured me all my life," he confesses, and what we see of him in the novel confirms this. So thoroughly has his "thought" devoured him that he has trouble communicating with those outside him. His language is strangely unsyntactic, and in his discussions, he seldom answers questions that are put to him; he does not seem to notice what the other person is saying. What is the idea that devours him? Albert Camus has said: *"Kirilov doit donc se tuer par l'amour de l'humanité. Il doit montrer à ses frères une voie royale et difficile sur laquelle il sera le premier. C'est un suicide pédagogique. Kirilov se sacrifie donc."* [8] Camus is partly right. Kirilov is killing himself out of love of humanity, but this is more than a "pedagogical suicide." He is not only killing God, he is usurping Christ's role. Christ died for man's sins; Kirilov will die for his misunderstandings. As a new man was created by Christ's sacrifice, so too a new man, washed clear of the fear of death and physically transformed, will inherit the earth. What Camus fails to understand is the dialectical nature of Dostoevsky's world, in which love of humanity can be hatred of humanity (without ceasing to be love), and sacrifice can be self-interest (without ceasing to be sacrifice). Kirilov is imitating Christ; he does sacrifice himself; and he does it out of love of man. But his self-imposed crucifixion is a grotesque imitation of Christ, as his love and sacrifice—despite his intention —are grotesque imitations of true love of man and true sacrifice. Kirilov does not believe in God, and he can—in Dostoevsky's logic—believe only in himself; since he believes only in himself, true love of mankind and true sacrifice are impossible.

Kirilov's logic is impeccable. As he tells Peter: "If God exists, then all is his will, and I can do nothing against his will. If God doesn't exist, then it is my will, and I am bound to express my self-will." If everything is his will, then he cannot be attached to anything, for to be attached is to depend on, and to depend on something is to restrict one's freedom. Kirilov's favorite expression consequently is *vse ravno*—"it doesn't matter." The "free man" must be indifferent to any emotion, value, or obligation. He is not free if he believes in socialism, progress, or in reason. Man's most enduring attachment has been God, and God is therefore his most rooted impediment to liberty. Indeed, all other attachments are derived from a belief in him; once God is dead (as an idea in man's consciousness), then, and only then, will man be free.

Despite his insistence that nothing matters, Kirilov seems to act as if it does. He loves children, feels sympathy for Shatov, loves life, keeps fit by exercising, and feels disgust for Peter. But these are only seeming contradictions. The new man must be indifferent to everything if he is really free, but Kirilov is not yet the new man. Only when he commits suicide and manifests his terrible freedom will he be free, or at least those who believe in his example and have killed the fear of God and afterlife will be free. Kirilov's sympathy for Shatov and his disgust for Peter are not contradictions in his reasoning but only signs that the man himself is not yet free. But there is a deception at the very core of his reasoning, and significantly it is Peter Verkhovensky who sees it and shows it up. Only Peter, with Stavrogin, is totally without deception.

Peter shows up the deceptive core of Kirilov's thinking during their curious meeting on the night Kirilov kills himself. Because he is afraid that Kirilov will lose courage, Peter tries to work himself up to a frenzied excitement—and hopefully suicide—by getting him to talk about why he must kill himself. Peter follows Kirilov's explanations with indifferent curiosity. After Kirilov explains why he will be God when he kills himself, Peter observes irritatedly, "You know what, to show my self-will, I should if I were in your place kill somebody else, and not myself." To which Kirilov answers, "To kill someone else would be the lowest point of my self-will. Such a suggestion could only come from a man with a soul like yours. I am not you; I want the highest point, and I will kill myself." By introducing high and low points of the will, Kirilov brings back the very values his act is supposed to liberate him from. On the one hand, he will prove his total indifference to any value—even that of friendship—by his act; and he must prove his indifference to any value, for otherwise he will be determined by the value he is not indifferent to. Yet he is insisting on the most important part of his will. Peter's casual remark exposed the deception at the core of his thinking, because Peter shows that the low point of his act is just as logical as the high point. To put it another way, Kirilov believes that with the death of God, man will be free to be good; but the logical consequence is that without God, man will be free to do his pleasure, and neither good nor evil will exist. Indeed, the living contradiction to his claim that the "high" part of man's "will" will follow on the killing of God is embodied in Peter. At one point in his irritated conversation with Peter, Kirilov exclaims: "Fool, I'm as big a scoundrel as you, as all, and not a decent fellow. There's never been a decent fellow anywhere." And Peter answers with a truth that is implied by Kirilov's reasoning, but one which he self-deceptively refuses to acknowledge: "So you've got it at last. How could you, Kirilov, with your intelligence, have failed to realize till now that all men are alike, that there aren't any better or worse, but that some men are more intelligent and others more stupid, and that if all are scoundrels (which incidentally is nonsense) there can be no people who are not scoundrels." Kirilov does not understand his "terrible freedom," and he cannot embody it. But one character in the novel understands it and embodies it in all its terrible and attractive aspects: Stavrogin.

Stavrogin

Stavrogin is mystery, power, and fatal attraction. While in the guard regiment and after rising into social circles that his mother had not even dreamed of, he suddenly commits a series of inconsequent and inexplicable actions: he indulges in wild bouts of vice; he runs over people with horses; he publicly insults a lady of high standing with whom he had had an affair; and he provokes duels for the pleasure of hurting others and ends up fighting two duels, guilty of starting both and killing one opponent and wounding another. He is tried and by special mercy deprived of his officer's rights and sent to a foot regiment. Because of heroism he is taken back into the officer's ranks, but once back he retires to carouse in dens with the dregs of society. What characterizes his behavior is inconsequence.

When at the age of twenty-five he comes back to Skvoreshniki, his actions are similarly irrational. For several months he behaves modestly in his home town, observing all the rules of social decorum. Then suddenly he commits three senseless and inconsequent acts: he pulls Gaganov about by the nose (because the old gentleman had a habit of saying that no one was going to pull him about by the nose), kisses Mrs. Liputin publicly, and bites the ear of the governor. These acts are all done "completely without any motive" (*sovershenno bez vsyakogo povoda*). He falls sick, and society explains these acts to itself by the sickness. The acts remind us of the spiteful and playful forays of the Underground Man, and they have a similar point. They are the testings of freedom; as the Underground Man had done, Stavrogin liberates himself from a fixed image of self by always doing the opposite. Contradiction and inconsequence become tools of revolt against one's nature, and consequently tools of one's freedom. Stavrogin first appears in the novel proper at the climax of Varvara Petrovna's Sunday gathering. By the time the gathering is over, Dostoevsky has managed to make Stavrogin the towering figure of fatal attraction, power, and mystery that he will remain throughout the novel. The metaphysical significance of Stavrogin is such that he must dramatically dominate everything about him, while he himself remains inactive. The whole scene at Varvara Petrovna's is a preparation for Stavrogin's appearance. Everything has reference to him; all mysteries lie in him; all complications start with him; and everyone's fate seems to depend on him. Stepan Trofimovich is suffering because he believes he will have to marry Dasha to cover up Stavrogin's sins; Liza has come because she suspects that Mary Lebyadkin is married to Stavrogin; and Varvara Petrovna trembles before his actions.

Mrs. Stavrogin has summoned—she never invites, and indeed talks only in the imperative—Stepan Trofimovich and Shatov to see her. Stepan's nervousness sets the atmosphere: he keeps jumping from his seat and babbling incomprehensibly. Shatov's glum presence sets the note of mystery. Mrs. Stavrogin's late arrival complicates the mystery. She brings with her Liza and the crippled Mary Lebyadkin; Mary has mysteriously attached herself to Mrs. Stavrogin, and Liza has mysteriously run after her. To the suspense of how Stepan Trofimovich's fate will be decided and the mystery of Shatov's presence is added the mystery of Mary Lebyadkin's attachment to Mrs. Stavrogin and Liza's attachment to Mary. The narrator tells us that "everyone was quiet and was waiting for some kind of denouement." Shatov is sunk in his corner, Stepan is wiping the perspiration off his brow, and Liza's eyes dart hysterically from Mrs. Stavrogin to Mary Lebyadkin.

As we learn later, Mrs. Stavrogin already suspects with sinking heart that her son is married to Mary Lebyadkin because of the anonymous letters she has received. But it is amazing how long Dostoevsky manages to postpone, not only the answer to the question of Mary's relation to Stavrogin, but the question itself. At first the reader has only Liza's inexplicable interest in the lame girl, and Mrs. Stavrogin's violent reaction to Mary Lebyadkin's innocent familiarity. Then Liza's mother arrives and scolds Liza for meddling in a scandal, and we know that some unpleasant truth is hidden in the complicating situation. Liza's mother finally cries out that the truth of the scandal has come out, and she points to Mary Lebyadkin. We are apparently about to unravel the truth that Liza's mother has pointed to. But Dasha enters the scene and suspends the unraveling; in the following conversation with Dasha, Mary Lebyadkin introduces a new complication by mentioning the money Dasha had "stolen" from her brother. What comes to light now for the first time is Stavrogin's connection with the situation, since it was he who had asked Dasha to give the money to Captain Lebyadkin. When we are ready to get back to the charge Liza's mother has made, Captain Lebyadkin appears to postpone matters again and to add further complications.

Lebyadkin serves as comic relief in a situation which Dostoevsky has built up in crest after crest of suspense. He lightens the air with his appearance. He has a flabby face, bouncing jowls, meaty hands, and is dressed incongruously in a new coat, gloves, linen, and hat. He trips over a carpet in running into the room, violates decorum by trying to pay Mrs. Stavrogin back for the money she had charitably given to Mary Lebyadkin; and when he tries to count out the money with trembling fingers, one of the bills falls to the floor. Lebyadkin is another of Dostoevsky's great clowns: though they are low in social esteem, they preserve a distorted and exaggerated sense of dignity.

Mrs. Stavrogin and Captain Lebyadkin talk to each other, but they do not communicate. Mrs. Stavrogin asks a question, and Lebyadkin takes the question into his own world, which is meaningless to her. The others present communicate no better. Stepan Trofimovich, communicating from his own private world, leaps up every once in a while to say something inappropriate to what is going on; Shatov sits sunk in his own thoughts, rising only to deliver at the end a blow that is caused by nothing apparent in the situation; Liza's laughs and stares are motivated by some private logic of her own. The social or public world is constantly being threatened by gestures and speech that well up from the individual and private worlds of those present.

When Mrs. Stavrogin is finally about to get to the bottom of her son's relationship to Captain Lebyadkin, or have Lebyadkin thrown out, it is announced that Stavrogin has arrived. With his arrival, everything seems to be at the point of being cleared up. Instead, Stavrogin's appearance is postponed, and Peter rushes in. As Peter hurries from person to person, shaking hands and chattering without end, Stavrogin appears framed in the doorway, silently surveying the scene. When he is noticed, his mother screams out at him the question that has so long been postponed: "I beg you to tell me at once, without moving from your place; is it true that this unhappy cripple—there she is—there—look at her!—is it true that she is—your lawful wife?" The question which was so long in being asked, and then so long in being put to the one person who could answer it, is again postponed. Instead of answering the question, Stavrogin walks silently across the room and kisses his mother's hand. Her question has had no effect upon him, despite the fact that it was suddenly and loudly put. We feel the wordless transfer of initiative from the stubborn and imperious Mrs. Stavrogin to her son, as indeed Stavrogin will take "control" of everything that he meets and surrounds him. Not an eyelash moves, and not one feature of his face changes. It is not only that he doesn't obey his mother's demand, he hardly seems to notice it. When he leaves, everyone bursts into excited conversation, as if wordlessly he had commanded silence while he was present. What follows is not only another postponement but a further complicating of the simple question of Stavrogin's relationship to Mary Lebyadkin. Peter explains Stavrogin's relationship to Mary as at worst (his explanations are always at worst) his having some fun. He quotes Kirilov's explanation: "You've chosen on purpose one of the most wretched human beings . . . a cripple, someone doomed to suffer disgrace and blows forever, knowing, too, that this creature was dying of comic love for you, and you're trying to mystify her on purpose simply to see what will come of it." Mrs. Stavrogin rejects this explanation in favor of one which sees Stavrogin's act as high-minded sacrifice for an unfortunate girl.

When Stavrogin returns, Shatov's blow ends the scene in mystery, as it had begun. Arising from the corner where he has sat during the whole scene, he goes over to Stavrogin and with his huge bony fist hits Stavrogin so hard that he rocks on his feet and blood drips from his mouth. Like Nastasya Fillipovna's throwing of 100,000 rubles into the fire, and Father Zossima's falling at the feet of a "murderer," we have in Shatov's blow one of those climactic gestures Dostoevsky likes to use to catch, like a camera click, the essential defining gestures of the situation. The physical pain is the smallest part of Stavrogin's triumph, for when he seizes Shatov's shoulders, a struggle goes on in the very citadel of his pride. The blow dishonors him, and he triumphs over his honor and his pride by the strength of his will. The struggle that takes place in him for several minutes is compared to someone holding onto a white-hot bar and by sheer will triumphing over the pain. Thus will Stavrogin "triumph" over everything he comes in contact with, freeing himself from dependence on anything. His marriage to Mary Lebyadkin is partly to stand it as he stands Shatov's blow and partly to liberate himself from commitment to beauty by accepting the ugliness of deformity. His plan to announce his marriage publicly is another "cross" he takes upon himself, not in sacrifice but in self-will. The truth is contained, I believe, in the affirmative answer Stavrogin refuses to give to Shatov's question: "Is it true that you declared that you saw no distinction in beauty between some brutal, obscene act and any great exploit, even the sacrifice of life for the good of humanity? Is it true that you found the same kind of beauty and equal enjoyment in both extremes?" In his next breath Shatov points explicitly to the core motive of Stavrogin and touches on the pulse of Dostoevsky's moral dialectic.

As so often at the crucial junctures of interpretation, the best translations lead one into thickets rather than clear glades. Dostoevsky says that Stavrogin married from a passion for suffering (*muchitel'stvo*), and this comes out as "You got married because of your passion for cruelty" in Magarshack, with the implied sufferer being someone else other than Stavrogin, which the context makes patently wrong.[9] Garnett translates the word as "martyrdom," and it is an example of her "interpretative" translating, which is often wrong but which here chances on a creative insight. Stavrogin is in his search for suffering imitating Christ's "martyrdom." Dostoevsky also says that Stavrogin married "from moral sensuality" (*po sladostrastiyu nravstvennomu*), which is perhaps a contradiction but which, nevertheless, points directly to the dialectic point of Dostoevsky's morality. Suffering and other moral qualities can be "self-indulgently" chosen. Magarshack obscures this point by translating it as "because of your moral turpitude," which sounds like some kind of conventional judgment. Garnett again is more faithful with "moral sensuality." Finally, Dostoevsky's "This was self-laceration" or "self-hurt" (*Tut byl nervny nadryv*) is translated unaccountably by Magarshack as "It was a case of morbid hysteria," which is wrong, widely interpretative, and pointedly insensitive to how Dostoevsky uses the term "*nadryv*."[10] Garnett translates this more faithfully as "It was a laceration of the nerves." Stavrogin represents the most complete

and the most frank—and perhaps the most courageous because undeceived—corruption of high moral truths. As the
passage above shows, he seeks suffering by marrying Mary
Lebyadkin and later announces his marriage so as to carry
"the cross" of his shame.

Stavrogin represents the totally free will, which in Dostoevsky's logic becomes the despotic will. The very act
of "freeing" is an act of "emptying." The will is threatened by every engagement, belief, and emotion. To prove
his freedom, Stavrogin must triumph over every attachment to life. As he tells Dasha in his final letter:

I've tried my strength everywhere. You advised me to do this
"that I might learn to know myself." As long as I was experi-
menting for myself and for others it seemed infinite, as it has
all my life. Before your eyes I endured a blow from your
brother; I acknowledged my marriage in public. But to what
to apply my strength, that is what I've never seen, and do not
see now in spite of all your praises in Switzerland, which I
believed in. I am still capable, as I always was, of desiring to
do something good, and of feeling pleasure from it; at the same
time I desire evil and feel pleasure from that too. But both
feelings are always too petty, and are never very strong.

Incidentally, the Magarshack translation again unaccountably leaves out "at the same time I desire evil and also feel
pleasure from that too" (*ryadom zhelayu i zlogo i tozhe
chuvstvuyu udovol'stvie*). This obscures the important leveling by Stavrogin of good and evil; and this leveling is a
logical consequence of the moral dialectic. Both good and
evil are one thing for Stavrogin: pleasure and the particular
pleasure of trying his will everywhere. The one time in the
novel that his "free" rejection of life breaks down is when
he runs off with Liza and spends the night with her. He
calls this an "impossible sincerity," for any attachment is a
contradiction to his self-willed freedom. The attempt to re-
attach himself to life is a failure, for he cannot really love
Liza.[11] She herself recognizes this.

Stavrogin represents the most complete and consistent embodiment of the principle of freedom without God. The Underground Man is the first step toward Stavrogin, but he is "attached" to life by anger, spite, revenge, and the whole range of negative emotions. Raskolnikov is really on the side of God, although he deceives himself that he wants freedom. Svidrigaylov and Rogozhin are not fully developed, and one is "attached" to sensuality, the other to Nastasya. Only Stavrogin stands undeceived, consistent, terribly and devastatingly free. The price of this freedom is necessarily to cut himself off from humanity. The necessary consequence of the free will without God, for Dostoevsky, is the death of the human being.

Peter asks Stavrogin to raise his banner because he knows that he is on Stavrogin's side, that his banner is Stavrogin's banner, and that his view of the world is Stavrogin's view of the world. He sees in Stavrogin his spirit's father, the inner principle which guides his own feverish activity. Both will later acknowledge this kinship; Peter will call Stavrogin his better half; Stavrogin will call Peter his clown. They are as much one as are spirit and act. The differences between them are aesthetic. Stavrogin is Satan in heroic defiance against God, proud unto damnation: Peter is Mephistopheles, the spirit that propagates the petty actions of evil. What Stavrogin conquers in his soul, Peter turns into practical action. As Stavrogin is the logical, undeceived outcome of the principle Kirilov attempted to reach, Peter is the logical outcome in action, and especially political action, of what is implicit in the views of the socialists.

The free will, Dostoevsky argues, leads to control over oneself and control over others. Stavrogin shows this force over himself, and against life, and Peter shows it against others. There is a correspondence between the inner drama of Stavrogin, and the outer drama of Peter. As Stavrogin kills spiritual life by controlling it, Peter kills physical life by controlling it. Dramatically, the developing inner chaos of Stavrogin is reflected in the developing outer chaos that

Peter moves. At the climactic point of self-destruction, the lines meet, and politics and metaphysic complement each other. Peter, Stavrogin's lower half, his devil, converts the movements of Stavrogin's soul into action, and brings to destruction the world that Stavrogin has brought into being. Peter is responsible for Shatov's and Kirilov's death, as Stavrogin had given them ideological life. Peter brings Liza and Stavrogin together, and as a consequence of Mary Lebyadkin's death, which he has arranged, he brings Liza to her death. Stavrogin in his suicide recapitulates in his private drama the death and destruction Peter causes in the public world.

The novel ends like Valhalla with the world that Stavrogin's spirit has brought to life set fire to by his spirit's clown, and Stavrogin himself going up with the flames. His suicide is the triumph of his will over life, even to the soaped cord which will foil any reflexive tricking of the body. Ippolit's suicide had been a fiasco; Kirilov's a deception; Stavrogin's free, conscious, and complete. It is his final triumph over life. The Stavrogin that appears in the expurgated confession chapter is unnecessary, and Dostoevsky wisely did not include it in editions of the novel after he was free of Katkov's objections. There is no inconsistency between this chapter and the Stavrogin that appears in the novel, as some critics have claimed. Those who see a repentant Stavrogin in his visit to Tikhon fail once again to understand the dialectical nature of Dostoevsky's world, for Stavrogin's "confession" is but another test of his strength, another virtue ineluctably corrupted by his strength. The portrait of Stavrogin in the confession chapter is morally consistent, but dramatically inconsistent. Throughout the novel we have a Stavrogin of silence and self-containment, a portrait that accords powerfully with the silent wasteland that his inner strength makes for him. The analytic Stavrogin of the confessional chapter mars this impassive, unattached air.

Stepan Trofimovich Verkhovensky

With the murder completed the socialists disintegrate in panic and fear. Lyamshin rushes off to confess, crawls on his knees before the authorities, and pours out all the details of the murders. Although he doesn't give up his "bright hopes," Virginsky is happy to be arrested, and happier to confess everything. Liputin is arrested in a brothel, with apparently not even the strength to put into effect his carefully laid plans for leaving the country. And yet the novel is not entirely without a hero and a ray of hope. Although Stavrogin and Peter represent the twin principles of "free will" without God, consistently and undeceptively applied, the source of both still lies in the liberalism of Stepan Trofimovich. The buffoon who orated against God, Russia, and the peasants in the name of some high liberalism at the beginning of the novel gathers stature as the novel progresses. His dignity begins when he recognizes that he had acted vilely toward Dasha when he had talked about covering up another man's sins by marrying her. Stepan Trofimovich finds his dignity in his "lowness." But Dostoevsky is realist enough to show this change occurring only faintly through the thicket of his old habits. Stepan Trofimovich remains in large measure Stepan Trofimovich: someone who knows very little about reality, who talks too much, and who cannot help embroidering everything he touches. His habits remain the same, but his perception of them, at times, has changed; he knows that he has been a babbling phony. When he sees his own falseness, he sees what is right. And he sees what his "high liberalism" has actually implied.

In his last pilgrimage he sets off to find the Russia he has never understood or indeed known. He appears suddenly out of the morning light and rain dressed outlandishly, as only his imagination could conceive: a great coat, big felt boots, umbrella, walking stick, and small bag. In a bookish gesture, he gets on his knees before Liza as the embodiment of everything that had been beautiful in his life. Then with a farewell to his past, he disappears in the fog. On the open road, which is the symbol of the reality that the garrulous Stepan had never known, he is pathetically comic. He doesn't know where he is going; he is afraid of being robbed; he doesn't know how to get into the peasant cart that stops for him; and he cannot recognize the beast that walks beside the cart as a cow.

Frightened, embarrassed, confused, he regains a shred of himself when, as with his old habit, he is taken care of by a woman. Then, the same braggart takes hold; he begins to talk to Sofia about how he loved the people and how he would sell Bibles with her. Although he hasn't read the Bible for thirty years, he will explain it to the people, and while explaining it, correct it. He becomes witty; his old habit of embroidering reality takes hold again: Mrs. Stavrogin turns out to be a brunette and Dasha a blonde, and each woman, having noticed the other's love, sacrifices herself. All three spend twenty years in high-minded sacrifice.

Still he recognizes, if only in glimmers, his own part in the sickness that has infected the town and, symbolically, all of Russia. He explains this sickness by the parable of the swine. The devils who beg Jesus to permit them to leave the sick man and to infect the swine are the accumulated sores and impurities which have infected Russia (the sick man) and which have entered the socialists, nihilists, revolutionaries, and "high liberals" (the swine). These in turn will destroy themselves (the swine who leap to destruction over the cliffs) and thus purify Russia. Stepan Trofimovich recognizes himself among the swine: "I perhaps worst of all." And in recognizing his responsibility he is no longer among them.

The Possessed *and History*

The Possessed is—despite Vivas and Payne—a finely constructed work of art, and the portrait of Stavrogin is an important advance in the refinement of Dostoevsky's moral dialectic. But *The Possessed* is also, as we are often reminded, history. Despite the fact that Dostoevsky took many of his plots from hints he found in newspapers, no other of his novels stems more directly from known events. We know, for instance, that both the central political intrigue and Peter himself are modeled on Nechaev and his own conspiratorial activity, that the fire and madness of the fête were probably provoked by the fires of the French commune, which took place while Dostoevsky was writing *The Possessed*, that Stepan Trofimovich is modeled on Granovsky,[12] that Pisarev was in mind when he wrote of the vulgar liberals who insisted that shoes were more important than Pushkin. Some argument has been made that Stavrogin himself was modeled on Bakunin,[13] and that the site of the actual murder, *Skvoreshniki*, is closely modeled on the park where the murder took place.[14] Yet as interesting and important as such parallels between novel and public event may be, *The Possessed* is not history reflecting itself in art, but art reflecting itself in history. The significance of the events Dostoevsky dramatizes is the significance that he gives them, and not the significance they have in some objective historical sense. It may be interesting to see what Dostoevsky kept unchanged and what he changed, but it is stupid to hold him accountable for literal fact. Yet he has been held accountable at times by critics here and abroad. A Soviet critic has said, for instance: "Dostoevsky knew little about the circumstances surrounding Nechaev, which he represented in the novel. He took his facts from newspapers, whose distorted information Shchedrin showed up in his article: 'The So-called Nechaev affair and the relationship of Russian journalism to It.' "[15] In America, Irving Howe has objected that Peter Verkhovensky is by no means representative of Russian radicalism. This is probably true, but the implication that Dostoevsky meant him to be a representative—or was obligated to make him a representative of Russian radicalism— is untrue. Dostoevsky explicitly rejected this intention and insisted that he was representing in *The Possessed* "what was possible," and not "what happened." What is possible for Dostoevsky is finally what is possible in human nature. Dostoevsky wanted to show where the roots of an affair of Nechaev's kind lay in the order of things, and he traced them back to a certain naïveté of liberalism, the roots of which, in turn, were to be found in the inclination of the soul. He says in his diary:

My Nechaev is not, of course, like the real Nechaev. I wanted to pose this question, and as clearly as possible in novel form give an answer to it: In our surprisingly progressive and contemporary society how do not only a Nechaev but Nechaevs come into being, and in what way does it happen that these Nechaevs are able to gather followers? [16]

And in a letter to Katkov:

One of the most important events of my story will concern the well-known murder of Ivanov by Nechaev in Moscow. I hurry to make this qualification: I have not known, and, except for what I have read in the newspapers, I do not know Nechaev or Ivanov or the circumstances of this murder. Even if I knew, I would not use them. I take only the completed act. My imagination can in the highest degree differ from what actually happened, and my Peter Verkhovensky can in no way resemble Nechaev; still, I believe that my imagination has created that person, that type, which corresponds to the crime.[17]

His imagination has created in *The Possessed* the type that corresponds to Nechaev's crime, and indeed through the socialists, Peter, Kirilov, and Stavrogin, the types that correspond to *crime* in general. He shows how the course of public events has its analogue in the soul of Stavrogin, and how in this soul the impulse to crime is paradoxically the impulse to freedom. All events have their roots deep in the soul's soil, where the first tendril of faith in God or self appears.

8

The Adolescent
and
The Dream of the Ridiculous Man

The Adolescent (1875) IS BY FAR THE WEAKEST of Dostoevsky's major novels. It is a grab bag of old themes, devices, and psychologizing. Very little is new, and there is a little bit of everything that Dostoevsky had dealt with before. The burning conviction that welds together seemingly disparate elements in the other novels is lacking. Old themes, character types, ideas, and devices jostle about in a somewhat disordered fashion. Only the portraits of Versilov, the father, and Arkady Dolgoruky, the son, are at the level of Dostoevsky's full creative powers.

The structure is poor. There are a number of plots vying for interest and tied together by improbable and melodramatic contrivances. Some of the structuring is reminiscent of the plotting in *The Insulted and the Injured* and the sentimental and gothic contrivances of the early works. The novel is filled with secret documents, mysterious letters, eavesdroppings, coincidences, portentous lawsuits, mysterious insults, and inexplicable motives. The portentous letter that Arkady carries sewn in the lining of his coat is the most conspicuous contrivance of all. Everyone wants to get his hands on it, and the game of "Who's going to get it" is overdone by the end of the novel. Some themes and subplots appear and disappear without finding their place in the organization of the work. The Dergachov-Kraft subplot, for instance, is never assimilated into the structure. It promises something of importance early in the novel; Arkady has one long discussion explaining his ideas and disagreeing with the socialist thinking of the members. But the group drops out of the novel and seems to have no real effect on Arkady's thoughts or actions. The group had a real prototype, "The Dolgushiny," who advocated a revolt against the order of things and a society based on equality, brotherhood, and life according to the law "of truth and nature." Dostoevsky planned originally a larger role for them, since they figure prominently in the notebooks. But the trouble he had in keeping them in the novel is somewhat symptomatic of the trouble he had in making structural sense of this compendium of themes and ideas.

The content is not much better. The novel is a patchwork of old themes, character types, and ideas. Versilov's love affair for an idiot girl reminds us of both Raskolnikov's love of the landlady's sick daughter and Stavrogin's love of Mary Lebyadkin; the slap Prince Sergey gives Versilov recalls the blow Stavrogin received from Shatov, and perhaps the blow the Underground Man dreams of giving Zverkov. Makar Ivanovich, a meek type, reminds us of Myshkin; Sonia, Arkady's mother, reminds us in her patient, suffering love for Versilov of Sonia in *Crime and Punishment*. The fatal attraction that Katerina Nikolaevna radiates goes back to Nastasya Fillipovna and perhaps to Katerina of *The Landlady;* Kraft's logical suicide reminds us of Kirilov; and Arkady's attempts to reconcile Katerina Nikolaevna and Anna Andreevna through his nobility reminds us of Julia von Lembke's conviction that everyone and everything would be reconciled with everyone and everything by the force of her nobility. Some of the themes look forward to *The Brothers Karamazov*. Ivan's demand for justice, here and now and not in the future when he will not be there, is anticipated in what Arkady says to the Dergachov group: "Why should I necessarily have to love my fellow man or your future humanity, which I shall never see, which shall not know of me, and which in turn will disappear without any trace or memory?" And Arkady's astonishment at the capacity of man "to cherish in his soul the highest ideal side by side with the basest motives" reminds one of Dmitry Karamazov's astonishment at the capacity of man to entertain at the same time the ideal of both Sodom and the Madonna.

If we look for some center in the multiple plots, the melodramatic play, and the compendium of Dostoevskiana, we come necessarily to the two characters, father and son, who are done well and who redeem to some extent the entire novel. Arkady is ashamed of his birth, embittered by his experiences at school and the conditions he lives in; he intends vaguely to take his revenge on society by becoming a Rothschild. He is convinced that money—and the power it gives—will make up for all his shortcomings. Ganya in *The Idiot*, it will be remembered, had the same idea, and Ptitsyn in the same novel had made himself successfully—at least partly—in the same image. The theme, which apparently attracted Dostoevsky, was something that he found difficult to sustain; for, as with Ganya, he drops it as a motive for Arkady after a few inconsequential experiments. Arkady is the center of action and his growth in understanding the world is the central line of action, but it is not always easy to understand his motives. From his earliest works Dostoevsky had used children as a test of the nature of men. Dostoevsky seems to argue that the ambivalent nature of children confirms the reality of both good and evil impulses of men. Arkady nurtures impulses of faith in people, nobility of action, and idealism, although from the point of view of a corrupt society, these are often naïve impulses. At the same time, however, he shows impulses of vanity, passion, meanness, and cruelty.

The "letter" that is used to tie together the various plots, and that Arkady carries about with him sewn in his lining confronts him with the choice of how to use power. The letter can ruin Katerina Nikolaevna; it can help Anna Andreevna, Versilov's legitimate daughter, by helping her ruthless plan to marry the doddering old Prince; and it can, if brought to his attention, hasten the death of the old Prince. Arkady dreams nobly of using it to do good: he plans to destroy it so as not to harm Katerina Nikolaevna, and he is convinced that his own noble gesture will inspire Katerina to equal nobility toward Anna Andreevna. But Arkady does not know himself. He puts off destroying the document and he does so because he enjoys the power the letter gives him; he even has a repressed and unconscious desire to force Katerina to submit to him. Lambert, his unscrupulous school friend, suggests this tactic to him, and Arkady is weak enough to accept the specious reasoning that he will not be forcing Katerina, since she is probably in love with him anyway. The full force of his self-deceptive motive is revealed in a dream where he makes lascivious advances to Katerina while Lambert eggs him on.

Arkady is the child in search of his father, or, what is the same thing, for Dostoevsky, the child in search of his faith. The novel is built on a series of analogical quests and attendant disappointments. Arkady does not find his ideal in the socialists he visits and argues with, nor in the nobility of the society, for the young Prince seduces his sister and is also a crook; nor does he find it in women, for Katerina is revealed finally to be a selfish, somewhat sadistic, and even trivial woman. Most disappointing of all, he does not find it in Versilov, where he seeks it most persistently and fervently.

Versilov is a liberal of the old stripe. He reminds us of Stavrogin and Stepan Trofimovich, and he embodies to a large extent the humanistic ideas Dostoevsky himself had flirted with in the late forties. He is the flower of Russian society, who in his espousal of "European" ideas comes to believe in culture as a substitute for God. The main point of Versilov's "Geneva ideas" is the concept of human virtue without Christ. From *The Winter Notes and Summer Impressions* on, Dostoevsky's works are filled—as are his letters, diaries, and articles—with exposing again and again the "sin" of the liberal fathers, who had given birth to the Nechaevs, the fires of the French commune, and the radicalism and moral confusion of Russia. The sin of the fathers lay in the belief of human life and human virtue without God. Versilov is a portrait of such a "father," embodying all its traits: its aristocracy, culture, wide knowledge, travel, high ideals, and idleness. What Versilov explicitly believes in may be misleading because he seems to espouse contradictory beliefs. He advises Arkady to believe in God, but also thinks it fine that Arkady cannot accept God; he believes in humanity, but thinks it impossible to love one's fellow man; the idea of civilization without the idea of God is inevitable for him, and he paints the picture of its dawning with tenderness and love. Yet he is nostalgic for the idea of God. Humanity, according to him, would, after abandoning God, eventually return to Him; for he sees Christ as aesthetically completing his view of history. Versilov's faith is not Dostoevsky's, and his Christ is not Dostoevsky's. Versilov has lost his living faith, though not his *idea* of God or his nostalgia for God. He is, in sum, the representative of the confused liberals of the forties, who thought that a rational humanism could reconcile God and socialism. Versilov's seeming belief in God has led some critics to see his high ideas as positive and even to identify them with Dostoevsky's. We need only remind ourselves that Stepan Trofimovich accepted God, but only as an adjunct to his aesthetic mind; Ivan accepts God, also, so as to have someone to blame the cruelties of history on. Indeed, the high-minded liberals of the forties often believed in God, as, indeed, their prototypes, the French utopian socialists, often believed in God. But "believing in God" in Dostoevsky's world can mean different things.

The failure to see once again the dialectical nature of terms like "God," "virtue," and indeed every important concept explains why critics like Ernest Simmons, and indeed many others, identify Dostoevsky's views with Versilov's. It is not enough to point out that Versilov once turned to God, or that he believes in virtue, or that he has suffered, or has looked for a great idea, or that he tries to do good deeds, or that he believes in the "golden age" of man's perfection. All of these acts can be dialectically their opposites, and their value is determined by man's choice. Indeed, Versilov's great yearnings and beautiful visions are contradicted by Versilov the man.

Versilov does "good" deeds, but he illustrates once again the consequences of Dostoevsky's moral dialectic: that a good deed without God can only be a self-interested act, and consequently an evil deed. His "good" deeds are always corrupted by his character. He marries the idiot girl that Prince Sergey has seduced, and he nobly takes over the care of the child, but he does so to spite Katerina Nikolaevna, who had rejected him. This contradiction between Versilov the man and his high-minded ideas is brought out most clearly for us and for Arkady in his motives toward Katerina, especially in the final scenes. There we find a petty, jealous, spiteful Versilov. Despite his "golden visions," his superior culture, and his belief in the essential nobility of man, he is moved by base motives. Acting in conspiracy with one of the basest characters in the novel, Lambert, he cooperates in a melodramatic attempt to humble the woman who has rejected him. She is herself cut of the same cloth. In an earlier meeting with Versilov, their relations are a mixture of cultured politeness and cruelty. She enjoys humbling him. When he asks if she has loved him, she answers that she has—but only for a short time. When he asks if she loves him now, she answers that she *almost* loves him. She is a master of the tantalizing answer, one that neither accepts nor rejects him completely. Despite all the contrived mystery about her, Katerina Nikolaevna is cruel, selfish, and trivial.

In these last scenes Versilov's double character is most apparent. He sees Katerina Nikolaevna as the embodiment of all virtue, and as a base and vicious woman; he sends her a letter calling her corrupt; later he sends a letter asking her to meet him. He loves her and hates her, protects her and tries to kill her. The metaphysical meaning of "doubling" has been, I think, widely misunderstood, even though it is one of Dostoevsky's most important devices. The split is a sign of a contradiction in the hero's nature, but it is both facile and misleading to speak of the split as the struggle of a good and a bad side, or of a conflict between "reason" and "feeling." The suffering which results from the split may be a sign of spiritual life, but the split itself is a sign of something wrong in the character. Good characters—Sonia, Myshkin, Makar, Father Zossima—are not split. In a double type—Golyadkin, the Underground Man, Raskolnikov, Versilov—the split is between what they *think* they are and what they really *are*. In Versilov this takes the form of a conflict between his high-minded, cultured liberalism and his actual acts, which are often cruel, petty, phlegmatic, and always self-interested. We must remind ourselves that no number of good intentions will change the essential choice that each character makes in the deepest recess of his being for or against God. And without faith in God, there is only faith in oneself. Doubling takes place for Dostoevsky in the mature novels, when the hero loses his faith in God but continues to believe in the "goodness" of his actions, in love, virtue, nobility, and any number of good motives. Over all of these, necessarily, will fall the shadow of self-interest, and what look like "good" and "bad" motives will be equally self-interested.

Versilov is the embodiment of the most essential deception that all of Dostoevsky's great characters face; this deception was at the core of the idea of "liberalism"; it had tainted his own thinking at the end of the forties; and to judge from critical appraisals, it is at the core of the thinking of most Dostoevsky criticism. This deception finds its most complete form in the dream of the "golden age," significantly the dream that was frequent in the literature of the French utopian socialists, the Russian utopians, and indeed in their radical followers: the golden age Vera dreams of in the fourth book of Chernyshevsky's *What Is to Be Done?* is not very different from the "golden age" Versilov, Stavrogin, and the Ridiculous Man dream of. Yet, strangely enough, the dream of the Ridiculous Man has without exception been taken as an expression of Dostoevsky's own ideal.

The Dream of the Ridiculous Man

According to Ernest Simmons, *The Dream of the Ridiculous Man* is a "restatement of Dostoevsky's faith in the 'Golden Age.'" This is true. Dostoevsky believed in the "Golden Age": that man's nature can be remade here and now. In the notebooks to *Crime and Punishment*, he considered giving Raskolnikov a vision of the Golden Age; he talks about it in his diary, and Zossima in *The Brothers Karamazov* describes it in words very similar to the Ridiculous Man's. Through faith in Christ—and the heart alone was the pledge of that faith—Dostoevsky was convinced throughout his career that man could be reborn into the kind of happiness, sinlessness, and joy the Ridiculous Man describes.

But if the "Golden Age" is something Dostoevsky cherished and wrote of in many works, there is a "Golden Age" that he looked upon with rage and revulsion. Vera's dream in the fourth book of Chernyshevsky's *What Is to Be Done?* of a happy, sinless, comfortable people brought to that state by "rational self-interest" (*razumny egoizm*) is dismissed with rage and indignation in *Notes from the Underground*. Shigalyov's dream of the happy and contented masses who will know no suffering or need is cruelly satirized in *The Possessed;* and the "Golden Age" which Ivan dreams of in "The Legend of the Grand Inquisitor" is bought at the price of self-deception and freedom. The Ridiculous Man's dream of a Golden Age had already appeared in almost the same form in Versilov's vision in *The Adolescent* and in Stavrogin's confession in *The Possessed.* Both Stavrogin and Versilov are men without faith, and they should have given Dostoevsky's interpreters the key to the possibility that the Ridiculous Man's dream is a dream of a Golden Age without faith. We need to remind ourselves that the tiny spot of light (the Ridiculous Man's star) turns into a red spider for Stavrogin, and that the sinking sun of the first day of European civilization turns into the last day of Russian civilization for Versilov. Indeed Dostoevsky insists on the paganism of the dream by placing it in antiquity and on the Greek archipelago.

The Golden Age, like every other important concept in Dostoevsky's world, is a dialectical concept: it can be sacrament or blasphemy, the vision of regeneration in Christ or the vision of degeneration in the imitation of Christ. *The Dream of the Ridiculous Man* is *blasphemy*, and yet it has been taken universally by Dostoevsky's interpreters as *sacrament.* If one can abstract the dream from the Ridiculous Man, then it is Dostoevsky's dream, for in every respect it is what Dostoevsky was convinced would follow upon a free choice grounded in the truth of Christ. But it cannot be abstracted, for no idea, no vision, no conviction in Dostoevsky's world can be abstracted. The dream of the Ridiculous Man is *his dream*, and it is as good as his motives, and his motives are self-interested. Dostoevsky has presented in this story what he has presented so often: he has placed some cherished truth in the mouth and being of a self-interested person. In the *Notes* he gave his argument against "compulsory rational happiness" to the Underground Man; in *The Possessed* he gave some of his most cherished ideas to the clown Lebedev; in *The Idiot,* some of his convictions to Ippolit. Dostoevsky criticism will always go wrong when it separates Dostoevsky's ideas from those characters who carry the ideas. In *The Dream of the Ridiculous Man* Dostoevsky shows, with great refinement, how even the most august truths can be corrupted to the service of the will.

The traditional interpretation is the following: the Ridiculous Man is saved from killing himself—motivated by his conviction that nothing matters—by the shaft of pity he feels for a small destitute girl. This shaft of pity contradicts his conviction that nothing in the world matters, and the dream he has of a "sinless" duplicate of the world is symbolic of his regeneration into "sinless" concern for others. Despite his love for these people, the Ridiculous Man, to be sure, cannot help corrupting them until through a process of evolution they become the same as the hating, self-justifying, warring, suffering, and corrupted people of the earth. But upon waking, he is filled with remorse for his deed and for his great loss, and the sign of his regeneration is his desire to preach the truth that he has come to recognize.

What we must not forget is that the dream is the Ridiculous Man's dream. Psychology has taught us that we are all the actors in our dreams, and W. D. Snodgrass has shown us, for instance, how Raskolnikov is every one of the actors in the dream of mare beating he has.[1] The Ridiculous Man similarly plays all the parts in his dream: he is the creator, corrupter, and redeemer of the "sinless" people. The shaft of pity he feels for the little girl is what gives birth to the dream of the golden age. But the pity that flickers in his heart is corrupted, and the dream tells us why he corrupts the Golden Age. He corrupts the Golden Age so that he can make it *his, and his alone.* The shaft of pity he feels for the small beggar is a threat to his conviction that nothing matters, and the dream is his way of coming to terms with the threat. And he comes to terms with the threat by killing the truth—hence the shot through his heart—and redeeming it in his own image. He corrupts the truth by making it his, and as is frequent in Dostoevsky's work, this corruption takes the form of a grotesque imitation of Christ. He begs the people he has corrupted to nail him to the cross, and even tries to show them how to make a cross. The corruption of "good" by the will always tends in Dostoevsky's work to be a corruption of the supreme act of good, Christ's sacrifice for man. Kirilov, we will remember, wants to sacrifice himself to redeem man, and Stavrogin's name itself is related to "cross" in Greek and to Satan in Russian (place-horns), catching in canting fashion the self's imitation and corruption of Christ.

The Ridiculous Man wants to suffer for the people he has corrupted, and when he awakens, he continues to want to suffer for the people about him. He invites abuse and suffers gladly the taunts and charges of madness that his "preaching" brings. Why? So that the truth that has threatened his control of the world—through indifference—will be his weapon for controlling the world. The truth is something that he alone knows, and something that he alone will always know. He has even been careful enough to forget it somewhat, and indeed even boasts a little that perhaps he made it all up. Life and preaching are to be his goals; not—it can be noticed—"life and living." Can there be any doubt as to what the point of the "preaching" is to be? It is to emphasize again and again his special status. It is in his martyrdom to feel again and again—his superiority in truth and everyone else's inferiority in falsehood. The Ridiculous Man has carried the blasphemy of truth to its highest point, the blasphemy of Christ.

In Dostoevsky's moral dialectic the highest goods can be corrupted to the deepest evils, and it is often hard to see the difference. But the difference is there, and it is absolute. Arkady Dolgoruky, in perhaps an unintentional yet meaningful ambiguity, says of his father, Versilov: "I considered him a preacher [*propovednik*]: he carried the Golden Age in his heart and he knew the future about atheism." The Golden Age—without Christ—is atheism. The Golden Age the Ridiculous Man dreams of is a Golden Age without Christ; even more, it is a Golden Age by which he attempts to make of himself a Christ.

9

The Brothers Karamazov

AFTER THE PRELIMINARY exposition *The Brothers Karama-zov* begins with one of Dostoevsky's great scenes. Ostensibly, a gathering in the Elder's cell to settle the grievance between Dmitry and Fyodor, the scene captures in image and dramatic gesture the polarities and dialectical oppositions of the novel. It is a magnificent introduction to the entire novel. Near the end of the scene, Dmitry Karamazov springs at his father and cries out in agonized rage, "Why does a man such as he live?" As Fyodor raises the cry of "father-killer," and the cell fills with commotion and disorder, the Elder rises from his seat, and supported by Alyosha, shakily walks up to Dmitry, where he falls to the ground and asks for forgiveness. The scene ends, and the novel begins with the hand of the child raised against the father. But only raised. For his cry of hate is muted into silence, and his gesture of violence is stayed by the long bow of expiation by the Elder. Like a camera click, the oppositions that Dostoevsky will dramatize in the novel are caught and stilled in the gestures of the father, son, and Elder: child against father; humility against hate; monastery against the world; expiation against threat. Only the novel itself will resolve the oppositions. When the scene ends, we do not know whether the son will destroy the father, or whether the act of humility will destroy the hate for him.

What is at stake is important: the right of the child to raise his hand against his father is for Dostoevsky the right of man to raise his hand against God. Later, Ivan will base his rebellion against God on the rights of children against the fathers who mistreat them, and by analogy the rights of men against the God who has mistreated them; the defense attorney at Dmitry's trial will argue that a child has the right to demand that a father prove his love, and that a child has the right to look upon a bad father as an enemy; and Dmitry will feel the stirrings of a new man within him when he accepts the suffering of children in his dream of the burnt-out huts. Finally, Alyosha will see in children the first signs of corruption and the first impulses of faith. Children are the moral touchstone of the novel.

In the same opening scene Ivan gives us the law by which a child is set against his father, and the law by which man humbles himself before man. *The law, in short, that propels Dmitry's spring and the law by which the Elder bows before the murderer are both given by Ivan.* The oppositions that are caught in the gestures of Dmitry and the Elder are both carried in the breast of Ivan. The external drama is Ivan's internal drama. In the ecclesiastical article Ivan had written, he maintains that the church cannot logically come to terms with the state and occupy a clearly defined but limited place in the state, as his ecclesiastical opponent had argued. According to him, the church must, to fulfill its true purpose, contain the whole state. The logic is impeccable, for the church, as the true representative of God, can no more give power to a temporal authority than God can. But while seemingly insisting on a theocracy of the most absolute kind, Ivan is also saying, as Miusov gleefully and quickly points out, that there is no natural law to compel man to love his fellow man. According to Ivan, if men have loved others, it is only because they have believed in immortality; and if you were to destroy the idea of immortality, you would destroy virtue and the love of others. If there is no immortality, all is permitted—and not only permitted, but enjoined. Every "right"-thinking and honest man will be obligated to express his self-interest, even to the point of crime. Miusov, who has been miffed by the attention Ivan's ecclesiastical article has provoked, gives the group this résumé so as to expose what he believes are contradictory views as well as Ivan's insincerity. The Elder Zossima knows that Ivan's views are not contradictory. He looks into Ivan's eyes and says, "If you so believe, you are blessed or most unhappy." With this statement, the Elder has drawn the logical consequences from Ivan's views. He sees that Ivan has logically drawn conclusions from two different premises, the most important and the most irreconcilable in Dostoevsky's whole work. If God exists, then what Ivan has written in his article about the church follows; if God and the attendant idea of immortality do not exist, then indeed there is only the law of self-interest, and man is obliged—if he is to live without deception—to express this law even to the point of crime. There is no contradiction in Ivan's views, but there is dreadful indecision, and this, too, the Elder sees. As the novel begins, the reader waits to see not only whether Dmitry's leap will reach his father or whether it will be stayed by the law of Zossima, but also whether Ivan, who carries both laws in his breast, will choose one or the other. *What is objectified in Dmitry against his father and in Zossima against both is internalized in Ivan against Ivan.*

Dmitry and Katerina

In the confession of an ardent heart, Dmitry tells Alyosha—he is our ears—what Katya means to him. But he tells only what he knows, and she means more to him than he knows. The relations between them bristle with paradoxes.

A high-minded, well-educated, rich girl insists on an engagement with an impoverished, dissolute army officer. When Dmitry basely repays her generosity by stealing her money and spending it on a wild orgy with another girl, Katerina rises nobly to forgiveness. Throughout the novel she stands ready to bear everything for his sake: vice, theft, unfaithfulness, insult, and even marriage to Grushenka. Despite all this, Dmitry not only is incorrigibly ungrateful but unaccountably sees her love and sacrifice as oppressive burdens. Katerina's "goodness" drives him to murder. The incriminating letter he writes Katya threatening his father's life makes this clear. In that letter he states that only by paying her back the money he had stolen from her could he preserve his honor, and if he could not get the money any other way, he would kill his father to get it. If the Elder's bow stays Dmitry's hand against his father, Katya's had originally moved it and continues to move it throughout the novel. The first meeting with Katerina begins with a bow, as low and as long as the Elder's bow of expiation. It is characteristic of Dostoevsky that he uses the same gesture for opposite meanings, as if to emphasize that the act remains without significance until we ourselves choose the significance.

On the simplest level it would appear that Katerina is sacrificing herself out of gratitude for Dmitry's noble gesture in saving her father and sparing her. This is the way that Alyosha understands her motives and her relations with Dmitry. As he goes to see Katya at her request early in the novel, he tells himself: "The girl's aims were of the noblest, he knew that. She was trying to save his brother Dmitry simply through generosity (*velikodushie*), though he had already behaved badly to her." And this is the way he understands it in his conversation with Dmitry, when his brother tells him about his first meeting with Katya: he assures Dmitry that Katerina loves him, and not Ivan. When Dmitry tells him about the 3,000 rubles that he had stolen from Katerina, Alyosha says:

"Katerina Ivanovna will understand it all," Alyosha said solemnly. "She'll understand how great this trouble is and will forgive. She has a lofty mind, and no one could be more unhappy than you. She'll see that for herself."

Yet even while Alyosha is convinced that Katerina's motives are lofty, pure, and sincere, he has moments of uneasiness. From the very beginning, something about her troubles him. On his way to his first meeting with her, even while paying justice to her fine qualities, "a shiver began to run down his back as soon as he drew near her house." When he sees her, he sees pride, self-confidence, and strong will in her face. Her black burning eyes are set beautifully in a thin, pale, almost yellow face, and he sees why Dmitry could easily fall in love with her. But he also sees unclearly something that makes it unlikely for Dmitry to love her for a long time. He tells his brother: "Perhaps you will always love her, but perhaps you will not always be happy with her." But he no sooner says this than he feels ashamed of himself. Later, when he goes to her with Dmitry's farewell message, he feels that his first impression must have been wrong. As she comes out to meet him, he sees in her face only simplicity, goodness, and sincerity.

Again and again Alyosha tries to take her as she sees herself, but each time he is stopped by a feeling he cannot understand. He swings from facing up to his doubt about Katerina's motives to feeling ashamed of having that doubt. Alyosha is our ears and our eyes, and the difficulty he has in understanding Katerina is our difficulty. And the difficulty is great. Engaged to Dmitry, Katerina regards him as a repugnant monster; determined to save him, she plots his ruin; frantic to keep him faithful, she provokes his betrayal of her. It is she who almost saves him at the trial, and it is she who most irrevocably ruins him legally by the letter she produces in which he had uttered threats against his father's life. Throughout her relations with Dmitry, her fitful character sweeps her from love to hate, generosity to spite, arrogance to submissiveness. She is all contradiction, flailing each action with its opposite. There is something in her relations with Dmitry that she cannot forgive, something that drives her to pursue him with an unrelenting, self-punishing love. She herself best expresses it in Mrs. Khokhlokov's drawing room before Ivan and Alyosha, when after a night of shame and rage at Grushenka's insult, she triumphantly announces that she will bear that too out of love for Dmitry:

"I've already decided, even if he marries that—creature" (she began solemnly), "whom I never, never can forgive, *even then I will not abandon him*. Henceforward I will never, never abandon him!" she cried, breaking into a sort of pale, hysterical ecstasy. "Not that I would run after him continually, get in his way and worry him. Oh, no! I will go away to another town—where you like—but I will watch over him all my life—I will watch over him all my life unceasingly. When he becomes unhappy with that woman, and that is bound to happen quite soon, let him come to me and he will find a friend, a sister. . . . Only a sister, of course, and so forever; but he will learn at least that that sister is really his sister, who loves him and has sacrificed all her life to him. I will gain my point. I will insist on his knowing me and confiding entirely in me, without reserve," she cried, in a sort of frenzy. "I will be a god to whom he can pray—and that, at least, he owes me for his treachery and for what I suffered yesterday through him. And let him see that all my life I will be true to him and the promise I gave him, in spite of his being untrue and betraying me."

It is this something that Alyosha finally understands as he listens to Katerina's final decision, even though he had been firmly convinced up to the previous night that she loved Dmitry: "Alyosha had till the evening before implicitly believed that Katerina Ivanovna had a steadfast and passionate love for Dmitry; but he had only believed it till the evening before." When he had awakened that morning—after dreaming of Grushenka all night—the word *nadryv* is on his lips. It is this word that startles him when it is used by Mrs. Khokhlokov about Katerina's love for Dmitry, and which—while listening to Katerina—sparks his illumination. For as he excitedly expresses it to the startled Katerina, her love for Dmitry is a love from *nadryv*, that is, a self-punishing love, delighting in its self-hurt, needing the hurt, and only masquerading as love. Ivan provides a further illumination: "Believe me, Katerina Ivanovna, you love only him. And the more he insults you, the more you love him—that's your 'laceration.' You love him just as he is; you love him for insulting you. If he reformed, you'd give him up at once and cease to love him. But you need him so as to contemplate continually your heroic fidelity and to reproach him for infidelity. And it all comes from your pride."

Alyosha and Ivan tell us what Katerina's love is, but they do not tell us why it is so. We can begin to understand why by going back—as indeed Katerina and Dmitry keep going back—to that first fateful meeting. The scene had ended with Dmitry's heroic and successful struggle to overcome the noxious Karamazov insect of passion within him. The tragic relations between them have their seeds in that success, or rather in the gesture that accompanies the "triumph" of Dmitry: Dmitry's long bow of respect, and Katerina's low bow of respectful gratitude. They know it, and the fateful bow is insisted upon by both of them in their conversations.

Katerina Ivanovna is convinced that Dmitry hates her, and he hates her because he had compelled her to bow to him. She explains the reason for "his hatred" for her in this way:

Oh, he has despised me horribly, he has always despised me, and do you know, he has despised me from the very moment that I bowed down to him for that money. I saw that. I felt it at once at the time, but for a long time I wouldn't believe it. How often have I read in his eyes. "You came of yourself, though."

Forgetting that it was she, not Dmitry, who had insisted on marriage, Katerina adds: "He was always convinced that I should be trembling with shame all my life before him, because I went to him then, and that he had a right to despise me forever for it, and so to be superior to me—that's why he wanted to marry me." Despite his contempt and monstrous ingratitude, "I tried to conquer him by my love, a love that knew no bounds. I even tried to forgive his faithlessness; but he understood nothing, nothing! How could he understand indeed? He is a monster!"

But the truth is that the hate and contempt that she ascribes to Dmitry is the hate and contempt she herself feels for him. This is, I think, clear to the reader who can pierce the rather transparent attempt to hide her own hate by giving the hate and all base qualities to Dmitry and all noble qualities to herself. In the notebooks to *The Brothers Karamazov* Dostoevsky makes the hatred she feels explicit. He writes of her in the first sketch of the scene: "Oh, he laughed at me because of that long, low bow. I hated him." [1] It is his bow, out of respect to her, that hurts. For with the bow Dmitry changes from one who abases and humiliates to one who respects and forgives. And she hates the long low bow she must return, for it acknowledges his triumph over her.

We can now understand Katerina's paradoxical and contradictory motives, for once we perceive the subtle deceptions she has drawn over her feelings, perhaps without knowing it, we can see that her motives and actions have followed consistently from what the bowing scene meant to her. Katerina wishes only to hurt because her meeting with Dmitry is compounded of nothing but hurt. She is humiliated in having to appeal for help to the repugnant sensualist, and she is humiliated in having to receive the respectful bow from him. The heroic sacrifice of Dmitry in overcoming the noxious Karamazov insect within him by his deep bow of respect is not an act of sacrifice executed in selflessness and taken in gratitude, but an act of sacrifice given and taken as a subtle and exquisite insult. It is sacrifice used as insult; and ravishment, by comparison, would have been kind. After Dmitry's respectful bow, Katerina carries away in her heart the intolerable burden of an act of sacrifice and the desire to repay it with an equally intolerable act of sacrifice. Is it any wonder, then, that she is obsessed, from this point on, with only one idea: to save Dmitry, to sacrifice herself wholly and fully, to repay the burning insult of sacrifice with the burning insult of sacrifice. The oscillations between arrogance and submissiveness, love and hate, and unselfishness and spitefulness are not the struggle of a proud nature between its good intentions and, as has been usually suggested, the selfish impulses of its spirit. The love no less than the hate, and the submissiveness no less than the arrogance, are needed to bring to her feet a Dmitry ruined and shamed before all, but contrite and nobly forgiven by her. As a consequence, she courts his betrayal, provokes his humiliations of her, works for his shame, and plots her own injury. The more sunken Dmitry is, the stronger her spirit is in lifting him; the deeper the injury to herself, the more lofty her forgiveness; and the more lofty her forgiveness, the sweeter her repayment of the insult of Dmitry's respectful bow.

Dmitry understands this. He understands why she gives him the 3,000 rubles when she knows that he will use it to carry Grushenka away. He knows that she gives him the money to destroy his honor and to provoke his humiliations of her. And he understands that she wants to be dishonored, so that her forgiveness will be all the nobler. How else is one to explain his agonized cry, "Katya, why have you destroyed me!" when at the trial he hears with dismay her generous account of their first meeting. As Katerina tells Alyosha, she is ready to bear all for his sake. Referring to the 3,000 rubles Dmitry had "stolen" from her, Katerina says: "Let him be ashamed of himself, let him be ashamed of other people's knowing, but not of my knowing. He can tell God everything without shame. Why is it he still does not understand how much I am ready to bear for his sake? . . . I want to save him forever."

What Katerina cannot bear is the possibility of a Dmitry who does not want to be forgiven. This is why, for instance, she becomes hysterical when Alyosha, after a meeting with Dmitry in the garden adjoining the Karamazov house, comes to convey to her Dmitry's "good-bye." Katerina is startled by the word "good-bye" and insists that Alyosha must have made a mistake in giving her the message. In the face of Alyosha's assurances that there has been no mistake, since Dmitry has asked him three times not to forget it, Katerina flushes and insists that Dmitry must not have said it deliberately but in a moment of reckless indecision. "He's merely in despair, and I can still save him," she infers exultantly.

It is at this point in the narration that translations blur this intention to trace back the drama of insult and repayment to Dmitry's respectful bow. The word "good-bye" (Magarshack has "good-bye" and Garnett "give his compliments") is in Russian the verb *klanyat'sya*, that is, "good-bye" by bowing. The Russian word expresses at once the sense of parting and recalls to Katerina the insulting respectful bow of the first meeting, when the same verb was used in a different aspect. The blurring in translation of Dostoevsky's intention is unfortunate since a phrase like "to bow out" would have caught, as does the Russian, both the sense of parting and a reminder of the fateful bow. Is it any wonder, then, that Katerina clings almost hysterically to the possibility of some mistake in Alyosha's message, which doubles the intolerable insult by recalling the first sacrifice and severing the possibility of repayment.

Dmitry, as the dissolute officer who struggled against the Karamazov sensuality within him, seemed unconscious of the enormity of the insult he had offered the proud girl, although in the ecstasy of self-satisfaction after she leaves, when he almost stabs himself with his sword, Dostoevsky hints that Dmitry has shared in the intention to insult. The Dmitry who reminds Katerina that she is rich and he but a poor rake, when she writes her letter of declaration of love for him, is also conscious of Katerina's motives. At times his awareness comes out sharply, though involuntarily, as when he retorts to Alyosha's assurance that Katerina loves him, and not Ivan: "She loves her virtue, and not me." He is always sorry for statements of this kind, ashamed of his base nature that erupts in criticism of Katerina, when morally he considers himself infinitely below her. Yet, despite his conscious intentions, he insists again and again in reminding her of the bow. In his last incriminating letter to her, he returns once again to the bow: "Farewell, I bow down to the ground [*Klanyayus' do zemli*] before you, for I've been a scoundrel to you. Forgive me! No, better not forgive me, you'll be happier, and so shall I! Better Siberia than your love." Better murder and prison than such love! Such love and sacrifice, and the bow that symbolizes them, are not purifying and uplifting but abasing and persecuting. They are not Zossima's love, nor is Katerina's bow Zossima's bow. Zossima's bow stays the hand of the murderer; Katerina's raises it. What is wrong with such a love?

Katerina loves Dmitry from *nadryv*, and in this word Dostoevsky catches the vortex of her emotions and motives; with this word he points to one of his most penetrating insights into human motives. Dostoevsky devotes all of Book Four of Part Two to examples of *nadryv*, pointing to something that Ferapont, Captain Snegirev, Katerina, and little Ilyusha have in common. Magarshack has ineptly translated the word as "heartache," Garnett less ineptly as "laceration." It is impossible to think of a translation more misleading than Magarshack's. It is romantic and trivial in connotation, and wholly inappropriate to what sears Katerina's breast. Garnett's translation is not much more helpful, but it is not the positive hindrance Magarshack's translation is.

The word comes from the verb *nadryvat'*, which means —apart from its literal meaning of tearing things apart, like paper—"to strain or hurt oneself by lifting something beyond one's strength." To this must be added Dostoevsky's special use of the word to mean a *purposeful* hurting of oneself, and to this, an explanation of the purpose. *Nadryv* is for Dostoevsky a purposeful and pleasurable self-hurt. Father Ferapont's ascetic deprivations are a self-denial from *nadryv*. He "hurts" himself, so that he can hurt the other monks; he needs the "indulgent" monks (which his exercises in asceticism create) as much as Katerina needs a fallen Dmitry. Father Ferapont's ascetic deprivations are weapons of humiliation of others and exaltation of self. Captain Snegirev's *nadryv* is more pathetic and less violent than Father Ferapont's, but it shares some of the same quality. He deliberately hurts himself—when he stamps on the money Alyosha offers him and which he needs so desperately—because of the beautiful and noble image he has of himself at that moment.

Nadryv is for Dostoevsky a primal psychological fact. It is the impulse in the hearts of men that separates one man from another, the impulse we all have to make the world over into the image of our wills. Katerina *loves* from *nadryv;* Father Ferapont *fasts* from *nadryv;* Captain Snegirev *loves honor* from *nadryv.* Dostoevsky shows this basic psychological characteristic working to corrupt what seem to be good motives. From the Underground Man on, one of the premises of Dostoevsky's mature dialectic has been that the Will will subvert the best and highest motives to its own purposes. *Nadryv* is Dostoevsky's mature pointing to the psychological impulse that works to corrupt everything to its own purposes.

Ivan has his *nadryv* also, for his hurt is his bruised sense of justice. He raises *nadryv* to a level of universal revolt against God.

Ivan

In the opening scene the Elder Zossima had looked into Ivan's eyes sympathetically and had seen the great choice Ivan had to make between the two irreconcilable principles he had defined. But Ivan refuses to make the choice; he attempts to reconcile the irreconcilable. And this is his great deception: his attempt to elevate the law of self-interest to the law of disinterestedness. If there is no immortality, then according to his own words, "all is permitted." Ivan believes that there is no immortality, but he wants to believe that only the good and the noble will be permitted.

Ivan's revolt against God is deep and powerful and *unanswerable*. The roots go deeper than reason; the antagonist is more powerful.[2] Ivan's revolt is based on the belly, on the sensibilities, on personal revulsion toward historical reality. Ivan knows that reason is a whore that will serve any purpose, that it can be used to prove God's existence as well as disprove it. Reason can justify the list of horrors that have been visited upon man; he knows this and dismisses it. Ivan knows only that suffering exists and that he wants the suffering avenged. After recounting his scrapbook of Russian atrocities against children, he dismisses what are conventional *rational* justifications:

"With my pitiful, earthly, Euclidian understanding, all I know is that there is suffering and that there are none guilty; that cause follows effect, simply and directly; that everything flows and finds its level—but that's only Euclidian nonsense, I know that, and I can't consent to live by it! What comfort is it to me that there are none guilty and that cause follows effect simply and directly, and that I know it—I must have justice, or I will destroy myself. And not justice in some remote infinite time and space, but here on earth, and that I could see myself."

Even if Ivan is wrong (what kind of rationalist is that?), he will remain with the sufferers and demand that they be avenged. "I would rather remain with my unavenged suffering and unsatisfied indignation, *even if I were wrong.*" If reason shows that there is no one to avenge, or that somewhere, someday, all will be explained, he will not be satisfied, but will stand by the facts and his own "irrational" feelings. It is fact, not reasoning, he wants. He tells Alyosha: "I want to stick to the facts. I made up my mind long ago not to understand. If I try to understand anything, I shall be false to the facts and I have determined to stick to the facts." And the facts are: Turks sticking babies with their bayonets; an enlightened father and mother tormenting their five-year-old daughter with excrement and locking her up in a privy all night because she had wet her bed; philanthropic Christians teaching Richard to bless God for the grace he has been taught to accept, as he goes to be beheaded for a crime society had forced him to commit; a General deprived of the administration of his estates because he had had a hound tear an eight-year-old boy to pieces for hurting the paw of one of his favorite dogs. Because of these facts, Ivan refuses to accept God's world, although he accepts God.

But he accepts God, so that he can dismiss him. God is a metaphysical concept; the world is a three-dimensional fact. And Ivan refuses to deal with anything but fact. He has a Euclidian mind, which can understand a Euclidian universe. But the idea of God is something beyond fact. To reject God would be to go beyond fact. He accepts God only in the sense that one accepts a hypothesis that cannot be proved. As Dostoevsky made abundantly clear in his letters, Ivan's acceptance of God is not a mitigation of his revolt, but simply a historic reality. To N. A. Lyubimov, he wrote:

In the text which I have just sent out I express the basic convictions of one of the most important characters in the novel. These convictions are precisely what I consider to be the synthesis of contemporary Russian anarchism: the denial not of God but of the meaning of his creation. Socialism began with the denial of the meaning of historical reality and ended in a program of destruction and anarchism. . . . My hero defends, in my opinion, an unanswerable position: the senselessness of the suffering of children and he deduces from that the absurdity of historical reality.[3]

And to K. P. Pobedonostsev, he said:

This book is the culmination of my novel and is called *Pro and Contra*. Its meaning is the following: blasphemy and its answer. The blasphemy is already finished and sent in; I'll send the answer in July. I took the blasphemy as I understood and felt it to be strongest, that is, as it exists in Russia today among (almost) all the higher classes, and particularly among the young. Our socialists today are not concerned with scientific and philosophic arguments against the existence of God (as were the whole last century and the first half of this century); these have been given up. Rather, they are interested in denying as strongly as possible the creation of God, his world, and his meaning. Only in these questions does contemporary civilization find meaning. In this way I flatter myself with the hope that even in such an abstract theme I have not betrayed realism.[4]

It simply doesn't matter whether God exists or not. Ivan accepts God's existence as you would accept the hypothesis of the universe supported by fishes. His acceptance implies its irrelevance, for the existence of God is an unreal question for the Euclidian mind. What is real, and what does matter is the world we live in, and that world is unacceptable because it is racked with senseless suffering. Ivan does not want rational justification, or Christian forgiveness. He wants justice, not justice at the last clanging of the world's gates, but justice here and now; such justice is the condition he poses for accepting God's world. But whose justice? Surely not the world's, for it is the world's justice that has condoned the birching of the eight-year-old, the tragedy of Richard's life, the terrors of the five-year-old in the privy; it is the world that has punished the General by taking away the administration of his estates from him.

Whose justice? The answer can only be—Ivan's justice.

And the dream of that justice is the dream of a world re-made in the image of him. This dream is the legend of the Grand Inquisitor.

The Grand Inquisitor

D. H. Lawrence first read "The Legend of the Grand Inquisitor" in 1913 at John Middleton Murry's recommendation. "The whole clue to Dostoevsky is in that Grand Inquisitor story," said John Middleton Murry. After finishing the piece, Lawrence asked Murry, "Why? It seems to me just rubbish." He found it to be an irritating "cynical-satanical" pose. But later he found it to be more true and more depressing with every reading. True and depressing because the Grand Inquisitor was right and Christ was wrong. His later interpretation is representative of a large body of critical opinion that sees the Grand Inquisitor as the victor of the duel with Christ:

> Since then I have read *The Brothers Karamazov* twice, and each time found it more depressing because, alas, more drearily true to life. At first it had been lurid romance. Now, I read *The Grand Inquisitor* once more and my heart sinks right through my shoes. I still see a trifle of cynical-satanical showing off, but under that I hear the final unanswerable criticism of Christ. And it is a deadly-devastating summing up, because borne out by long experience of humanity. It is reality versus illusion, and the illusion was Jesus, while time itself retorts with reality.[5]

And:

> And we cannot doubt that the Inquisitor speaks Dostoevsky's own final opinion about Jesus. The opinion is, badly, this: Jesus, you are inadequate, men must correct you. And Jesus in the end gives the kiss of acquiescence to the Inquisitor, as Alyosha does to Ivan.[6]

Lawrence takes his stand with the Grand Inquisitor and, thus, with the spirit of darkness and destruction. He takes his stand reluctantly (note the "more drearily true"), for he would like man different. He is perceptive enough to recognize that in taking his stand with the Grand Inquisitor, he accepts man as weak, slavish, and self-deceptive; that he gives up immortality, true freedom, and salvation. But he takes his stand because these are the facts and the rest is illusion. Even more, Lawrence tries, as those who have chosen the truth of the Grand Inquisitor have characteristically tried to do, to bring Dostoevsky over to his side.

We know that Lawrence's interpretation is not what Dostoevsky intended, at least consciously, but it is interesting that the truth of the Grand Inquisitor should have been chosen—and attributed to Dostoevsky—by so many distinguished critics and by critics of different philosophical background and culture. Leo Shestov's whole book *Dostoevsky i Nietzsche* is dedicated to proving that Dostoevsky was really on the side of his godless heroes, and Rozanov is similarly convinced that Dostoevsky was on the side of the Grand Inquisitor. In the *Legend of the Grand Inquisitor* Rozanov says:

When Dostoevsky died, he did not carry the secret of his soul to the grave with him. Before his death, he left us, as if by some instinct revealing his soul, an astonishing scene by which we can see that the words of Alyosha to Ivan "And you are with him" can be definitely applied to the author himself, who so clearly is on his side.[7]

The revolt of so many distinguished readers against Dostoevsky's conscious intention is, whatever else, a testimony to the force and persuasiveness with which Dostoevsky was able to state the other case.

Before the Grand Inquisitor is through talking, the Christ of all the people is the Christ of the chosen few; the Christ who had come to suffer for man has come only to make him suffer; and the Christ of compassion and love is the Christ of indifference and unconcern. The word "revolt" for the Grand Inquisitor's stand is not strong enough; Guardini's "aggression" is better, but it is even more than that. It is *despoilment,* for what Christ had stood for, now the Grand Inquisitor stands for. It is not Christ who loves all the people, who suffers for them and sacrifices not only his life but perhaps his eternal life for them. It is the Grand Inquisitor. This reversal is clearly implied in the final text, and in the notebooks to *The Brothers Karamazov* Dostoevsky made the contrast explicit. There the Grand Inquisitor tells Christ: "We are more humane than thou. We love the earth." [8] And, "I love humanity more than thee." [9] The Grand Inquisitor does not merely oppose his truth to Christ's truth, but he is the truth Christ had failed to erect. He is light and truth; Christ is darkness and falsehood. In the notebooks, the Grand Inquisitor goes so far as to identify Christ with the forces of hell and evil: "I have only this to say to you: you have been disgorged from hell; you are a heretic." [10]

The Grand Inquisitor's argument is not based on idle rhetoric or cheap tricks. Nor is it contradictory as some have claimed. Logic is on his side, not Christ's, although the truth of each is finally subject to more than logic. Lawrence, Shestov, Guardini, Rozanov, and many other distinguished critics have taken the side of the Grand Inquisitor against Christ because his argument is powerful and indeed unanswerable. And they do this despite the fact that Dostoevsky made the case he wanted to make for Christ. There is no weakness in Christ's argument, and there is no weakness in the Grand Inquisitor's argument. Mochul'sky's argument that the Grand Inquisitor is wrong because he argues from love of mankind, yet portrays mankind as weak and slavish is clearly a *non sequitur.* One can love what is weak and slavish, and perhaps love more deeply. Those who try to help out Dostoevsky by showing that the Grand Inquisitor's argument is self-contradictory do not understand the Grand Inquisitor, and they do not understand Dostoevsky. Dostoevsky made the only case he could for Christ, and the truth of Christ he presents does not demolish the Grand Inquisitor's truth any more than the Grand Inquisitor's truth demolishes Christ's truth. We are concerned here with two ways of understanding man's nature, and they are discontinuous; one cannot stand in refutation by the other because there are no common assumptions. This will become clear by seeing and understanding the nature of the Grand Inquisitor's truth, which is consistent and complete and deep in its appeal.

Christ had bade men to follow his example, the essence of which was contained in his rejection of Satan's three temptations in the wilderness: (1) to turn stones to bread, (2) to prove his divinity by performing a miracle, (3) to agree to the worship of earthly power. It is curious, as an aside, that many important critics have failed to understand what the three temptations are as Dostoevsky understands them, even though a single careful reading will make this clear. For some perverse reason—Magarshack and Rahv are examples—many critics persist in seizing upon the words "miracle, mystery, and authority" as the three temptations, whereas for Dostoevsky these are clearly the instruments of the second temptation only: man's eternal desire for *proof* or certainty before giving his faith. The eternal instruments of this deceptive proof are miracle, mystery, and authority. Rahv's understanding is representative: "The three powers with which Satan had tempted Him in the wilderness are miracle, mystery, and authority, the sole means of vanquishing the conscience of men forever and holding it captive for their own good." [11]

The three temptations are the three great limitations of a *free faith*. Christ's example is of a faith freely given, standing without the support of bread, miracles, or the need of collective earthly power. Christ had bade men believe in him with the same faith. But Christ had, according to the Grand Inquisitor, cruelly misunderstood the nature of man, for fifteen centuries had proved that man by his very nature was incapable of what Christ had asked. Men

had always cried—and were crying in Dostoevsky's time—
"feed us and then we will be virtuous," [12] and men had always asked not for the anxiety and fear of choosing freely
but for the certainty of miracles, mystery, and authority,
and they had always been afraid of being alone, craving
always the sheeplike comfort of worship with everyone
else. Christ had asked men to be alone and unafraid in the
presence of things unseen, supported only by the free movement of the heart, but men had always chosen material
comfort, the certainty of proof, and the assurance of collective worship.

But man's nature was such that Christ's demands were
beyond his strength, and Christ's demand of a free faith
could only visit upon him pointless sufferings. Fifteen centuries had proved that only a handful of men were strong
enough to follow Christ's example, and that the rest could
never follow it. From this it follows—and the Grand Inquisitor makes this charge again and again—that Christ had
acted as if he had not loved man, as if he had cared only
for the few strong and free and not for the millions upon
millions who had not been able to bear his terrible freedom. It also follows that Christ had either misunderstood
man's nature or understood it and visited needless sufferings upon man. If the first, then he was not Christ; if the
second, then he had been gratuitously cruel.

If the Grand Inquisitor were simply opposing man's
slavery to Christ's freedom, man's sheeplike desire for the
peace and comfort of body and conscience to Christ's
dignity of suffering body and conscience; man's weakness
to Christ's strength, then there could be little appeal in his
argument against Christ. Even we of the twentieth century
have not yet grown callous enough to prefer weakness to
strength and slavery to freedom. No, the appeal of the Grand
Inquisitor lies deeper, and those like Lawrence and Shestov,
who have cast their lots with the Grand Inquisitor, have
sensed this appeal. They too would prefer the strength
and beauty and freedom of Christ, but with the Grand In-

quisitor they have seen that it is not a question of *what man would like to be* but *what he is and can be*. For them, all of history has shown man to be as the Grand Inquisitor has painted him, not as Christ had demanded him to be.

It is the failure to see the fundamental, sincere, and believable appeal of the Grand Inquisitor's argument—as I am convinced Dostoevsky saw it—that has led his supporters to argue in support of Christ on false premises. It is useless to argue on the grounds of which is the more attractive picture of man and to grant on that basis the truth to Christ. The Grand Inquisitor would be the first to grant that Christ's view of man is more attractive than his own, but he would correctly maintain that this does not establish the truth of Christ one bit. Mochul'sky, for instance, argues correctly that without Christ there is no essential manhood, humanity, or love. But he fails to see that this does not prove that there *are* such things as essential manhood, humanity, and love.[18] The Grand Inquisitor is not wrong because he sees man as weak and slavish, or because he is contemptuous of man. Nor does he contradict himself when he speaks of working for man's happiness, while seeing him as weak and slavish. He loves man for what he is, not for what he is not, and the accepts the melancholy fact of man's weakness because it is a fact. The Grand Inquisitor is wrong only if his view of human nature is wrong, and neither logic nor the facts of history are against him. The testimony of things seen are overwhelmingly on his side. But Christ never based his truth on the testimony of things seen, but on the testimony of things unseen. The demand for proof is the second temptation, and what he offers men is the freedom and struggle to reject the demand for proof. What he offers them is the same as what he demands of them. He asks them to rise above their natures, to make over their natures in his image, and they can do that only as he had done it: in loneliness, terror, and anxiety. Men crave what he asks them to give up: the firm foundations of conduct that will assure them that they are

acting rightly; the assurance that they are right beforehand, so that they may be relieved of the terrors and anxiety of a free conscience, and so that they may have the
comfort of knowing that others and, best of all, all others
are doing the same thing. But Christ asks something different: though all men be against you, though history prove
it impossible, choose what the heart whispers as possible,
even though this choice will most certainly be in loneliness, anxiety, and despair, with no other guide than Christ.
This choice—against logic, and history and the examples
of others—is Christ's freedom. Why is it freedom? Because
for Dostoevsky freedom is what is determined by nothing
else. A free choice based on the condition of earthly comfort, on the assurance beforehand from miracle, mystery,
and authority, or on the condition that your neighbor believes as you do, is not a free choice. A free faith for Dostoevsky is a faith without conditions; it is a faith that knows
only the free movement of the heart.

Dostoevsky had never before offered himself and his
readers a choice so stark, because he had never granted
so much to his antagonists before. He had not granted so
much in *Notes from the Underground*, where the bulls
had been portrayed as callous, stupid, and slavishly attracted to the laws of nature; nor in *Crime and Punishment*,
where he had been eager to prove Christ right and Raskolnikov wrong; and he had not granted so much in *The
Possessed*, where the antagonist of freedom, the socialists,
are cruelly crushed by satire, and the antagonists of Christ,
Stavrogin and Kirilov, are led down the path to self-destruction. The Grand Inquisitor's monologue is an argument
against Christ, and it is an argument against almost everything Dostoevsky had written up to this point. For the
Grand Inquisitor grants Dostoevsky every premise he had
worked so hard to establish, only to show that the nature
of man Dostoevsky had defined supports not Christ but
the imitation of Christ. Man is a rebel, as Dostoevsky had
shown in *Notes from the Underground*, but he will tire

of his rebellion; he hungers for immortality, but he will accept and, indeed, can endure only the pretense of immortality; he hungers for freedom, but can suffer only the illusion of freedom; he will find neither peace nor equality in socialism, but he will accept socialism because it will give him a *false* peace and equality.

This is Dostoevsky's final statement against God. It is Dostoevsky confronting himself with the candor and courage to place everything he had built up into the balances again. It is his final confrontation with the testimony of things seen and with man's desolating weakness and infinite capacity for self-deception. Only the words he wrote from prison to a friend remain at the end to sustain him, as they had all his life, and to sustain his world: "If anyone proved to me that Christ was outside the truth, and it really was so that the truth was outside Christ, then I should prefer to remain with Christ than with truth." [14]

Smerdyakov

Who is the Grand Inquisitor? He is, of course, first and foremost, Ivan. He is Ivan's hypothetical dream; he is Ivan remaking the world. In his conversation with Alyosha before narrating the poem, he says—as does the Grand Inquisitor—"The kind of love Christ had for people is a miracle that is not possible on earth." When Ivan finishes his catalogue of tales of suffering, he poses for Alyosha precisely the question of remaking God's world without suffering. And this is what the Grand Inquisitor does. Ivan, like the Grand Inquisitor, bases his revolt on the unjustified suffering in the world, a case made stronger by restricting his example to the suffering of children. Like the Grand Inquisitor, he bases his revolt on the evidence of his Euclidian mind, that is, on the testimony of things seen. Both Ivan and the Grand Inquisitor are identified with Satan in the notebooks, and both sum up and express in its most complete form the various antagonists of God that had appeared in Dostoevsky's novels.

Is there an answer to Ivan and the Grand Inquisitor in *The Brothers Karamazov*? Formally, the answer is given in the chapters on the Elder Zossima, although these chapters have often been found wanting. But it is wrong to look only at these chapters for the answer. The full answer is in the words of the Elder Zossima, the character of Alyosha, in Dmitry's regeneration, in the rallying of the boys about Alyosha's truth, and, most powerfully of all, in the consequences of the Grand Inquisitor's views on Ivan. "The Legend of the Grand Inquisitor" is Ivan's dream of a world built on enlightened, virtuous self-interest; but Smerdyakov is the real embodiment of the world built on self-interest. The Grand Inquisitor is what Ivan would like; Smerdyakov is what he is forced to confront. Ivan is both the Grand Inquisitor and Smerdyakov. Ivan makes the poem of the Grand Inquisitor, and he *makes* Smerdyakov, for Smerdyakov's views are formed largely by the long conversations he has with Ivan.

As the dream of the hard, necessary, and tragic conflict against an unjust Christ fades and Ivan turns to go home, reality presses upon him. He is overwhelmed, for some unknown reason, by a vague, nasty feeling, the cause of which he cannot drive away or make clear. It becomes clear when he sees Smerdyakov languidly cooling himself on a bench outside the Karamazov property. At first sight, Ivan understands "that the lackey Smerdyakov lay in his soul and it was precisely he whom his soul could not bear." When he first addresses Smerdyakov, he wants to say: "Get away, miserable idiot. What have I to do with you? But to his astonishment, he asks: "Is my father still asleep, or has he waked?" From the first question, Dostoevsky makes clear what the relations between Ivan and Smerdyakov are and what they will be. It is Ivan who speaks first and he who waits for Smerdyakov's answers; it is Ivan who becomes irritated, excited, perturbed; Smerdyakov is calm and assured. It is Ivan who is deferential; Smerdyakov is almost contemptuous. Ivan is alternately attracted and repelled: he hates the smirking, contemptible lackey, and yet he cannot tear himself away from him. He cannot, because Smerdyakov lies in his soul; it was Ivan who taught Smerdyakov how to see the world, and now it is Smerdyakov who teaches Ivan. Smerdyakov maintains a tone of "I'm only saying what both of us already understand," and he ends up speaking for Ivan: "If I were in your place I should simply throw it all up rather than stay on in such a position."

Reality confronts Ivan with Smerdyakov, and Smerdyakov confronts Ivan with Chermashnya. Ivan's moral problem concerns what appears to him to be a nonsensical and irrelevant decision to go to Chermashnya. But, though simple, the decision represents the moral choice Ivan has to make, and Chermashnya takes on symbolic overtones. The first syllable of the word, *Cher*, is the root of the Russian word "dark," and the practical reason why Fyodor is pressing Ivan to go to Chermashnya is to sell a wood. Chermashnya is a "dark wood." This dark wood points symbolically to the Karamazov corruption. If Ivan goes to Chermashnya and sells the wood for Fyodor, he will save his father 3,000 rubles, precisely the amount Fyodor is using to lure Grushenka to him, and precisely the amount that the desperate Dmitry needs to liberate himself from Katya and to take Grushenka away. Dmitry is convinced that the wood belongs to him, because it is part of the inheritance that Fyodor has stolen from him. The "dark wood" is a point of struggle between father and son, and it lies at the core of the decision Ivan must make: whether to accept his responsibility for his father or whether to turn his back on him. In "The Legend of the Grand Inquisitor" Ivan could reconcile the irreconcilable, but in real life, he must choose. He can prevent the murder, or he can let it happen, and no amount of subtleness can obscure this simple moral decision. The meaning of Smerdyakov's smirking, leering

suggestions is clear to the reader, if not to Ivan. Smerdyakov is telling Ivan that if he goes to Chermashnya it will
be a signal for Smerdyakov to kill Fyodor.

After leaving Smerdyakov, Ivan is filled with vague feelings of hate, spite, and revenge. He cannot understand his
motives. He wants to go out, for some reason, and beat
up Smerdyakov; he is filled with hate and spite even against
Alyosha; and he cannot sleep. He gets up twice to listen to
the restless movement of his father, imagines how he must
be peering into the dark and eagerly awaiting Grushenka,
and his curiosity fills him with self-revulsion. Later, he
will remember it as the vilest act of his life, because his
imagination was already anticipating his father's death, and
in imagining it, wanting it. He will understand that on that
night he wanted his father's death, and in wanting it, he
was already his father's murderer.[15] The next morning, at
his father's prompting, he promises to stop off at Chermashnya on his way to Moscow. At the relay station, however,
he "morally" triumphs by changing his mind and going
straight to Moscow. The change has no moral significance
at all. It made no difference whether Ivan went to Chermashnya or to Moscow; it only made a difference whether Ivan
stayed by his father's side.

Ivan comes back to Skotoprigonevsk five days after his
father's death, and a day after Fyodor is buried. Ivan did
not give his address to anyone, and it takes five days to
find him. But distance and ignorance does not modify the
ugly truth in his heart; the vague suspicion that tortured him
remains with him, and on the first day of his return he
goes to see Smerdyakov. He sees him for the second time
two weeks later, and for the third and last time a little over
a month afterwards. Smerdyakov is like some epicenter of
his moral being, from which he cannot tear himself away
and to which he must return. Ivan wants to be convinced
that Mitya is the murderer, and he is convinced again and
again, but each time the evidence—even though seemingly
irrefutable—does not satisfy him. Smerdyakov convinces

him on the first interview that he could not possibly have been the murderer and that there has been no "plot" between them and indeed no preparation for the crime. If a clever man were planning a crime, Smerdyakov tells Ivan, he would not leave such a clue as to tell another of it beforehand. Ivan is so satisfied after this interview that he tells Smerdyakov: "I don't suspect you at all, and even consider it ridiculous to do so; on the contrary, I am grateful to you for having put me at peace." But he is not set at peace; neither the official arraignment of Dmitry, nor Smerdyakov's assurances, nor the document Katerina shows him—after the second meeting with Smerdyakov—can quiet him. In the third meeting with Smerdyakov, he learns what he dreads knowing, but must know: that Smerdyakov has murdered Fyodor, that he, Ivan, knew it would happen, wanted it to happen, and encouraged Smerdyakov to do it. When Smerdyakov tells him that, the face of Smerdyakov—physically wasted by sickness and his yellow eyes sunken—appears to him to be that of a phantom. At that moment Ivan understands that the repulsive thing Smerdyakov represents is in himself, and the objective Smerdyakov is indeed unreal.

When he hears the ugly truth from Smerdyakov that he is the murderer, the ditty of a drunken peasant, "Vanka Has Gone off to St. Petersburg," rings through his mind. And it rings through his mind because the ditty reminds him of the hardness of his heart, where the impulse to murder had come and where it still lay. This is the refrain that a drunken peasant was singing when Ivan had picked his way through the snowstorm on his way to the third meeting with Smerdyakov. He had collided with the peasant, pushed him to the ground, and had indifferently left him to freeze to death. Ivan recognizes that he is the murderer of his father, because his heart is indifferent—as it was to the peasant—to the fate of his fellow man. On his way back, Ivan finds the peasant again and attempts to make up for his hardness. He has made up his mind to confess the next day, and he spends almost an hour seeing to it that the peasant is well cared for. But it is his head that moves his actions, and not his heart. He is too satisfied with his deed and too conscious of the clarity of his mind.[16] Ivan's heart first moves only after the Devil's last visit to him and after he learns of Smerdyakov's death. Alyosha comes to give him the news that Smerdyakov had hanged himself, and Ivan notices that Alyosha is cold. Feeling sympathy for him, he says, "Alyosha you are frozen, you've been out in the snow. Would you like some tea? Are you cold? If you want, I'll order some tea? *C'est à ne pas mettre un chien dehors.*"

Ivan dreamed of a world in which "all was permitted" and of a hero who, like the Grand Inquisitor, would by sacrifice and suffering build a better world. But the living embodiment of his dream is a knavish, cowardly, simpering cook who dreams, not of sacrificing himself for the happiness of all men, but of establishing a restaurant in Moscow, wearing lacquered boots, and, if possible, trading Russia, a nation of scoundrels, for a wiser nation, France. Ivan had deceived himself, but in his deception lay the seed of a better Ivan. The sign of the better Ivan is the suffering he undergoes before the ugly truth of his part in the murder.

As Smerdyakov stands behind the figure of the Grand Inquisitor, so too the sponging, shabby, low-thinking Devil who visits him in his room stands behind the august antagonist of Christ. There is even some evidence that Smerdyakov and the Devil are one; as Smerdyakov withdraws from life—he strikes Ivan as a phantom in his last talk with him—the Devil appears. The Devil appears for his third meeting with Ivan—the only one that is dramatized—at precisely the moment that Smerdyakov dies. Ivan tells us that his conversation with the Devil takes an hour—he can tell this by the wet towel he put to his brow to dispel what he thinks is a hallucination—and Alyosha arrives to tell Ivan that Smerdyakov has hanged himself an hour before.

Father Zossima and Alyosha

To Ivan's law of "all is permitted," the Elder Zossima answers that "All are responsible for all." This may seem like pretty weak ammunition against the onslaught of the Grand Inquisitor, but the two arguments are incommensurate. What does the law of "all are responsible for all" mean? It means that every person has the obligation, or rather the constant and never ending opportunity, of changing the world and himself by accepting and suffering the outrages of the world. Our responsibility lies most in suffering the beast of self-will in ourselves; we confront this beast at every moment, and we can conquer it only by denying it wholly and unconditionally. The impulse to assert our wills expresses itself in endless variety, but most directly in the hurt we inflict on others. The impulse can also spring from, and corrupt, our good impulses: from the pity we give others, from our demands for justice, from love, reason, virtue, and even from our faith in God. For Zossima—and for Dostoevsky—there can only be one answer: a total acceptance of others, all others. There is only one right way to accept (the wrong ways are endless), and that is to humble oneself before all others; and there is only one way to humble oneself (the wrong ways are endless), and that is to see oneself as endlessly and hopelessly more sinful than all others. At the first impulse to see oneself as less sinful than anyone, the will and the self spring to birth, bringing with them separation, hardness, and the endless duels of Dostoevsky's world. *This is why the hardest thing—and the most beautiful—is not to forgive but to accept forgiveness.* To forgive is to imply that one has the right to forgive, but to accept forgiveness is to acknowledge one's need of forgiveness. The Elder even goes so far as to say that one must humble oneself before all nature, asking forgiveness even of the birds. All nature is one unity, and the smallest act reverberates through all of it. This is a thought that will be repeated by Sartre and other existentialists much later: "Everything is like an ocean; everything flows and touches. You touch the universe in one place, and like a lyre, it trembles in another place." If one were able to humble oneself before all others, Dostoevsky seems to say, the world would be beautiful, because in denying oneself, one would be gaining all others. Although suffering is a key to Elder Zossima's and Dostoevsky's religious ideal, it is not an end. Again and again, in both his fictional and nonfictional writings, Dostoevsky insists on the *joy* of religious consummation.

The mysterious stranger whom Father Zossima guides to rebirth learns that "the love of humility is a terrifying strength," and it is a love that is bought by hard work and struggle. The struggle for that kind of love is embodied in Alyosha. Zossima is his spiritual father—the embodiment of the law "all are responsible for all"—and Fyodor is his natural father, the embodiment of the law "all is permitted." Alyosha's spiritual illumination, the dream of the miracle of Cana, occurs when his natural father is being murdered. Alyosha lives in two worlds, and his ceaseless trips between the Karamazov house and monastery point to this split. His heart is filled with anxious compassion for the fates of his brothers and his father; he also feels the Karamazov lust Dmitry speaks of, the rebellion Ivan feels (he tells Lise that perhaps he doesn't believe in God), but he is most seriously tempted by his love for the Elder. This man, in his eyes the most worthy of all men, suffers in the eyes of the world—and temporarily in his eyes—shame and disgrace.

Everyone had expected the Elder to receive at his death a special sign from heaven as a reward for his sanctity, and according to popular tradition the sign was to manifest itself in the nondecomposition of his body. When the body not only decomposes and smells—but does so even more quickly than the body of an ordinary sinner—many gloat in the hardness of their hearts, but Alyosha despairs in the mildness of his heart. But the despair is as much wrong as is the cynicism and glee. Alyosha needs help to bring him out of a bruised, self-pitying love which refuses to accept what is not his to judge. This help comes from a sinner, Grushenka, who offers him her onion of compassion. What Grushenka touches is completed in the vision of the Cana of Galilee. After returning from Grushenka's, he returns to the coffin of his Elder, where, with the monotonous praying of Father Paissy filling the air, he falls asleep and has his vision. Dostoevsky has called this scene the most essential in Book Seven of Part Three and perhaps the most essential in the novel.[17] As Alyosha prays, his heart becomes filled with sweetness, and the "self-pitying, aching, torturing pity he had felt that morning no longer afflicted his soul." The miracle he had wanted for his Elder is effected in his heart and symbolically in the dream he has of Christ's turning of the vessels of water into wine at the marriage of the Cana of Galilee. Here Christ creates a miracle for the joy of others, and not for himself, "not to show his own terrible power, but to visit gladness upon men." The miracle Alyosha experiences in his heart is the change from his own "hurt" feelings to the shared joy of others. The Elder, who has been humbled, takes the hand of Alyosha, who has rebelled against the humbling, and together they are wedded in Christ's joy, the joy of forgiveness by the acceptance of forgiveness. "All that is true is beautiful, and all that is beautiful is completely filled with forgiveness," Alyosha whispers to himself in understanding.

The Beast Pen

When Ivan makes his decision to leave his father's side for Chermashnya-Moscow, he leaves the way clear for the murder to take place. Smerdyakov has his simulated fit; Grigory has his attack of lumbago; Marfa prepares her remedy, rubs him down, and together they drink what is left; Dmitry runs off in foolish quest of the 3,000 rubles he needs to save his honor and to stay his hand from murder; he tries to borrow it from Samsonov, Grushenka's keeper, where he is dismissed; then he goes to Mme. Khokhlokov's, where she advises him to seek his fortune in gold mining; and finally he goes to Chermashnya, where he makes a futile and frustrating trip to sell the dark wood. When Dmitry returns to town, he learns that Grushenka is not where she told him she would be—at Samsonov's—and he assumes that she has gone to Fyodor's. He grabs a pestle, and with murder in his heart leaps over the Karamazov fence. All his hate is centered on the repulsive old man who has stolen his inheritance, who has destroyed his self-respect before Katerina, and who is now (symbolically with the same 3,000 rubles) stealing the woman he is in love with. He is crazed with desire for Grushenka, with hate for his father, and he is oppressed by Katerina's sacrificial love.

When Dmitry leaps over the fence into the Karamazov garden, Dostoevsky brings to completion a symbolic pattern of detail that he has built up throughout the novel. It begins with the basic postures of father and son: the father crouching behind the high fence that surrounds the Karamazov house, trying to lure Grushenka with the bait of 3,000 rubles, and the son crouching, as if in a lair, in the adjoining garden waiting to see if the bait will be taken. A series of fences rib the back alleys of the town, and they all seem to lead to the high-fenced Karamazov garden. Alyosha has to scramble over them on two occasions in order to see Dmitry. The first time he has to tuck up his cassock and needs Dmitry's strong arm to help him over; the second time (after he has been weakened by his lack of faith) he scampers over the fence without Dmitry's

help, significantly at the same spot. What finally draws together the "topographical" symbolism of the town is the
name of the town itself, which is mentioned only a few
times. The name is Skotoprigonevsk, a place-name adapta-
tion of the Russian word *skotoprigonny*, that is, "beast cor-
ral" or "beast pen." The Karamazov garden is the posi-
tional center of the town's corruption, and one's own corruption is measured by the distance from this center. The
core of the Karamazov corruption lives in the pen: Fyodor,
Smerdyakov, and Ivan; Dmitry lives just outside the garden
and symbolically just outside the corruption; and Alyosha
is a moving link between them, the world of the monastery
and the world of the beast pen.

Dostoevsky seems to have this pattern of detail very
much in mind when he brings the threatened murder—so
long held in suspension—to a climax. When Dmitry leaps
over the fence to kill his father, Dostoevsky is careful to
mark it as precisely the place where Stinking Liza had
climbed over so as to lay the visible progeny of Fyodor's
sensual corruption, Smerdyakov, at his father's feet. When
Marfa awakens on that fateful night to Grigory's groans,
she thinks of the groans of Stinking Liza on the night she
had given birth to Smerdyakov. Dostoevsky insists on
linking the birth of Smerdyakov with the death of Fyodor,
and his intention is clear. Smerdyakov, the visible embodiment of Fyodor's sensual corruption, returns to kill the
progenitor.

Dostoevsky completes the spatial symbolism with the
murder and its aftermath: all the Karamazovs in the beast
pen are destroyed, and indeed destroy each other and themselves; all those outside the beast pen are saved. Dmitry leaps
in and out over the high fence, saved by the forgotten
softness of his heart; Alyosha is only a visitor from another world to the pen. Fyodor dies by what he had pro-
duced, and Ivan is driven crazy by what he, too, had pro-
duced, Smerdyakov's mind.

The Trial

The novel ends with more than a hundred pages devoted to the trial. The long exposition at the beginning of the novel, which had set the stage for the drama of the Karamazov crime, is now balanced by the long exposition of "who did it" and why. The crime commands the attention of all Russia; it provokes curiosity, ambition, romance, and, perhaps most of all, the sacred rage of liberalism. There is something for everyone in the crime and in the trial. For the ladies in the galleries there is the piquant scandal of father and son fighting over the town wench and of a highborn woman struggling with the town wench over the town brawler. For the liberal elements from Moscow and St. Petersburg, there is the sacred cause of liberating Russia from outworn prejudices and ushering her into a new era of enlightened humanitarianism. For Fetyukevich, the defense attorney, there is the opportunity to show off his incomparable talents, for everyone is convinced that Dmitry is guilty, and the evidence is overwhelmingly against him. For the reader and for Dostoevsky, there is the awesome problem of the right of a child to raise his hand against his father, and by analogy the right of humanity to raise its hand against God.

Everyone judges according to his own measure. The ladies are convinced that Dmitry is guilty, and because he is guilty they are certain he will be acquitted. In this way the drama and excitement will be greater, and the lawyer from St. Petersburg will be better able to display his talents. Fetyukevich judges according to his measure too: what he argues for must be right. The liberals come to judge by the measure of the new humanitarianism, according to which Dmitry must be acquitted if Russia is to progress. The peasants come to judge also, but their measure is the true measure.

The legal process is essentially irrelevant to what happens at the trial, to what is true, and to what influences the jury. Despite his adroitness, skill, and brilliant tactics, the defense attorney discovers no new facts; they come by themselves. Katerina's startling revelation that Dmitry wrote to her on the eve of the murder threatening to kill his father and Ivan's confession of the murder come as interruptions, and not as results of the legal process. The legal process is an obstacle to the facts, for the participants must rend the decorum of the court to have their say, and the truth is disbelieved and the lies believed. All Fetyukevich succeeds in doing is besmirch the character of every witness he examines. Katerina's confession of Dmitry's guilt is false and believed; Ivan's confession is true and disbelieved. The legal process brings forth only technique, ambition, and triviality. It is as if there were no place in the trial except for sneers, innuendoes, assassinations of character, and rhetoric. Rakitin can have his say, but Dmitry must shout in defiance of decorum to have his say. Rakitin is listened to and even applauded, but Ivan is looked upon as insane.

After the disorders, the bell ringings, the rhetoric, and showmanship, there remains the silence of the jury. We are told about their composition [18] at the beginning of the trial, and even the narrator has some doubts that the truth will be weighed wisely in such company. We hear nothing more of them until they deliver their judgment. When they speak, their words are an outrage to all present: to Fetyukevich's irresistible rhetoric, to the ladies' anticipation of a beautiful ending and to the progress of Russia toward some humanitarian dawn. The jury finds Dmitry guilty without qualification on every count. It is as if everything that had gone on had not touched them, and as if the whole trial had served no purpose. Fetyukevich had touched everyone but the jury. The judgment is final, unadorned, unwavering, positive, and brutal, and to everyone present—and perhaps to the reader—completely baffling. Nor can we congratulate them for ignoring the rhetoric and sticking to the facts, for—and this must increase the outrageousness—they are wrong as to the facts. They have judged an innocent man guilty. They are wrong, and Fetyukevich is right. Whatever his motives, he comes close to understanding how the crime actually took place, who committed it, and why it was done. One can go through all the points of contention and find that the prosecutor is wrong on almost every count and Fetyukevich right. In fact, not only is Fetyukevich right with most of the facts but his final appeal is based on a position that sounds like a summation of Dostoevsky's ideas. When Fetyukevich argues that if the court sends Dmitry to prison it will only harden him into resentment and will make him feel justified in his crime, he is saying almost the same thing that Dostoevsky said in *The House of the Dead*. And when he pleads with the court to show mercy and love, he argues for the kind of forgiveness that Dostoevsky would seemingly countenance. What is wrong with his appeal? Like the Grand Inquisitor, Fetyukevich uses the words of Christ for a different end. As the Grand Inquisitor and Ivan have argued, he argues that children have a right to turn against their fathers when they feel themselves wronged. There is a difference, and it is significant: Ivan cannot live with his conclusions; Fetyukevich is untouched by his argument. In fact, Fetyukevich goes so far, in championing the rights of "wronged" children before their fathers, by calling Dmitry's alleged murder of Fyodor a parricide only by prejudice.

The peasants know better. They reflect the ancient stubborn faith of the people in their conviction that man is responsible for his acts, and that his responsibility lies in the movement of his heart. Dmitry, for them, is guilty because he had raged against his father, and because in his heart he had desired the death of his father. Dmitry recognizes the truth of their judgment, and he accepts it. He has felt the stirrings of a new man within him, and the sign of that new life, the condition of it, is the recognition of his guilt. Dmitry wants to suffer, not in tribute to his strength in bearing it, but for God's sake. He accepts the suffering of the children in the burnt-out huts, whereas Ivan refuses to accept the suffering of children. Ivan uses the sufferings of children as a premise of revolt, Dmitry as a recognition of his responsibility.

Dmitry as purified by suffering seems to come to understand clearly, near the end of the novel, the insult he had offered Katerina. This is why he asks, through Alyosha, that Katerina come to his hospital room and forgive him. He knows that she has hurt him grievously and that it is her testimony that has probably condemned him to Siberia, but he has come to know that only forgiveness by her and not by him can cleanse her soul. His own readiness to be "forgiven" is a sign of the new man which has arisen within him. When she appears at the door of his hospital room—an appearance that recalls her first visit to him—she is momentarily wrenched out of the trap of self-willed hurting and being hurt by the sincerity of a changed and purified Dmitry. For a few minutes the astonished Alyosha witnesses one of those rare scenes, evocative of the moment that had flashed through the duel between the Underground Man and the prostitute, when love and sacrifice are no longer weapons for punishment but bonds for discovered souls. It is a moment when the pressure of self-conscious hate explodes into selflessness, so thin is the edge between the deepest hurt and deepest love. But only for a moment —Dostoevsky was too much of a realist for this to endure for more than a flash of the spirit. Rebuffed by Grushenka, Katerina returns with bitter satisfaction to the trap of her old self. With eyes flashing and voice strangled with resentment, she leaves the last pages of the novel approving the insult of Grushenka.

The novel begins with the hand of the child raised against the father; it ends with the cheers of children for another Karamazov. The "boys" are gathered about the coffin of Ilyusha, united in their love for him and in their admiration for Alyosha. With Alyosha, they are confident in the beauty of life, the reality of immortality, and the hope in the future. Dostoevsky began *The Brothers Karamazov* as a novel about children; he visited pedagogical institutions; his first notes on the novel had to do with children. Despite this, the long chapters on the boys are only vaguely connected with the narrative proper. Alyosha is our primary link with the boys; as he is a link between the world of the Karamazovs' and the world of the monastery, so, too, is he a link between the worlds of the adults and of the children. He suffers the anger and physical attack of Ilyusha, the intellectual exhibitionism of Kolya, and by suffering he quiets their anger against the world. What we find in the children's world are the incipient passions of the adult's world. Ilyusha's anger and shame before his father's disgrace reminds us of Dmitry's honor; Kolya's learning reminds us of Ivan's; and his cruelty to Perezvon, Ilyusha's dog, reminds us of Smerdyakov's cruelty. But there is a difference. Kolya may revolt against his family, but he is quickly won over to love and admiration; he may illustrate some of the same hard vanity in knowledge that Ivan did, but his armor is quickly pierced by a little love. Ilyusha may show a tendency to *nadryv*—by attacking a crowd of boys and by attacking Alyosha so that he may be punished. But he seeks to bear punishment for his father, whereas Dmitry uses his honor as justification to threaten his father. One spark of love is enough to consume the paper forts the boys have built about themselves. Alyosha is the igniting force, for he makes their defenses unnecessary. The boys may fight and even hate, but the instinctive wells of love and compassion have not dried up, and they are quickly reunited in the despair of Ilyusha over his lost dog and in the love and faith over his dead body. The shadow of the adult world hangs over them, but it is quickly dispelled, and Alyosha, a child himself in the mildness and quickness of his heart, strives to keep them that way.

The fates of the brothers at the end of the novel are

still in the making, pointing to the continuation of *The Brothers Karamazov* Dostoevsky had planned. Ivan burns in the fever of a divided self; Dmitry has taken up the cross of his guilt; Alyosha stands at the threshold of the world in which he will reside. But perhaps the most unfinished aspect of this last great work of Dostoevsky is the stark choice he has dramatized in the "Legend of the Grand Inquisitor" between the truth of the Grand Inquisitor and the truth of Christ, between the craving of man for certitude and the terrible anxiety of a free and conditionless faith. This is a choice that for Dostoevsky can be made only in the lonely anguish of each man's heart, and it is a choice that has split Dostoevsky's critics into two irreconcilable groups, each insisting that Dostoevsky is on his side. We know on which side Dostoevsky wanted to be, and there is nothing more we can prove. He too, I am sure, suffered the anguish of the choice which he dramatized so brilliantly, so convincingly, and so clearly that we too as readers must, as we admire the drama, give assent to one or the other: Christ or the Imitation of Christ. And it matters little what we say, for the choice will be made without our words.

Notes

Chapter One

1. V. G. Belinsky, "Vzglyad na russkuyu literaturu 1846 goda," in *F. M. Dostoevsky v russkoy kritike*, ed. A. A. Belkin (Moscow, 1956), p. 32. "No v 'Dvoynike' est' eshche i drugoy sushchestvenny nedostatok: eto ego fantastichesky kolorit. Fantasticheskoe v nashe vremya mozhet imet' mesto tol'ko v domakh umalishennykh, a ne v literature, i nakhoditsya v zavedovanii vrachey, a ne poetov."

2. *Ibid.*, p. 33. "V iskusstve ne dolzhno byt' nichego temnogo i neponyatnogo."

3. Belinsky, "Peterburgsky sbornik," in *F. M. Dostoevsky v russkoy kritike*, p. 27.

4. N. K. Mikhaylovsky, "Zhestoky talant," in *F. M. Dostoevsky v russkoy kritike*, p. 345. This article was first published in 1882.

5. *Ibid.*, p. 364.

6. A sample is the following: "On, v litse Makara Alekseevicha, pokazal nam, kak mnogo prekrasnogo, blagorodnogo i svyatogo lezhit v samoy ogranichennoy chelovecheskoy nature." *Peterburgsky sbornik*, p. 15.

Chapter Two

1. K. Mochul'sky, *Dostoevsky, zhizn' i tvorchestvo* (Paris, 1947), p. 173. French translation available: *Dostoïevski, l'homme et l'œuvre* (Paris, 1962).

2. Leonid Grossman, "Dostoevsky i Evropa," *Russkaya mysl'* (Nov. and Dec., 1915), p. 58.

3. Georgi Chulkov, "Dostoevsky i utopichesky sotsializm," *Katorga i ssylka, 51* (1929), 29.

4. Nicholas V. Riasanovsky, "Fourierism in Russia: an Estimate of the Petrashevtsy," *American Slavic and East European Review*, XII (1953), 289–302.

5. Leonid Grossman, *Put' Dostoevskogo* (Leningrad, 1924), p. 81.

6. I. Belchikov, "Pokazaniya F. M. Dostoevskogo po delu Petrashevtsev," *Krasny arkhiv, 45* (1931), 140.

7. *Ibid.*, pp. 141–142.

8. *Ibid.*, p. 123.

9. F. M. Dostoevsky, *Dnevnik pisatelya* (Paris, 1951), Vol. 1, p. 359.

10. *Ibid.*, Vol. 3, p. 28.

11. *Ibid.*, Vol. 4, p. 52.

12. Vladimir Solovyov, *Tri rechi, 1881–1883* (Berlin, 1925), p. 13. "Khudshie lyudi myortvogo doma vozvratili Dostoevskomu to chto otnyali u nego lyudi intelligentsii."

13. Mochul'sky, p. 161.

14. Ernest J. Simmons, *Dostoevsky: The Making of a Novelist* (London, 1950), p. 84.

Chapter Three

1. The phrase that he uses is "edinstvo zakonov prirody." He says: "Not very long ago, it seemed that so-called organic chemicals (for example, acetic acid) exist only in organic bodies; but now it is known that in some circumstances, these acids appear in inorganic bodies, so that organic combinations of elements and non-organic combinations appear and exist according to the same laws." *Antropologichesky printsip v filosofii* (Moscow, 1948), p. 37. In an earlier essay (1858) entitled "Russky chelovek na rendez-vous," Chernyshevsky applies the law of one nature to annihilate the differences between people:

"Every man is like every other man. In each, there is what there is in the other. And the closer you examine human nature, the more you become convinced of this axiom. Differences seem important only because they lie on the surface and they hit the eye, but underneath this appearance lies a complete identity of one nature with all others." *Polnoe sobranie sochinenii* (St. Petersburg, 1906), Vol. 1, p. 94.

2. "The phenomenon that we call the will is itself one of the links in the chain of facts and phenomena bound by cause and effect." *Antropologichesky printsip,* p. 60.

3. "Moral science is different from so-called natural science only because the premises of moral science began to be worked out later than those of natural science and have not yet been worked out as fully." *Ibid.,* p. 36.

4. "People talk as if animals do not reason; that's pure nonsense. You pick up a stick before a dog; the dog picks up its tail and runs away; why? It ran away because it reasoned syllogistically: when I am hit with a stick, I feel pain; this man wants to hit me with a stick; therefore, I will run away from him so as not to feel pain from his stick." *Ibid.*

5. *Ibid.,* p. 65.

6. Valkovsky says: "Ya naverno znayu chto v osnovanii vsekh chelovecheskikh dobrodeteley lezhit glubochayshy egoizm. I chem dobrodel'nee delo—tem bolee tut egoizma. Lyubi samogo sebya—vot odno pravilo kotoroe ya priznayu."

7. Chernyshevsky says: "Voobshche nadobno byvaet tol'ko vsmotret'sya pristal'nee v postupok ili chuvstvo, predstavlya-yushchiesya beskorystnymi, i my uvidim, chto v osnove ikh vse-taki lezhit ta zhe mysl' o sobstvennoy lichnoy pol'ze, lichnom udovol'stvii, lichnom blage—lezhit chuvstvo nazyvaemoe egoizmom."

8. N. A. Dobrolyubov, *Zabitye lyudi* in *F. M. Dostoevsky v russkoy kritike* (Moskva, 1956), pp. 39–95. See pp. 54–56.

Chapter Four

1. N. K. Mikhaylovsky, "Zhestoky talant," *Dostoevsky v russkoy kritike,* p. 317.

2. The word *obida* is usually translated as "insult," but because of its social connotations, "insult" is too restrictive.

3. In 1837, Dostoevsky was on his way to a military engineering school in St. Petersburg, and he witnessed a scene that remained in his memory for the rest of his life. In his *Diary of a Writer* (January, 1876) he tells of seeing a State Courier beat his coachman with his fist, and the coachman beat the horses. The rhythm of hurt passing from one being to another was an early instance of what was to be a premise of his mature psychology.

4. Dostoevsky was aware of the power of an outraged will early in his life. In a letter to his brother, October 31, 1838, he recounts how he failed an examination and how he would have to repeat a year. "Up to now I have not known what it means to have one's self-love hurt. I would have blushed if such a feeling had possessed me. But you know; I would like to destroy the whole world in one flash now." *Pis'ma*, I, 49.

Chapter Five

1. Alberto Moravia, "The Marx-Dostoevsky Duel," *Encounter*, VIII (November, 1956), 3–12.

2. Dostoevsky wrote a column in *Time* (*Vremya*) dealing, from time to time, with criminal news. In commenting on the "Lassener" case he explained his intention in this way: "We hope to please the reader from time to time with accounts of famous criminal trials. They are more interesting than any novel because they illuminate dark corners of mankind's soul, corners which art doesn't enjoy touching, and if it touches them does so only in passing. We will choose the most interesting cases. In the current case, the trial concerns a phenomenal man: puzzling, terrifying, and interesting. Low instincts and cowardice before need made him a criminal, but he has tried boldly to put himself forth as the victim of his age. He is boundlessly vain, vanity carried to the utter extreme." Quoted in L. Grossman, "Kompozitsiya romane Dostoevskogo," *Vestnik Europy* (Sept. 1916), pp. 125–126.

3. K. Mochul'sky, *Dostoevsky: Zhizn' i tvorchestvo*, Paris, 1947, pp. 232–233.

Chapter Seven

1. Letter to M. I. Katkov, October 20, 1870. *Pis'ma*, Vol. II, pp. 288–289.

2. Letter to A. N. Maykov, March 14, 1871. *Pis'ma*, Vol. II, p. 333.

3. Letter to A. A. Romanov, February, 1873. *Pis'ma*, Vol. III, p. 50.

4. Irving Howe, "Dostoevsky: The Politics of Salvation," *Kenyon Review*, XVII (Winter, 1955), 42–68.

5. Philip Rahv, "Dostoevsky in *The Possessed*," in *Image and Idea: Fourteen Essays on Literary Studies* (Norfolk, Conn.: New Directions, 1949), pp. 86–110. First published in *Kenyon Review* in 1936.

6. As an example, see the following from A. L. Volynsky, *Kniga velikogo gneva* (St. Petersburg, 1904), pp. 3–127: "Stavya Boga v zavisimost' ot narodnogo kharaktera i dazhe dopuskal, chto kazhdy sil'ny narod imeet svoego 'osobligo Boga,' chto, 'u vsyakogo naroda svoe sobstvennoe ponyatie o zle i dobre i svoe sobstvennoe zlo i dobro,' Shatov lishaet religioznuyu ideyu osnovnogo smysla i znacheniya." (P. 65.)

7. Dostoevsky even went so far as to call this the theme of his novel. "He who loses his people and his nationality, he loses his faith in his country and in God. If you want to know, this is the theme of my novel. It is called *The Possessed*." Letter to A. N. Maykov, October 21, 1870, *Pis'ma*, Vol. II, p. 291.

8. Albert Camus, *Le Mythe de Sisyphe* (Paris: Gallimard, 1942), p. 147.

9. The relevant passage from Dostoevsky is: "Znaete li pochemu vy togda zhenilis', tak pozorno i podlo? Imenno potomu, chto tut pozor i bessmyslitsa dokhodili do genial'nosti! O, vy ne brodite s krayu, a smelo letite vniz golovoy. Vy zhenilis' po strasti k muchitel'stvu, po strasti k ugryzeniyam sovesti, po sladostrastiyu nravstvennomu. Tut byl nervny nadryv."

10. See discussion of the meaning of *nadryv* on pp. 159–160.

11. George Steiner sees the night that Stavrogin and Liza spend together as evidence of Stavrogin's sterility. See *Tolstoy or Dostoevsky* (New York: Knopf, 1959), p. 184.

12. Dostoevsky wrote to Strakhov: "I need this book [Stankevich on Granovsky] like air, and I need it as quickly as possible; it is most necessary for my novel, and I cannot do without it." *Pis'ma*, Vol. II, p. 256, dated Feb. 26, 1870 and March 10, 1870.

13. L. Grossman, "Dostoevsky v rabote nad Bakuninym,"

Katorga i sylka (1925), Nos. 14–16, pp. 74–91. See also "Speshnev i Stavrogin," *Katorga i sylka* (1924), No. 4, pp. 130–136.
14. Park Petrovskogo Razumovskoy Akademii.
15. E. N. Konshina, *Zapisnye tetradi F. M. Dostoevskogo* (Moscow, 1935), p. 8.
16. *Dnevnik*, Vol. I (1873), p. 351. "Litso moego Nechaeva, konechno, nepokhozhe na litso nastoyashchego Nechaeva. Ya khotel postavit' vopros, i skol'ko vozmozhno yasnee, v forme romana, dat' na nego otvet: kakim obrazom v nashem perekhodnom i udivitel'nom sovremennom obshchestve vozmozhny—ne Nechaev, a Nechaevy, i kakim obrazom mozhet sluchit'sya, chto eti Nechaevy nabirayut sebe pod konets Nechaevtsev?"
17. Letter to Katkov of October 20, 1870, *Pis'ma*, Vol. II, pp. 288–289. "Odnim iz chisla krupneyshikh proisshestvii moego rasskaza budet izvestnoe v Moskve ubiistvo Nechaevym Ivanova. Speshu ogovorit'sya: Ni Nechaeva, ni Ivanova, ni obstoyatel'stv togo ubiistva ya ne znal i sovsem ne znayu, krome kak iz gazet. Da eslib i znal, to ne stal-by kopirovat'. Ya tol'ko beru sovershavshysya fakt. Moya fantaziya mozhet v vysshey stepeni raznit'sya s byvshey destvitel'nostiyu i moy Petr Verkhovensky mozhet, niskol'ko ne pokhodit' na Nechaeva; no mne kazhetsya, chto porazhennom ume moem sozdalos' voobrazheniem to litso, tot tip, kotory sootvetstvuet etomu zlodeystvu.

Chapter Eight

1. W. D. Snodgrass, "Crime for Punishment: The Tenor of Part One," *Hudson Review*, XIII (Summer, 1960), pp. 202–253.

Chapter Nine

1. "On smeyalsya za zemnoy poklon. Ya nenavidela ego," *F. M. Dostoevsky, Materialy i issledovaniya*, ed. A. S. Dolinin (Leningrad, 1935), p. 306.
2. A conventional view is the following: "Ivan gord svoim razumom i emu legche otkazat'sya ot bozh'ego mira chem ot razuma. Esli mir ne opravdan razumom ego nel'zya prinyat'," K. Mochul'sky, *Dostoevsky: zhizn' i tvorchestvo* (Paris, 1947), p. 505.

3. Letter to N. A. Lyubimov of May 10, 1879, *Pis'ma*, IV, 53.
4. Letter to K. P. Pobedonostsev of May 19, 1879, *ibid.*, pp. 56–57.
5. D. H. Lawrence, "The Grand Inquisitor," *Selected Literary Criticism*, ed. Anthony Beal (London, 1955), p. 233.
6. *Ibid.*, p. 234.
7. V. V. Rozanov, *Legenda o velikom inkvizitore F. M. Dostoevskogo*, 3rd ed. (St. Petersburg, 1906), pp. 167–168.
8. "My chelovechnee tebya. My lyubim zemlyu." *Materialy i issledovaniya*, ed. Dolinin, p. 129.
9. *Ibid.*, p. 129.
10. "Mne stoi lish skazat' odno slovo chto ty izverzhen iz ada i eretik," *Materialy i issledovaniya*, ed. Dolinin, p. 133.
11. Philip Rahv, "The Legend of the Grand Inquisitor," *Partisan Review*, Vol. 21 (May–June, 1954), p. 255.
12. In a letter to V. A. Alekseev, June 7, 1876, Dostoevsky interpreted "stones to bread" to mean the social problem of environment. "Kamni i khleby' znachit tepereshny sotsial'ny vopros, sreda," *Pis'ma*, III, 211.
13. K. Mochul'sky, *Dostoevsky: zhizn' i tvorchestvo*, pp. 510–511.
14. Letter to N. A. Fonvizina, Feb. 20, 1854, *Pis'ma*, I, 142. "Eslib kto mne dokazal, chto Khristos vne istiny, i deystvitel'no bylo by chto istina vne Khrista, to mne luchshe khotelos' by ostavat'sya so Khristom, nezheli s istinoy."
15. *Materialy i issledovaniya*, ed. A. S. Dolinin, p. 95. He is referred to here and elsewhere as "ubiitsa."
16. "Odnako kak ya v silakh nablyudat' za soboy! podumal on v tu zhe minutu eshche s bol'shim naslazhdeniem."
17. "Kana Galilleyskaya-sama sushchestvennaya vo vsey knige, a mozhet byt' i v romane." Letter to Lyubimov, Sept. 16, 1879, *Pis'ma*, IV, 114.
18. Entry in the notebooks: Sostav prisyazhnykh, 4-kh chinovnikov, 2-kh kuptsov, 6 meshchan i krestyan, ili obratno." *Materialy i issledovaniya*, p. 336.

Notes on the Writing and Publishing of the Main Works Discussed

FOR THE FOLLOWING MATERIAL I have relied largely, but not exclusively, on the biographical data compiled by Leonid Grossman in *F. M. Dostoevsky* (Moscow, 1958), Vol. 10.

Poor Folk (Bednye Lyudi)

Poor Folk was written in 1844 and 1845. On May 24, 1845, Dostoevsky wrote to his brother Michael: "I finished it about November [1844], but in December I decided to revise it completely; I did the revision and then in February, I began to clean it up, smooth it out, put in and take things out. About the middle of March I was finished and satisfied with it." But in a letter of May 4 of the same year, he wrote his brother that he was still revising it. In May of 1845 the novel was read by Grigorevich and Nekrasov. Nekrasov took the manuscript to Belinsky, who similarly became enthusiastic about it. The novel was first published in *The Petersburg Miscellany* (*Peterburgsky sbornik*) in 1846, but long before that it had become a literary event because of the powerful influence of Belinsky.

The Double (Dvoynik)

Dostoevsky worked on *The Double* in the summer of 1845 and finished it about January of 1846. On the first of February,

1846, he wrote to his brother Michael: "I have just finished the tale of my scoundrel, Golyadkin, that is: I finished it about the twenty-eighth of January. Horror! I wanted to finish it in August, and it stretched out to February." *The Double* was published in *The Fatherland Notes* (*Otechstvennye zapiski*) in February, 1846. The original title was *The Double: The Adventures of Mr. Golyadkin*. Dostoevsky wrote to his brother Michael of its reception: "The first impression was one of uncontrolled enthusiasm, talk, hubbub. The second reaction was critical; that is, both our friends and the general public found Golyadkin to be boring and lifeless. It seemed to some to be so stretched out as to be unreadable." Dostoevsky was disappointed in its reception, and was convinced for the rest of his life that the central idea was important and with proper revision could be made more effective. He planned to revise *The Double* for the 1860 edition of his works. In 1859, having returned recently from Siberia, he wrote his brother from Tver: "About the middle of December I'll send you or bring you a revised *Double*. Believe me that this revision and the preface to it will be worth a new novel. They will see finally what *The Double* really is. . . . Why should I lose an excellent idea, an important social type, whom I first discovered and put forth?" In the notebooks covering the years 1861–1864, Dostoevsky included plans for revising *The Double*. He planned to make Golyadkin a Fourierist, a member of the Petrashevsky circle, and to give him dreams of starting an uprising in Russia. Golyadkin Jr. was to work for the police. For the Stellovsky edition of his works, 1865–1866, Dostoevsky was so busy writing *The Gambler* and *Crime and Punishment* that he was not able to use his plans and notes, and he restricted his revisions to shortening several parts and to making some stylistic changes. This small revision did not satisfy him, and he continued to look upon *The Double* as harboring an important idea that he had never really exploited properly. As late as November, 1877, he wrote in his *Diary of a Writer:*

"This novel positively did not come off, but the idea was clear [*svetlaya*] enough, and indeed I never brought to literature a more important [*seryoznee*] idea. But the form of the novel never came off. About fifteen years later I revised it for a collected edition of my works, but again it did not come off. If I were to take up this idea again, I would give it a completely different form. But in 1846 I did not find this form and I couldn't master the material."

Mr. Prokharchin (Gospodin Prokharchin)

Dostoevsky began *Mr. Prokharchin* in the spring of 1846 and finished it in September of the same year. It was first published in *The Fatherland Notes* in October of 1846. The censors went over it with a heavy hand, and whole passages were cut out. Dostoevsky wrote to his brother: "Prokharchin has been badly mangled in one place. These 'monsieurs' even prohibited the word *chinovnik* [government worker] in one place, and God only knows why. . . . Everything living has disappeared. Only a skeleton of what I wrote remains. I renounce my work."

The Landlady (Khozyayka)

Dostoevsky wrote *The Landlady* from the fall of 1846 to the fall of 1847, and he first published it in *The Fatherland Notes* in October and December of 1847. In 1847 he wrote his brother: "I am writing *The Landlady*. It's coming out better than *Poor Folk*. It's the same kind of work. Inspiration has seized my pen and everything comes straight from the soul. It's nothing like *Prokharchin*, which made me suffer all summer." The novel, however, was badly received by Belinsky and other contemporary critics. Only in our century has Grossman attempted to elevate it to a work of importance.

Netochka Nezvanova

Netochka Nezvanova was first published in *The Fatherland Notes* in the January, February, and May issues of 1849. The original title was *Netochka Nezvanova, the Story of a Woman* (*Netochka Nezvanova, Istoriya odnoy zhenshchiny*). He worked on the tale for more than two years and placed great hopes in it. He was writing *The Landlady* and *Netochka Nezvanova* at about the same time, although the first appeared earlier. The failure of *The Landlady* came as a complete surprise to him, but true to his habit, he accepted the critics' opinion of it as poor. This only increased his hopes that *Netochka Nezvanova* would be great. In February of 1849 he wrote to Kraevsky, one of the editors of *The Fatherland Notes:* "I know very well, Andrey Alexandrovich, that the publication in January of the first part of *Netochka Nezvanova* is very good; it is so good that I know that *The Fatherland Notes* can publish it without shame. It is an important work. It is not only I, but everyone, who is saying this." The journal edition consisted of three parts: "Childhood," "New Life," and "Mystery." With his arrest, the work—which even in the journal edition was unfinished—was broken off. When preparing the work for the 1860 edition, Dostoevsky realized that he could not continue this work—because of other obligations—and he therefore changed the original journal edition in some respects. The three parts were changed to numbered chapters; an episode describing Netochka's acquaintanceship with a boy named Larya, who like her was cared for by the Count, was deleted; and material concerning another character, Fyodor Ferapontovich, who had at one point in the story taken care of Larya and who is one of the "beaten" people in the novel, was also deleted. Having decided not to continue *Netochka Nezvanova,* Dostoevsky eliminated those people and episodes which pointed to further, unwritten portions of the story.

The Uncle's Dream (*Dyadyushkin son*)

Dostoevsky first published *The Uncle's Dream* in the March number of *The Russian Word* (*Russkoe slovo*) in 1859. We don't know exactly when he began work on the novel. But in January, 1856, he wrote Maykov that he was at work on a comic novel, and in the fall of the same year, he wrote to his brother that he had entire episodes of a large novel finished. At the beginning of 1859 he sent the novel to *The Russian Word.* Dostoevsky did not rate this story highly. In September, 1873, he wrote to M. P. Fyodorov: "I have decided that I can't possibly do any revision. Fifteen years have passed since I read *The Uncle's Dream.* Now, I've reread it, and I find it bad. I wrote it when I was in Siberia, when I was just out of prison, and I wrote it with one aim in mind, to get my literary career going again. I was at the time terribly afraid of censors."

A Friend of the Family (Selo Stepanchikov i ego obitateli)

Dostoevsky wrote *A Friend of the Family* in 1858 and 1859, and he first published it in November and December of 1859 in *The Fatherland Notes*. He left off writing it at one point to finish *The Uncle's Dream*. He finished it about the middle of 1859, and at that time he wrote: "The novel I'm sending off to Katkov, I consider much better than *The Uncle's Dream*. There are two important characters in the novel; they are even new, since they have appeared nowhere else. But how am I to finish the novel? I'm rather fed up with it, and indeed it's even worn me out, literally. [*Uzhasno on mne nadoel, dazhe izmuchil menya, bukval'no.*]" The novel was first promised for Nekrasov's *The Russian Word* (*Russkoe slovo*), but Nekrasov broke the promise because he was disappointed with its content. Although Dostoevsky set the novel in the country, he hardly touched on the peasant question or on conditions in the country, which Nekrasov had hoped he would treat.

Dostoevsky had a very high opinion of the work. In the letters he wrote: "There are two enormously typical characters in the novel; I worked on them for five years, and in my opinion they are done extremely well. These characters are fully Russian and up to now hardly touched on in Russian literature. . . . I am sure that there is much in my novel that is weak and bad. But I am also sure—do what you will with me —that there are beautiful parts in it. I have poured them out of my soul. There are scenes of high comedy, scenes that Gogol himself would subscribe to."

The House of the Dead (Zapiski iz myortvogo doma)

The publication of *The House of the Dead* is complicated. The introduction and the first chapter appeared in *The Russian World* (*Russky mir*) on September 1, 1860, and then publication was suspended. Publication was resumed in the first part of 1861; the introduction and the first four chapters were published, and then again publication was cut off. The censors believed that Dostoevsky was not showing the horrors of punishment sufficiently, and they feared that the reader might get a distorted impression of prison life from the novel. The full text of *The House of the Dead* was first published in *Time* (*Vremya*). The first four chapters were published in April, 1861, and the rest was published from September, 1861 to December, 1862. Chapter Eight of Part Two was originally suppressed by the censors, but subsequently published.

Dostoevsky apparently began *The House of the Dead* shortly after getting out of prison. A "Siberian Notebook" has been left by him with folk sayings and expressions, and this notebook first served as a basis for *The House of the Dead*. This was published in *Links* (*Zven'ya*), VI (1936), 415–438. There is even some evidence that Dostoevsky began to write *The House of the Dead* in the prison hospital with the permission of the doctor. One of the first letters to his brother after getting out of prison is a sketch of the new novel. In it he gives the attitude of the "people" toward the gentry: "You, gentry, are hard-nosed; you have pecked us to death. You have tortured us and become worse than any of us."

Turgenev, writing in 1861 from Paris, called it Dantesque and praised it for its sensitive and true psychology. Hertsen wrote: "One must not forget that these years bequeathed us one terrifying book, in its own way a *carmen horrendum*, which will always appear at the entrance of Nikolay's reign, like the famous sign over the entrance to Dante's hell. This is *The House of the Dead* of Dostoevsky. It is a terrifying narrative and the author himself probably did not suspect that in sketching his fellow prisoners with his pen in chained hands, he was creating from the moral atmosphere of one Siberian prison camp frescoes *à la Buonarotti*." Pisarev wrote in *The Destroyed and Those Who Are Being Destroyed* (*Pogibshie i pogibayushchie*) in 1866: "It is hardly necessary to point out to the thinking reader that prisoners, cut off from all their normal rights, still continue to feel and think as do all men. But all readers are not thinking readers, and for that reason it is necessary to point out the human traits of our prisoners. And it is dangerous also."

The Insulted and the Injured (Unizhennye i oskorblyonnye)

The first mention, apparently, of intention to publish *The Insulted and the Injured* is to be found in a letter of the third of November, 1857, written from Semipalatinsk, but Dostoevsky did not work on it until 1860–1861. He first published it in *Time* in January and July, 1861. The original title was *The Insulted and the Injured: From the Notes of an Unsuccessful Writer.* In the same year a revised separate edition came out. Some of the melodramatic scenes were left out, and some of Valkovsky's speeches were shortened. Subsequent editions during Dostoevsky's lifetime contained only stylistic changes.

In an article in *Epoch*, Apollon Grigorev charged that the editors of *Time*, and editors in general, were driving Dostoevsky's talent like a post horse. He was troubled by the injury that serial publication under the pressure of deadlines was doing to Dostoevsky's talent. Dostoevsky answered this sympathetic complaint in *Epoch* in 1864, and said that with the exception of *Poor Folk* and several chapters of *The House of the Dead*, he had published all of his work so that some chapters were in preparation while he was working on others. He had grown accustomed to working so, and he had worked on *The Insulted and the Injured* in the same way. He insisted that no one was driving him, so that if there was anyone at fault it was he himself.

The novel got a mixed reception, with the emphasis on the negative. Chernyshevsky found it good: "Of all the pieces in the number, the most important, and deservedly so, is the novel of Dostoevsky." Dobrolyubov failed to see in his "The Beaten People" (*Zabitye lyudi*) adequate motivation for most of what happens in the work: "Why does Natasha lose her will and reason, and why does Ivan Petrovich politely give in to the nitwit Alyosha? Why does old Ikhmenev, after bearing every kind of suffering, refuse to forgive his daughter so as not to give in to the Prince and his son? Why does Nelli accept so wildly the favors of Ivan Petrovich and then go off and beg so as to use the money she collects for some cup she has broken? Where is the cause of all these implausible, strikingly strange relations among people? Where is the root of this incomprehensible disjunction between what should be natural and reasonable and what is shown?"

Notes from the Underground (*Zapiski iz podpol'ya*)

Notes from the Underground was first published in *Epoch* (*Epokha*). The first part was published in the January and February numbers in 1864 and the second part in April, 1864. Dostoevsky wrote the *Notes* under very difficult conditions: while his first wife was dying and while he was oppressed by debts and the threatened loss of his journal. His first wife died on April 15, 1864, and Dostoevsky wrote his brother on March 20, 1864: "I sat down to work on my novel. I want to get it off my back as soon as possible, but I still want to do it as well as possible. It has been harder to write than I thought it would be. Still it is absolutely necessary that it be good: I personally want it to be good. The tone now seems too strange, sharp, and wild; perhaps it will not right itself; if not, the poetry will have to soften it and carry it off." On April 5, 1864, he wrote to his brother, addressing himself to the relationship between the two parts of the novel: "You understand what a musical *transition* is. It's exactly the same here. In the first part, there seems to be only idle talk; but then suddenly the talk ends up in a catastrophe." Dostoevsky complained to his brother that the next to last chapter of Part One had been mangled and distorted by the censor: "It would be better not to publish at all the next to last chapter (the most important, where the central idea is expressed), than to publish it as it is, that is, in bits and pieces and self-contradictory. But what can I do? The pig of a censor! Where I have scoffed at everything and where I blasphemed at times for appearances—that is permitted, but where I deduce from all this the necessity of faith and Christ, that is forbidden."

In the May number of *The Contemporary* (*Sovremennik*), 1864, Shchedrin satirized the *Notes* in this tone: "At first he talks of various trifles: how he is sick and spiteful, how everything is unstable in this world, how his back hurts and how one cannot be sure if the summer will be good for mushrooms or not, and finally how every person is worth nothing and will not become good until he recognizes that he is worth nothing. . . ." A. Grigorev, on the other hand, praised the *Notes* highly and advised Dostoevsky to continue writing in the same vein. In general, the reception tended to point out negatively the fantastic element in the *Notes*.

Crime and Punishment (Prestuplenie i nakazanie)

Dostoevsky first published *Crime and Punishment* in *The Russian Messenger* (*Russky vestnik*) in 1866 from January to

December. The first separate edition came out in 1867 with some stylistic changes. Editions came out also in 1870 and 1877 during Dostoevsky's lifetime without significant changes. Three of Dostoevsky's notebooks pertain to *Crime and Punishment*. These notes were published in full in 1931 by I. I. Glivenko, *Iz arkhiva F. M. Dostoevskogo, "Prestuplenie i nakazanie."*

On June 8, 1865, Dostoevsky wrote to Kraevsky about a novel called "The Drunkards," which is the first mention of the novel that was to become *Crime and Punishment*. In September of 1865 he wrote his famous letter to Katkov, outlining the plan of the novel:

The idea of the novel cannot, as far as I can see, contradict the tenor of your journal; in fact, the very opposite is true. The novel is a psychological account of a crime. A young man of middle-class origin who is living in dire need is expelled from the university. From superficial and weak thinking, having been influenced by certain "unfinished" ideas in the air, he decides to get himself out of a difficult situation quickly by killing an old woman, a usurer and widow of a government servant. The old woman is crazy, deaf, sick, greedy, and evil. She charges scandalous rates of interest, devours the well-being of others, and, having reduced her younger sister to the state of a servant, oppresses her with work. She is good for nothing. "Why does she live?" "Is she useful to anyone at all?" These and other questions carry the young man's mind astray. He decides to kill and rob her so as to make his mother, who is living in the provinces, happy; to save his sister from the libidinous importunities of the head of the estate where she is serving as a lady's companion; and then to finish his studies, go abroad and be for the rest of his life honest, firm, and unflinching in fulfilling his "humanitarian duty toward mankind." This would, according to him, "make up for the crime," if one can call this act a crime, which is committed against an old, deaf, crazy, evil, sick woman, who does not know why she is living and who would perhaps die in a month anyway.

Despite the fact that such crimes are usually done with great difficulty because criminals always leave rather obvious clues and leave much to chance, which almost always betrays them, he is able to commit his crime, completely by chance, quickly and successfully.

After this, a month passes before events come to a definite climax. There is not, nor can there be, any suspicion of him. After the act the psychological process of the crime unfolds. Questions which he cannot resolve well up in the murderer; feelings he had not foreseen or suspected torment his heart. God's truth and earthly law take their toll, and he feels *forced* at last to give himself up. He is forced even if it means dying in prison, so that he may once again be part of the people. The feeling of separation and isolation from mankind, which he felt immediately after the crime, tortured him. Human nature and the law of truth take their toll. The criminal decides to accept suffering so as to redeem his deed. But it is difficult for me to explain in full my thinking.

Near the end of November, Dostoevsky wrote his friend Baron Vrangel that he had decided on a new plan and that he had burned everything he had written. Later, while the book was being serialized, *The Russian Messenger* wanted him to cut out the chapter in which Sonia and Raskolnikov read the Bible together. On July 10, 1866, for instance, he wrote to A. P. Milyukov:

Well, as it appeared, Lyubimov had another thoroughly insidious idea. It was this: that one of these four chapters must not be published. This was decided by Lyubimov and confirmed by Katkov! I talked it over with them, but they still insist on it. About the chapter itself, I can't rightfully tell. I wrote it in positive inspiration, but it may be that it is bad. They aren't concerned with its literary excellence, but only with its *morality*. I'm in the right on this point. There is nothing immoral in this chapter; in fact, the very opposite is true. But they see it differently, and in fact see even traces of nihilism in the chapter.

Dostoevsky was able to insist on his point of view, and the chapter was retained largely in its original form. In the notebooks on *Crime and Punishment* Dostoevsky fluctuates between various kinds of points of view (some of the notes are even written from the first-person point of view), and between alternative courses of action for Raskolnikov after the killing of the landlady: he has Raskolnikov contemplating another crime and seeing a vision of Christ. He also considers three different endings: the redemption of Raskolnikov in prison (as in the final text), suicide, and fleeing abroad.

The novel was immediately popular and established Dostoevsky as a major writer. Nevertheless, much of the liberal press greeted the book with sharp criticism, especially of its "great men" theory; and some of the liberal press saw Raskolnikov's portrait as a caricature of the radicals. Pisarev, perhaps the most "individualistic" of the radicals, welcomed the book and wrote in *The Struggle of Life* (*Bor'ba za zhizn'*) that the novel described a struggle against poverty and that poverty had motivated Raskolnikov to commit the crime.

The Idiot (*Idiot*)

The Idiot was first published in *The Russian Messenger* from January to February, 1869. Dostoevsky began the book in Geneva in September, 1867, and finished it in Florence in January, 1869. The notes that Dostoevsky left us on the novel are copious, for the novel went through many plans and versions. The notes were published in 1931 in *Iz arkhiva F. M. Dostoevskogo, Idiot. Neizdannye materialy*, Moscow-Leningrad, 1931. In the early plans there is a heavy reliance on the Umetsky case. The Umetskys were a family that misused their children; the older daughter, Olga, tried to set fire to the parents' house several times. The circumstances and trial were played up in the newspapers of the time, and Dostoevsky had access to Russian newspapers and read them avidly and daily. In the early versions of the novel, the idiot is described as a double character: alternately humble and proud, holy and satanic. Dostoevsky describes him in the notebooks: "The last degree of pride and self-interest. He does vile things in spite and thinks that that is the way they must be done." Of the main theme of the novel, Dostoevsky says: "The main idea of the novel: so much power, so much passion in our modern generation and nothing to believe in. Limitless idealism and limitless sensualism." The conception of the idiot we meet in the final text appears in the later plans. In a famous letter to A. N. Maykov on January 12, 1868, Dostoevsky explains his plan to express a positive and beautiful character in *The Idiot:* "For a long time an idea has tortured me, but I was afraid of writing a novel about this idea, because it is too difficult and I am not up to it. But the thought is very tempting, and I love it. This idea is *to depict the wholly beautiful man* [*izobrazit' vpolne prekrasnogo cheloveka*]. There isn't anything more difficult to do, especially in our age." His desire to depict the "positive and beautiful man" was to some extent a reaction to the positive types that the radicals were depicting in their novels, especially beginning with the portrait of Rakhmetov in

What Is to Be Done? by Chernyshevsky. On the subject of "beautiful" types, Dostoevsky also wrote to S. A. Ivanova: "Of the positive types in Christian literature there is only Don Quixote. But he is positive only because he is at the same time comic. Dickens' Pickwick (an infinitely weaker conception than Don Quixote, but nevertheless an immense conception) is also comic and is successful for that reason. We sympathize with the comic figure who is beautiful but doesn't know it. This provoking of sympathy is the secret of humor. Jean Valjean is also a powerful attempt; he awakens sympathy because of the terrible misfortunes he has to suffer and because of the injustice of the society he lives in. I have nothing like these, nothing at all, and consequently I fear dreadfully that it will be a positive failure."

Dostoevsky was not satisfied with the novel when he finished it. On January 25, 1869, he wrote S. A. Ivanova: "I am not satisfied with the novel; I have not expressed a tenth of what I wanted to express; nevertheless, I don't renounce the novel; and I still love the idea, even though it may be unsuccessful." He had a hard time writing the novel; it went through many versions, and the completion came slowly.

The novel was read widely on publication, and most readers found the first part particularly good. Maykov complained about its "fantastic quality" and couldn't get over the fact that the main character was an idiot. Shchedrin saw the task Dostoevsky set himself as so important that the social questions of the day paled by comparison, but he felt that Dostoevsky contradicted himself by criticizing so viciously the radical elements that were striving for the same goals. According to S. T. Semenov, Leo Tolstoy was supposed to have called Myshkin a gem.

The Possessed (Besy)

The Possessed was first published in *The Russian Messenger* in 1871–1872. It came out in a separate edition in 1873. Dostoevsky began the novel apparently as a political pamphlet. In a letter to Strakhov of March 24, 1870, he wrote: "I have great hopes for the piece I'm writing for *The Russian Messenger,* not from an artistic but from a tendentious point of view. I want to express several thoughts, even if the artistic side suffers.

These thoughts have accumulated in my mind and heart and
have to be expressed. Let it be a pamphlet, but at least I'll have
my say."

The Possessed was conceived and begun while he was abroad.
The sources of the novel are principally two: the Nechaev
murder, which occurred on November 21, 1869, and Dostoevsky's thoughts and notes on "The Life of the Great Sinner,"
which had begun under the title of "Atheism" in 1868. The plan
for "The Life of the Great Sinner" is the search of a modern
man for faith, passing through all the fashions and vices of the
age and finally finding Christ. His early plans are to be found
in E. Konshina's edition of the notebooks to *The Possessed,*
which was published in 1935. Of the main conception of "The
Life of the Great Sinner," Dostoevsky wrote to Maykov on
March 25, 1870: "The main question which will appear in all the
parts is the same one I've tortured myself with consciously and
unconsciously all my life: the existence of God. The hero during his whole life is alternately an atheist and a believer, a
fanatic and sectist and then again an atheist." One of the
plans was to have the great sinner meet the monk Tikhon,
and this meeting occurs between Stavrogin and Tikhon in the
suppressed chapter on Stavrogin's confession. Some of the
material for "The Life of the Great Sinner" was subsequently
used in *The Adolescent* and *The Brothers Karamazov.*

In addition to his use of the Nechaev case—which Dostoevsky
insisted he had no intention of using as historical fact—Dostoevsky also leaned heavily on real-life prototypes for some of
the characters in *The Possessed.* T. N. Granovsky, the famous
historian (1813–1857) was the prototype for Stepan Trofimovich
Verkhovensky; Turgenev was satirized in Karmazinov; Shigalyov in the first notes is called V. A. Zaytsev (1842–1882), a
radical follower of Chernyshevsky and Dobroliubov; Virginsky
is at first called Uspensky in the notebooks, after P. G. Uspensky
(1847–1881); and Dostoevsky was thinking of Chernyshevsky's
ideas on love and marriage in *What Is to Be Done?* in the
caricatured portrait of the cuckold Virginsky, who refers
enthusiastically to Chernyshevsky's novel at one point. Finally,
Grossman has made out a case for Stavrogin as a satire of
Bakunin.

Radical critics received the novel negatively, as one would

expect. One critic in *Act* (*Delo*), A. P. Tkachev, saw in *The Possessed* the total bankruptcy of Dostoevsky's talent. Most critics accused him of distorting facts and of having a fantastic conception of nihilism. At the turn of the century *The Possessed* was taken up as prophecy by the symbolist critics, like Merezhkovsky and Volynsky, as indeed it was taken up in America during the forties and fifties.

The Adolescent (Podrostok)

Dostoevsky worked on this novel from February, 1874, to November, 1875, and published it in *The Fatherland Notes* in 1875. It appeared as a separate edition in 1876. Notes to the novel were published in A. S. Dolinin's *V tvorcheskoy laboratorii Dostoevskogo* in 1847.

Dostoevsky had published most of his major and mature novels in the conservative journal *The Russian Messenger,* and in publishing *The Adolescent* in *The Fatherland Notes,* a very liberal journal under the editorship of Nekrasov, he was sharply departing from his usual practice. Dostoevsky himself suggested that the novel be published there, evidently hoping in some small measure to unite conflicting elements in Russian society.

The novel drew heavily on contemporary events. A February, 1874, trial in St. Petersburg of counterfeiters of railroad stock provided a source for what was finally a minor incident; the Dolgushintsy sect and the trial they underwent in July of 1874 provided the source for some of the radical characters Dolgoruky visits and talks with. This sect called for the overthrow of the Czar in the name of "freedom, equality, and brotherhood." Details of this group are to be found in A. Kunklya's book *Dolgushintsy,* published in Moscow, 1932. Their part in the notes is prominent but is sharply reduced in the final version.

In the final text there are four suicides, but in the notes many more were planned: The Adolescent's sister Liza, her small brother, the young Prince Sokolsky, and even the Adolescent—after being accused of theft—were all to commit suicide.

In the early notes Dostoevsky pointed to the main idea of the novel: "Degeneration is the important and clear idea of my novel." In the notes he found nothing in contemporary society that was "general" or "uniting"; everywhere vanity and money ruled. In his diary (one of the earliest entries) he described his hero this way: "He has been hurt [*obizhen*], and the hurt rankles in him, although he knows to the point of suffering that he himself is guilty; he has several hard-to-bear memories of his illegitimate birth, of his mother, whom he had hurt, of his meeting with his lawful brother, who out of pride and arrogance refused to recognize him. His soul is filled with poison, and he has a colossal and monstrous plan to make others pay for what he will not face in himself."

One critic, Avseenko, writing in *The Russian World* (*Russky mir*) in 1875, accused Dostoevsky of extreme naturalism and at the same time of fantastically depicting the abnormal and the sickly. *The Russian Messenger*, Dostoevsky's "parent" journal, found the novel "dirty" and beyond the pale of decency. It pointed particularly to the incident in which an impoverished maiden advertises out of desperation for lessons and receives instead indecent proposals. Shchedrin and Nekrasov valued highly the first two chapters of the novel. P. Tkachev, who wrote two large and excoriating articles on *The Possessed*, and who represented the opinions of the radicals, found *The Adolescent* much better. In fact, writing in *Act* (*Delo*), he found it better than *Crime and Punishment*. He saw in Dostoevsky's characterization of "degenerate society" a new crop of "beaten people." Playing on Dobrolyubov's phrase *zabitye lyudi*, he sees Dostoevsky's world populated with people oppressed by outdated and meaningless ideas.

The Brothers Karamazov (Brat'ya Karamazovy)

Parts One and Two and up to the ninth book of Part Three of *The Brothers Karamazov* were published in *The Russian Messenger* in 1879. The rest of the book was published in the same journal in 1880. The novel came out as a separate edition in 1881. Dostoevsky's wife Anna gave the manuscript of *The Brothers* to Dostoevsky's son Fyodor, who died in 1921, and the manuscript was apparently irretrievably lost. There are a few galley fragments in the Pushkin Library. Notebooks to the novel were first published in German, *Die Urgestalt der*

Brüder Karamasoff (Munich, 1928), and then in Russian in 1935 in A. S. Dolinin's *F. M. Dostoevsky, Materialy i issledovaniya* (Leningrad, 1935).

One of the sources of the novel is the life of one of the prisoners Dostoevsky met in Omsk. His name was Ilinsky, and he had been condemned for killing his father. Later he was found not to be guilty. Some of the material for *The Brothers* appears in the notebooks for *The Adolescent:* the first sketch of the Grand Inquisitor, a description of Stinking Liza, and the three temptations of the Devil. For the portrait of Zossima, Dostoevsky relied on the book *Zhitie i podvigi startsa skhimonakha Zosimy* (Moscow, 1860). The name of the monk in real life was Zakhariya, and like Zossima in the novel, he was an officer who, after a moral crisis, renounced his vain life. Other sources for the novel are childhood memories: one of the estates the family owned was called Chermasnya, and an idiot who roamed the village was called Stinking Liza; the Book of Job, which he read and a copy of which he marked up while working on *The Brothers;* material he had written for the unfinished work "The Life of the Great Sinner"; visits to various pedagogical institutions, an account of which may be found in his diary; and, of course, the political and cultural events of the time and his great and varied readings.

According to his wife's memoirs, Dostoevsky was deep in thought on *The Brothers* by the beginning of 1878, but by the middle of March, 1878, he had not yet begun to write the novel, as is seen by his letter to V. V. Mikhaylov of March 16, 1878. His three-year-old son died May 16, 1878, and this event interrupted his thinking of the novel. At Anna's suggestion he went to Optina Pustyn' monastery with Vladimir Solovyov on June 18, 1878, and spent four days there. On July 11, he wrote S. A. Yurev that he had begun the novel. In late summer and fall he worked hard on the novel, according to his wife's memoirs. He finished the work at the beginning of November, 1880, three months before his death.

The novel was immediately and widely popular. Dostoevsky looked upon it as another rise of his creative powers. Lunacharsky found that Dostoevsky did not have faith in man as a social animal; some of the contemporary critics saw a certain abstractness in his portraiture, though they praised them. But, on the whole, the novel was welcomed by conflicting camps, a last testimony to Dostoevsky's dream—as he expressed it in his "Pushkin Speech"—that the warring elements of Russian thought would be reconciled.

Biographical Data

All dates are according to old Russian calendar except when events take place abroad.

October 30 1821. Dostoevsky is born in Moscow in the right wing of the Marinsky hospital, where his father was a surgeon. The building today is preserved as the Dostoevsky Museum.

January 29, 1837. Death of Pushkin produces a powerful effect on Dostoevsky.

February 27, 1837. His mother dies.

May, 1837. Dostoevsky, with his brother Michael, goes to St. Petersburg to enter a military engineering school. On the way, they witness the scene at a posting station in which a courier hits the driver and the driver hits the horse. Dostoevsky wrote in *The Diary of a Writer* in January, 1876: "This disgusting picture remained in my memory for the rest of my life."

January 16, 1838. Dostoevsky enters the Engineering Institute.

August 9, 1838. Dostoevsky writes his brother about his heavy reading. Among those mentioned are Hoffman, Balzac, Goethe, and Hugo.

October 30, 1838. Dostoevsky writes his father to inform him that he will have to repeat the first year of the studies at the Engineering Institute. He fails algebra and blames it on the spite of one teacher.

June, 1839. His father, Mikhail Andreevich Dostoevsky, is killed by his own serfs. After the death of his wife, the father, a cruel man by nature, had begun to drink more and abused his peasants more and more. His peasants castrate him and pour alcohol down his throat, but call a priest to permit him to confess and receive the last rites.

February 16, 1841 (at the house of his brother Michael). Dostoevsky reads from two dramas he had written, *Maria Stuart* and *Boris Godunov.* Neither has come down to us.

August 12, 1843. Dostoevsky finishes the engineering course and is assigned to work in a military department in St. Petersburg.

December, 1843. During the Christmas holidays, he translates Balzac's *Eugénie Grandet.*

September, 1844. He gives up his job with the government.

September 30, 1844. He writes to his brother Michael that he has finished a novel of the size of *Eugénie Grandet.* He is referring to *Poor Folk.*

Fall, 1844. Dostoevsky meets D. V. Grigorovich. They room together.

Winter, 1845. He works hard on revision of *Poor Folk.* It is believed that he suffers his first attacks of epilepsy while walking with Grigorovich at that time.

May, 1845. He reads the manuscript of *Poor Folk* to Grigorovich. Grigorovich and Nekrasov stay up until four o'clock in the morning reading *Poor Folk* and crying over it. On the following morning the manuscript is given by Nekrasov to Belinsky. Belinsky is also enthusiastic about the manuscript, and calls Dostoevsky to see and talk with him.

Summer, 1845. Dostoevsky begins work on *The Double.*

November, 1845. Dostoevsky writes in one night the story "A Novel in Nine Letters."

January 15, 1846. Poor Folk is published in *The St. Petersburg Miscellany (Peterburgsky sbornik).*

January 28, 1846. Dostoevsky finishes *The Double.*

February 1, 1846. The Double is published in *The Fatherland Notes (Otechestvennye zapiski).*

March, 1846. Belinsky analyzes and criticizes *Poor Folk* and *The Double* in *The Fatherland Notes,* No. 3.

Spring, 1846. Dostoevsky meets Petrashevsky for the first time.

October–November, 1846. Dostoevsky writes his brother that he is working on *The Landlady* and outlines plan of *Netochka Nezvanova.*

January, 1847. "The Novel in Nine Letters" is published in *The Contemporary (Sovremennik).*

April, 1847. Dostoevsky begins to frequent the Petrashevsky meetings.

April–June, 1847. Dostoevsky publishes pamphlets in *The St. Petersburg Chronicle (Peterburgskaya letopis')* in *The St. Petersburg News (S. Peterburgskie vedomosti).*

January, 1848. A Strange Wife is published in *The Fatherland Notes.*

February, 1848. A Faint Heart (Slaboe serdtse) is published in *The Fatherland Notes.*

March, 1848. Belinsky sharply criticizes *The Landlady* in an article entitled "A Survey of Russian Literature in 1847" *(Vzglyad na russkuyu literaturu 1847 goda, vtoraya stat'ya),* published in *The Contemporary,* No. 3.

April, 1848. "The Stories of a Veteran (from the notes of an anonymous writer): I. One who has been retired. II. The Honest Thief" is published in *The Fatherland Notes,* Vol. 4.

September, 1848. The Christmas Tree and the Wedding (Elka i Svad'ba) is published in *The Fatherland Notes,* Book 9.

December, 1848. White Nights and *The Jealous Husband, an Unusual Event (Revnivy muzh)* are published in *The Fatherland Notes,* Vol. 12.

January, 1849. Dostoevsky tells Maykov that the most active of the Petrashevsky members (Durov, smaller circle) have plans for starting a secret printing press.

January–February, 1849. The first two parts of *Netochka Nezvanova* are published in *The Fatherland Notes.*

April, 1849. Dostoevsky reads Belinsky's letter to Gogol at one of the Petrashevsky meetings.

April 22, 1849. The "Third Section" orders arrest of Dostoevsky.

April 23, 1849. Dostoevsky is arrested, his room is searched, and he is conducted to the Petropavlovskaya Prison.

September 30–November 16, 1849. Trial for arrested Petrashevsky members.

December 22, 1849, 7 o'clock in the morning. Mock execution takes place on Semenovsky Square. Sentence commuted to four years of prison and four years in the Siberian army as a private.

December 24, 1849. With other prisoners Dostoevsky, in chains, leaves for Tobolsk.

January 23, 1850. Dostoevsky is signed in at prison at Omsk. He stays there as a prisoner until about the fourteenth of February, 1854.

March 2, 1854. Dostoevsky is signed in as private in the seventh Siberian battalion stationed at Semipalatinsk.

Spring, 1854. One of the first books he reads is Turgenev's *A Sportsman's Sketches.* He reads it with great enthusiasm. Also, he becomes acquainted with Aleksandr Ivanovich Isaev and his wife, Maria Dmitrievna.

November 20, 1855. Dostoevsky becomes a low-ranking officer (*unter-ofitser*).

March 24, 1856. Dostoevsky writes E. I. Totleben, asking for permission to leave the army and permission to publish.

October 1, 1856. For good service Dostoevsky is promoted to second lieutenant (*praporshchik*).

February 6, 1857. Dostoevsky marries the widow Maria Dmitrievna Isaeva.

April 17, 1857. Rights of a nobleman are returned to Dostoevsky.

August, 1857. The Small Hero (*Malen'ky geroy*), written by Dostoevsky in the summer of 1849 while in prison, is published in *The Fatherland Notes.* The story is signed M-i.

March 26, 1858. Dostoevsky is released from army service, and he is put under secret observation. The secret observation will not be lifted until the last year of his life.

May 31, 1858. He writes to his brother Michael that he is writing two novels: *The Uncle's Dream* and *A Friend of the Family* (*Selo Stepanchikovo*).

July 2, 1858. Dostoevsky leaves Semipalatinsk for Tver (now Kalinin).

September 22, 1859. Dostoevsky is in Tver and is forbidden to go to the capital.

November 25, 1859. Dostoevsky learns that his request to live in the capital has been approved.

December, 1859. A little after the middle of the month Dostoevsky returns to St. Petersburg, approximately ten years after he left it in chains.

January, 1860. A two-volume collection of Dostoevsky's works is published by N. A. Osnovsky.

July 8, 1860. Dostoevsky's brother Michael receives permission to publish a monthly, *Time* (*Vremya*).

January, 1861. The first issue of *Time* comes out. First part of *The Insulted and the Injured* is published in this issue.

April, 1861. The publication of *The House of the Dead* (*Zapiski iz myortvogo doma*) is transferred from *The Russian World* (*Russky mir*), where it had been in trouble with the censors, to *Time.*

July 9, 1861. Publication of *The Insulted and the Injured* in *Time* is completed.

August, 1861. Dobrolyubov publishes his article on Dostoevsky's works "The Beaten People" (*Zapitye lyudi*) in *The Contemporary.*

December, 1861. M. Antonovich writes a negative article on the contents and direction of *Time.* The article is entitled "On the Soil—Not in the Agricultural Sense but in the Spirit of *Time.*"

January, 1862. The second part of *The House of the Dead* begins to be published in *Time.*

June 7, 1862. Dostoevsky goes abroad for the first time. He visits Germany, France, and England. He meets Hertsen in Paris and Bakunin in London. Later he visits Switzerland and Italy. His impressions of this trip are published in February and March, 1863, in *Time* under the title: *Winter Notes and Summer Impressions* (*Zimnye zapiski i letnie vpechatleniya*).

August, 1863. Dostoevsky goes abroad for the second time. He meets A. Suslova in Paris; they go off together to Italy; meet briefly in Baden-Baden, and then again in Italy. A. Suslova wrote a book about their relations: *Gody blizosti s Dostoevskim.*

September 5–8, 1863. Dostoevsky meets Turgenev in Baden-Baden.

January 24, 1864. Dostoevsky's brother Michael gets permission to publish a new journal *Epoch.* Permission to publish *Time* had been canceled in the previous year because of an article on the Polish question which was interpreted by a censor as anti-Russian.

March 21, 1864. The first issue of *Epoch* and the first part of *Notes from the Underground* are published.

April 15, 1864. Dostoevsky's first wife, Maria Dmitrievna Issaeva, dies.

July, 1864. Dostoevsky publishes an article anonymously in *Epoch* entitled "Mr. Shchedrin, or Division among the Nihilists" (*"Gospodin Shchedrin ili raskol v nigilistakh"*).

November 28, 1864. Dostoevsky publishes anonymously in the Volume 9 of *Epoch* an article entitled "So as to Finish: A Final Discussion with *The Contemporary*" (*Chtoby konchit': Poslednee ob'yasnenie s "Sovremennikom"*).

April, 1865. Dostoevsky proposes to A. V. Kovrin-Krukovskaya and is refused. Account of this is given in the memoirs of S. V. Kovalevskaya.

June, 1865. The journal *Epoch*, published by Michael and run by Fyodor, ceases publication because of lack of funds.

August, 1865. Dostoevsky goes abroad for the third time.

September, 1865. A. P. Milyukov tries to get Dostoevsky an advance for *Crime and Punishment* (of which Dostoevsky sent him a plan) from various publishers, but without success.

September, 1865. Dostoevsky writes Katkov outlining plan for *Crime and Punishment.*

January to December, 1866. *Crime and Punishment* is published in *The Russian Messenger* (Vol. numbers I, II, IV, VI, VII, VIII, XI, XII).

October 4, 1866. Anna Grigorevna Snitkina comes to work with Dostoevsky as a stenographer. Dostoevsky had promised an unscrupulous publisher Stellovsky a new novel by November 1, 1866, for an advance. If he did not meet the deadline, he would lose the rights to all the novels he had published. The novel he dictates to A. G. Snitkina is *The Gambler (Igrok).*

October 5–29, 1866. Every day from noon to four o'clock Dostoevsky dictates *The Gambler* to A. G. Snitkina.

November 1, 1866. Dostoevsky takes the finished novel to Stellovsky, does not find him home, and, at Anna's suggestion, registers the novel at the local police station.

November 8, 1866. Dostoevsky proposes to Anna and is accepted.

February 15 1867. Dostoevsky marries Anna.

April 14, 1867. Dostoevsky and his wife go abroad where they stay more than four years.

May, 1867. Pisarev publishes an article on *Crime and Punishment* in *Act (Delo)* under the title of "Everyday Aspects of Life" (*Budnichnye storony zhizni*). The title was changed to "Struggle for Life" (*Bor'ba za zhizn'*) in his collected works.

August 24, 1867. Dostoevsky sees Holbein's "Christ in the Tomb" in Basel.

September 9–12, 1867. First Congress of the League of Peace and Freedom meets in Geneva. Dostoevsky attends a meeting on September 10.

September 26, 1867. First notes for the novel *The Idiot*.

January, 1868. Publication of *The Idiot* begins in *The Russian Messenger*.

May 24, 1868. His daughter Sofia dies in Geneva.

September 26, 1869. Dostoevsky's daughter Lyubov is born in Dresden.

December 8 and 21, 1869 (old style). Plan for "The Life of the Great Sinner" is sketched in his notebooks.

January–February, 1870. *The Eternal Husband* is published in *Dawn (Zarya)*.

April 6, 1870. Dostoevsky writes Maykov from Dresden that he is working on a large tendentious novel directed against the nihilists. The novel is *The Possessed (Besy)*.

July 8, 1871. Dostoevsky returns to St. Petersburg after more than a four-year absence.

February, 1873. N. K. Mikhaylovsky publishes in *The Fatherland Notes* an article entitled "Literary and Journalistic Notes" (*Literaturnye i zhurnal'nye zametki*), which sharply criticizes Dostoevsky's editorship of *The Citizen*, his novel *The Pos-*

sessed, and *The Diary of a Writer*. Dostoevsky answers this article in *The Diary of a Writer*, February 19, 1873, and in an article entitled "Two Observations of the Editor" (*Dve zametki redaktora*), published in *The Citizen*, July 2, 1873.

January, 1874. Dostoevsky informs Meschersky that he is giving up the editorship of *The Citizen*.

January, 1875. Publication of *The Adolescent* (*Podrostok*) begins in *The Fatherland Notes*.

May–June, 1875. Dostoevsky goes to Ems.

August 10, 1875. A son, Aleksey (*Alyosha*), is born to Dostoevsky.

December 27, 1875. Dostoevsky visits an institution for young criminals.

July 20–21, 1877. Dostoevsky spends two days with his sister, V. M. Ivanova, in Darovoe. This is his mother's estate, which passed to his sister and where Dostoevsky spent some of the summers of his youth. On the estate is a woods called Chermashnya, which was Dostoevsky's favorite site as a child.

December 24, 1877. Dostoevsky records in his notebooks the following projects to complete: (1) Write a Russian *Candide*, (2) Write a book about Jesus Christ, (3) Write my memoirs, (4) Write a poem about the forty-day requiem (*sorokovina*).

May 16, 1878. Dostoevsky's son Aleksey dies.

June 26–27, 1878. Dostoevsky visits the monastery Optina Pustyn' with Vladimir Solovyov. He sees the holy monk Father Ambrose three times and speaks with him twice.

June 8, 1880. Dostoevsky makes his "Pushkin Speech" in Moscow. Everyone is enthusiastic.

September 26, 1880. L. Tolstoy writes Strakhov that *The House of the Dead* was the best book of the century, including the work of Pushkin. Strakhov tells Dostoevsky of this.

November 8, 1880. Dostoevsky sends off the Epilogue to *The Brothers Karamazov* to *The Russian Messenger.*

January 28, 1881. At eight-thirty in the evening Dostoevsky dies.

February 1, 1881. Funeral and burial of Dostoevsky take place.

Bibliography

THE BIBLIOGRAPHY THAT FOLLOWS is far from complete, but it is full enough to be representative of works on Dostoevsky in Russian and English and to give a fair idea of what has been done in different areas of study. The readings have been grouped under rubrics such as "Basic Sources," "Prerevolutionary Russian Criticism," "Criticism," and other appropriate subrubrics. These classifications will, I hope, be an aid to finding easily and quickly various kinds of works, and will constitute a preliminary analysis of the content of the readings. Although some overlapping is inevitable, no work has been put under more than one classification.

I. Bibliographies

RUSSIAN

Dostoevskaya, Anna. *Bibliografichesky ukazatel'* (St. Petersburg, 1906). An itemized list of 4,232 objects in the Dostoevsky museum: books, portraits, documents.

Nechaeva, Vera S., ed. *Opisanie rukopisey F. M. Dostoevskogo* (Moscow, 1957). An exhaustive listing of manuscripts and locations.

Seduro, Vladimir. *Dostoevsky in Russian Literary Criticism* (New York, 1957), pp. 346–399. This bibliography is very good on Soviet works on Dostoevsky; selective on prerevolutionary works.

Tomashevsky, B. V., ed. *F. M. Dostoevsky, Polnoe sobranie khudozhestvennykh proizvedenii*, Vol. 13 (Moscow and Leningrad, 1930), pp. 617–625.

ENGLISH
Beebe, Maurice, and Christopher Newton. "Dostoevsky in English: A Selected Checklist of Criticism and Translations," *Modern Fiction Studies*, IV (1958), 271–291. An excellent source for English works on Dostoevsky; it may be supplemented by the annual bibliographies put out by *PMLA*.

II. Basic Sources

EDITIONS
Grossman, L. P. *et al.*, *F. M. Dostoevsky, Sobranie sochinenii*, 10 vols. (Moscow, 1956–1958). The Tomashevsky is now something of a rarity, whereas this edition is at the present time widely available. The edition does not contain letters, diaries, publicist writings or notebooks, but it does include most of Dostoevsky's fiction.
Tomashevsky, B. V., and K. I. Khalabaev. *F. M. Dostoevsky Polnoe sobranie khudozhestvennykh proizvedenii*, 13 vols. (Moscow and Leningrad, 1926–1930). This is the most complete edition of Dostoevsky's works.

ENGLISH TRANSLATIONS
The translations of Constance Garnett and David Magarshack are the best. The Garnett translations are still a notch better, everything considered, than the Magarshack and other translations.

LETTERS (RUSSIAN)
Dolinin, A. S., ed. *Pis'ma*, 4 vols. (Moscow, 1928, 1930, 1934, and 1959). This is the most complete edition of the letters Dostoevsky wrote.

LETTERS (ENGLISH)
Various editions of selected letters in English are available. All of them are highly selective, and all together they represent only a fraction of what is contained in the Dolinin edition.

LETTERS (FRENCH)
Four volumes of Dostoevsky's letters, complete through 1871, have been published: *Correspondance de Dostoïevski* (Paris, 1951, 1959, 1960, 1961).

Hill, Elizabeth, and Doris Mudie, ed. and trans. *The Letters of Dostoevsky to his Wife* (New York, 1930).

Koteliansky, S. S., and J. Middleton Murry, ed. and trans. *Dostoevsky: Letters and Reminiscences* (New York, 1923).

Mayne, Ethel Colburn, ed. and trans. *Letters of Fyodor Michailovitch Dostoevsky to his Family and Friends* (London, 1914). This volume includes reminiscences (selections) of Grigorovich, Milyukov, Martynov, Vrangel, and Kovalevskaya; and contemporary literary judgments by Pobedonostsev, Aksakov, Turgenev, and Tolstoy. A new edition (New York, 1961) of this volume is available, with an introduction by Avrahm Yarmolinsky.

REMINISCENCES (RUSSIAN)

Cheshikhin-Vetrinsky, V. E., ed. *F. M. Dostoevsky v vospominaniyakh sovremennikov, pis'makh i zametkakh* (Moscow, 1912).

Dostoevskaya, Anna. *Dnevnik A. G. Dostoevskoy, 1867 goda* (Moscow, 1923).

Dostoevsky, A. M. *Vospominaniya Andreya Mikhaylovicha Dostoevskogo* (Leningrad, 1930).

Grigorovich, D. B. *Literaturnye vospominaniya* (Leningrad, 1928).

Grossman, L. P. *Vospominaniya* (Moscow, 1925).

Milyukov, A. P. *Literaturnye vstrechi i znakomstva* (St. Petersburg, 1890).

Suslova, A. P. *Gody blizosti s Dostoevskim* (Moscow, 1928).

Vrangle, A. E. *Vospominaniya o F. M. Dostoevskom v Sibiri* (St. Petersburg, 1912).

REMINISCENCES (ENGLISH)

Koteliansky, S. S., trans. and ed. *Dostoevsky Portrayed by His Wife; the Diary and Reminiscences of Mme. Dostoevsky* (New York, 1926).

Mayne, Ethel Coburn. See reference under *Letters (English)*.

DIARIES AND NOTEBOOKS (RUSSIAN)

Dolinin, A. S. *F. M. Dostoevsky, materialy i issledovaniya* (Leningrad, 1935). Along with other important archival material, this volume contains the notebooks to *The Brothers Karamazov*.

BIBLIOGRAPHY

Dolinin, A. S. *V tvorcheskoy laboratorii Dostoevskogo* (Moscow, 1947). Notebooks for *The Adolescent* (*Podrostok*).

Dostoevsky, F. M. *Dnevnik pisatelya*, 3 vols. (Paris: YMCA Press, 1951).

Glivenko, I. I. *Iz arkhiva Dostoevskogo, Prestuplenie i nakazanie* (Moscow and Leningrad, 1931). Dostoevsky's notebooks for *Crime and Punishment*.

Grossman, L. P. *Pervaya zapisnaya knizhka. Sibirskaya tetrad'*, *Zven'ya*, VI (1936), 413–438.

Konshina, E. N. *Zapisnye tetradi F. M. Dostoevskogo* (Moscow and Leningrad, 1935). Notebooks to *The Possessed*.

Lossky, N. *Dostoevsky i ego khristianskoe miroponimanie* (New York: Chekhov, 1953). Contains notebook of Dostoevsky written at the bier of his wife.

Sakulin, P. A., and N. F. Belchikov, eds. *Iz arkhiva F. M. Dostoevskogo, Idiot, neizdannye materialy* (Moscow, 1931). Dostoevsky's notebooks to *The Idiot*.

Strakhov, N. N. *Biografiya, pis'ma i zametki iz zapisnoy knizhki Dostoevskogo* (St. Petersburg, 1883).

DIARIES AND NOTEBOOKS (ENGLISH)

Brasol, Boris, trans. *The Diary of a Writer*, 2 vols. (New York, 1949).

Note: French translations of the notebooks to the major novels are available as part of the Gallimard editions of the novels.

OTHER SOURCE MATERIAL

Belchikov, N. F. "Kak pisal romany Dostoevsky," *Pechat' i revolyutsiya*, II (1928), 88–93. Contains unpublished variant of *Netochka Nezvanova*.

Belchikov, N. F., ed. *Pokazaniya F. M. Dostoevskogo po delu Petrashevtsev, Krasny arkhiv*, 45–46 (1931), 130–146 and 160–178. Source material of the Petrashevsky trial.

Belchikov, N. F., ed. *Dostoevsky v protsesse Petrashevtsev* (Moscow and Leningrad, 1936).

Brodsky, N. L., ed. *Dokumenty po istorii literatury i obshchestvennosti* (Moscow, 1922). Contains Stavrogin's confession and the plan of the "Life of the Great Sinner."

Dolinin, A. S., ed. *Dostoevsky, stat'i i materialy*, I and II (St. Petersburg, 1922, and Moscow and Leningrad, 1925).

Grossman, Leonid, ed. *Tvorchestvo Dostoevskogo* (Odessa, 1921).
Grossman, Leonid. "Dostoevsky i pravitel'stvennye krugi 1870 godov," *Literaturnoe nasledstvo*, XV (1934), 83–162.
Koteliansky, S. S., and V. Woolf. *F. M. Dostoevsky, Stavrogin's Confession and the Plan of the Life of a Great Sinner* (Richmond, England, Hogarth Press, 1922).
Oksman, Yuri G. *Fel'etony sorokovykh godov; i gazetnaya proza* (Moscow, 1931).

III. Reception in the West

Discussions and bibliography concerning Dostoevsky's reception and early reputation may be found in the following works:

Brewster, Dorothy. *East-West Passage: A Study in Literary Relationships* (London, 1954), pp. 226–232.
Hemmings, F. W. J. *The Russian Novel in France, 1884–1914* (New York, 1950).
Muchnic, Helen. "Dostoevsky's English Reputation, 1881–1936," *Smith College Studies in Modern Languages*, XX (1939). Excellent survey.
Teitelbaum, Salomon. "Dostoevsky in France of the 1880's," *American Slavic Review*, V (Nov., 1946), 991–1008.

For examples of early Western reception of Dostoevsky's works, the following are useful sources:

Murry, J. Middleton. *Fyodor Dostoevsky, a Critical Study* (London, 1916). An example of almost hysterical enthusiasm for Dostoevsky as a "prophet."
Vogüé, E. M. de. *Le roman russe* (Paris, 1886). An English translation of this is available: Sawyer, H. A., New York, 1916, pp. 203–278.

IV. Prerevolutionary Russian Criticism

The best selected source of representative prerevolutionary critical opinion in Russian is found in *F. M. Dostoevsky v russkoy kritike*, ed. A. A. Belkin (Moscow, 1956). The volume includes selections from Belinsky, Annenkov, Dobrolyubov, Pisarev, Saltykov-Shchedrin, Uspensky, Antonovich, Mikhaylovsky, Gorky, and Lunacharsky. Vladimir Seduro's *Dostoevsky in Russian Literary Criticism* (New York: Columbia Univ. Press, 1957), is a good bibliographical source of prerevolutionary works on Dostoevsky.

I shall list below, in chronological order, a selected list of the most important works on Dostoevsky up to the revolution.

Belinsky, V. G. "Peterburgsky sbornik," *Otechestvennye zapiski*, XLV, No. 3 (1846), 1–30. Reprinted in *Sobranie sochinenii*, III (Moscow, 1948), pp. 61–86.
Belinsky, V. G. "Vzglyad na russkuyu literaturu 1846 goda," *Sobranie sochinenii*, III (Moscow, 1948).
Belinsky, V. G. "Vzglyad na russkuyu literaturu 1847 goda," *Sobranie sochinenii*, III (Moscow, 1948).
Annenkov, P. V. "Zametki o russkoy literature proshlogo goda," *Sovremennik*, XIII (1849).
Dobrolyubov, N. A. "Zabitye lyudi," *Sovremennik*, IX (1861). May be found in *Polnoe sobranie sochinenii*, II (Moscow, 1935).
Pisarev, D. I. "Pogibshie i pogibayushchie," *Luch* (1866). In *Polnoe sobranie sochinenii*, V (St. Petersburg, 1897), 254–314.
Pisarev, D. I. "Bor'ba za zhizn'," *Polnoe sobranie sochinenii*, VI (St. Petersburg, 1897), 283–344. First published in 1867 under the title "Budnichnye storony zhizni" in *Delo*.
Strakhov, N. N. "Prestuplenie i nakazanie F. M. Dostoevskogo," *Otechesvennye zapiski*, CXXI (1867), 544–556.
Chernyshevsky, N. G. "Moi svidaniya s F. M. Dostoevskim," N. F. Belchikov, ed. *Chitatel' i pisatel'*, XXIX (1928).
Saltykov-Shchedrin, M. E. "Svetlov, ego vzglyady, kharakter i deyatel'nost'," *Otechesvennye zapiski* (April, 1871). In *Polnoe sobranie sochinenii*, VIII (Moscow, 1937).
Mikhaylovsky, N. K. "Kommentarii k 'Besam'," *Otechestvennye zapiski* (February, 1873). In *Sochineniya*, I (1896), 840–872.
Uspensky, G. I. "Prazdnik Pushkina," *Otechestvennye zapiski*,

Vol. 6 (June, 1880). In *Polnoe sobranie sochinenii*, VI (Moscow, 1953).

Uspensky, G. I. "Secret," *Otechestvennye zapiski*, VII (1880). In *Polnoe sobranie sochinenii*, VI (Moscow, 1953).

Antonovich, M. A. "Mistikoasketichesky roman: 'Bratya Karamazovy'," *Novoe obozrenie*, III (March, 1881), 190–239.

Mikhaylovsky, N. K. "Zhestoky talant," *Otechestvennye zapiski* (Sept.–Oct., 1882). In *Sochineniya*, V (1897), 1–78.

Solovyov, Vladimir. *Tri rechi v pamyat' Dostoevskogo, 1881–1883, Sobranie sochinenii*, III (St. Petersburg, 1912), 186–223.

Rozanov, V. V. *Legenda o velikom inkvizitore F. M. Dostoevskogo, Russky vestnik* (1890). In book form, St. Petersburg, 1894. May be found in the third edition of his works, St. Petersburg, 1906.

Merezhkovsky, D. S. "O 'prestuplenii i nakazanii' Dostoevskogo," *Russkoe obozrenie*, II (1890), 155–186. In *Polnoe sobranie sochinenii*, XIII (St. Petersburg and Moscow, 1911), 210–236.

Solovyov, E. F. *Dostoevsky, ego zhizn' i literaturnaya deyatel'nost'* (St. Petersburg, 1898).

Bely, Andrey. "Dostoevsky: po povodu 25 letiya so dnya smerti," *Zolotoe runo*, II (1906), 8–90.

Berdyaev, N. A. "Veliky inkvisitor," *Voprosy filosofii i psikhologii*, I (1907), 1–36.

Ivanov, Vyacheslav. "Dostoevsky i roman-tragediya," *Russkaya mysl'*, V and VI (1911), 46–61 and 1–17. In *Borozdy i mezhi* (Moscow, 1916).

Merezhkovsky, Dmitry Sergeevich. *L. Tolstoy i Dostoevsky* (Moscow, 1914).

V. Criticism

Critical works listed below have, for convenience, been divided into rubrics like "General Criticism," "Psychology," and "Influence and Contemporaries." Soviet and Western works have been alphabetized together. I have tried to list English works more fully than Soviet works, because I feel the specialist in Russian literature will more easily find what is useful to him without this aid. As an aid to those who would like a shorter and more selective list, I have put an asterisk next to works of special significance.

BIOGRAPHY

Antsiferov, H. *Byl' i mif* (St. Petersburg, 1924).

Bennett, Arnold. "Tourgenieff and Dostoevsky," *Books and Persons* (New York, 1917), pp. 208–213.

*Carr, Edward Hallett. *Dostoevsky (1821–1881)*, a New Biography (Boston and New York, 1931).

Carr, Edward Hallett. "Was Dostoevsky an Epileptic?" *Slavonic Review*, IX (Dec., 1930), 424–431.

Dostoevsky, Aimée. *Fyodor Dostoevsky, a Study* (London, 1921).

Fiske, John C. "Dostoevsky and the Soviet Critics, 1947–1948," *American Slavic and East European Review*, IX (Feb., 1950), 42–56.

Fülop-Miller, René, "Dostoevsky's Literary Reputation," *Russian Review*, X (Jan., 1951), 46–54.

*Fülop-Miller, René, "The Lost Dostoevsky Manuscripts," *Russian Review*, X (Oct., 1951), 268–282.

*Grossman, Leonid. *Put' Dostoevskogo* (Leningrad, 1924).

*Grossman, Leonid. *Zhizn' i trudy F. M. Dostoevskogo, biografiya v datakh i dokumentakh* (Moscow and Leningrad, 1935).

*Grossman, Leonid. *Dostoevsky* (Moscow, 1962).

Kirpotin, V. Ya. *Molodoy Dostoevsky* (Moscow, 1947).

Magarshack, David. *Dostoevsky* (New York, 1961).

Nikol'sky, Yury. *Turgenev i Dostoevsky, istoriya odnoy vrazhdy* (Sofia, 1921).

O'Connor, Frank. "Dostoevsky and the Unnatural Triangle," *The Mirror in the Roadway: A Study of the Modern Novel* (New York, 1956), pp. 199–222.

Payne, Robert. "Dostoevski: The Last Days," *New World Writing*, No. 14 (New York: New American Library, 1958), pp. 223–247.

*Payne, Robert. *Dostoevsky* (New York, 1961).

Slonim, Mark. L. *Tri lyubvi Dostoevskogo* (New York, 1953).

Slonim, Marc. *The Three Loves of Dostoevsky* (New York, 1955).

BIBLIOGRAPHY

Solovyov, Evgeny. *Dostoevsky, his Life and Literary Activity*, trans. C. J. Hogarth (London, 1916).

Troyat, Henri. *Dostoievsky* (Paris, 1940).

Troyat, Henry. *Firebrand; the Life of Dostoevsky* (New York, 1946).

Volotskoy, Mikhail Vasil'evich. *Khronika roda Dostoevskogo 1506–1933* (Moscow, 1933).

Wilson, Edmund. "Dostoevsky Abroad," *The Shores of Light* (New York, 1952), pp. 408–414.

Yakushin, Nikolay I. *Dostoevsky v Sibiri; ocherk zhizni i tvorchestva* (Kemerovo, 1960).

Yarmolinsky, Avrahm. *Dostojewsky: A Life* (New York, 1934).

Yarmolinsky, Avrahm. *Dostoevsky, His Life and Art* (New York, 1957).

General Critical Works

*Bakhtin, M. M. *Problemy tvorchestva Dostoevskogo* (Leningrad, 1929). A brilliant work, although the principal idea is pushed too far.

Bem, A. L., ed. *O Dostoevskom*, 3 vols. (Prague, 1929, 1933, 1936).

Bem, A. "Lichnye imena u Dostoevskogo," *Sbornik v chest' na Prof. L. Miletich* (Sofia, 1933), pp. 409–434.

*Brodsky, N. L., ed. *Tvorchesky put' Dostoevskogo* (Leningrad, 1924). Articles included: K. K. Istomin. "Iz zhizni i tvorchestva Dostoevskogo v molodosti." V. Vinogradov. "Syuzhet i arkhitektonika romana Dostoevskogo 'Bednye Lyudi v svyazi s voprosom o poetike natural'noy shkoly." M. G. Davidovich. "Problema zanimatel'nosti v romanakh Dostoevskogo." A. P. Skaftymov. "Tematicheskaya kompozitsiya romana 'Idiot.'" A. Gizetti. "Gordye yazychnitsy (K kharakteristike zhenskikh obrazov Dostoevskogo)." D. Darski. "Dostoevsky-myslitel'."

Bitsilli, P. *K voprosu o vnutrenney forme romana Dostoevskogo* (Sofia, 1946).

Chulkov, Georgi I. *Kak rabotal Dostoevsky* (Moscow, 1939).

Curle, Richard. *Characters of Dostoevsky: Studies from Four Novels* (London, 1950).

Engel'gorrot, B. M. "Ideologichesky roman Dostoevskogo," *Dostoevsky, stat'i i materialy*, ed. Dolinin (Leningrad, 1924).

Ermilov, Vladimir Vladimirovich. *F. M. Dostoevsky* (Moscow, 1956). This is a bad book, but it is itself interesting historically, since it shows a party conformist struggling to accommodate Dostoevsky to Communist ideology. There is an English translation by J. Katzer of the Moscow Foreign Languages Publishing House. The translation is unreadable.

Fanger, D. L. "Dostoevsky Today: Some Recent Critical Studies," *Survey*, XXXVI (1961), 13–19.

Faure, Elie. *Les constructeurs: Lamarck, Michelet, Dostoievsky Nietzsche, Cézanne* (Paris, 1951).

Fayer, Harry Mischa. *Gide, Freedom, and Dostoevsky* (Burlington, N.H., 1946).

Gibian, George. "Dostoevskij's Use of Russian Folklore," *Journal of American Folklore*, LXIX (1956), 239–253.

Gibian, George. "The Grotesque in Dostoevsky," *Modern Fiction Studies*, IV (Autumn, 1958), 262–270.

Gide, André Paul. *Dostoievsky*, Paris, 1923. This is an interesting work on Dostoevsky. It tells us very little about Dostoevsky, but much about what Dostoevsky meant to Gide. There is an English translation with an introduction by Arnold Bennett, London, 1952.

*Grossman, Leonid. "Kompozitsiya v romane Dostoevskogo," *Vestnik Evropy* (Sept., 1916), 121–155.

*Grossman, Leonid. "Problemy realizma u Dostoevskogo," *Vestnik Evropy*, II (Feb., 1917), 65–99. An excellent work on the craft of Dostoevsky. Grossman occupies himself in tracing out the sources of Dostoevsky's realism: his life, his times, and Gothic literary tradition.

Grossman, Leonid. "Dostoevsky i teatralizatsiya romana," *Bor'ba za stil'* (Moscow, 1927), pp. 147–153. In the same volume: "A. G. Dostoevskaya i ee 'Vospominaniya'," pp. 243–266.

*Grossman, Leonid. *Poetika Dostoevskogo* (Moscow, 1925). This includes several of the items listed above and others. Important pieces in the volume are: "Kompozitsiya v romane Dostoevskogo," "Bal'zak i Dostoevsky," "Zhivopis' Dostoevskogo," "Stilistika Stavrogina," and "Iskusstvo romana u Dostoevskogo."

*Grossman, Leonid. "Dostoevsky i Evropa," *Russkaya Mysl'* (Nov.–Dec., 1915), 54–93.

Kazin, Alfred. "Dostoevsky and the Age of Anxiety," *The Inmost Leaf: A Selection of Essays* (New York, 1955), pp. 253–256.

Kirpotin, F. M. *Dostoevsky* (Moscow, 1960).

Lavrin, Janko. *Dostoevsky, a Study* (New York, 1947).

Lloyd, John Arthur Thomas. *Fyodor Dostoevsky* (New York, 1947). This work has some interesting things to say about Dostoevsky's reputation in the world.

*Lukacs, Georg. *Der russische Realismus in der Welt Literatur* (Berlin, 1948). What he has to say about Dostoevsky is provocative.

Lunacharsky, A. V. "Dostoevsky kak khudozhnik i myslitel'," *Krasnaya nov'*, IV (1921), 204–212.

Mackiewicz, Stanislaw. *Dostoevsky* (London, 1947). This work of a distinguished Polish critic has had some influence on Soviet critics.

Markovitch, Milan. "Le problème du style dans 'Les frères Karamazov' de Dostoievski," *Stil und Formprobleme*, IV (1959), 402–406.

Matlaw, Ralph E. "Thanatos and Eros: Approaches to Dostoevsky's Universe." *Slavic and East European Journal*, IV (1960), 17–24.

Matlaw, Ralph E. "Recurrent Imagery in Dostoevsky," *Harvard Slavic Studies*, III (Cambridge, Mass., 1957), 201–225.

Merejkowski, Dmitri. *Tolstoi as Man and Artist with an Essay on Dostoievski* (New York, 1902).

*Mochul'sky, Konstantin Vasil'evich. *Dostoevsky: zhizn' i tvorchestvo* (Paris, 1947). This is perhaps the best all-around introduction to the works of Dostoevsky. French translation: *Dostoïevsky, l'homme et l'œuvre* (Paris, 1962).

Ortega y Gasset, José. "Notes on the Novel," *The Dehumanization of Art* (Garden City, N.Y., 1956).

Pachmuss, Temira. "The Technique of Dream Logic in the Works of Dostoevskij," *Slavic and East European Journal*, IV (1960), 220–242.

Pachmuss, Temira. *F. M. Dostoevsky: Dualism and Synthesis of the Human Soul* (Carbondale, Ill., 1963).

Parker, Fan. "The Revival of Dostoevskij on the Soviet Stage," *Slavic and East European Journal*, XVI (1958), 33–41.

Pereverzev, Valerian Fedorovich. *Tvorchestvo Dostoevskogo* (Moscow, 1922).

Poggioli, Renato. "Dostoevsky or Reality and Myth," *The Phoenix and the Spider: A Book of Essays about Some Russian Writers and Their View of the Self* (Cambridge, Mass., 1957), pp. 16–32. First published in the *Kenyon Review* in 1952.

Pogozheva, L. "Mechta Dostoevskogo o zolotom veke," *Krasnaya nov'*, II (1941), 173–181.

Powys, John Cowper. *Dostoievsky* (London, 1946). A rather eccentric work, but interesting material on "play theory" and Dostoevsky.

Proust, Marcel. "Dostoevsky," *On Art and Literature 1896–1919*, trans. Sylvia Townsend Warner (New York, 1958), pp. 380–381.

Rahv, Philip. "Fiction and the Criticism of Fiction," *Kenyon Review*, XVIII (Spring, 1956), 295–298.

Roe, Ivan. *The Breath of Corruption; an Interpretation of Dostoievsky* (London, 1946).

Rosen, Nathan. "Chaos and Dostoevsky's Women," *Kenyon Review*, XX (1958), 257–277.

Sajkovic, Miriam. *F. M. Dostoevsky: His Image of Man* (Philadelphia, 1962). A recent work of very dubious usefulness.

Shklovsky, Viktor Borisovich. *Za i protiv; zametki o Dostoevskom* (Moscow, 1957). Disorganized, eccentric, but fascinating in small insights at times.

Shklovsky, Viktor Borisovich. *O teorii prozy* (Moscow, 1925).

Simmons, Ernest J. *Dostoevski; the Making of a Novelist* (London, 1950). Available now in Vintage paperback.

*Sokolov, A. N., ed. *Protiv burzhuaznykh i revizionistskikh kontseptsii istorii russkoy literatury* (Moscow, 1963). An interesting small book in which some of the staff of the philological faculty of Moscow University take to task the interpreters of Dostoevsky in the West.

Steinberg, A. *Sistema svobody F. M. Dostoevskogo* (Berlin, 1923).

*Steiner, George. *Tolstoy or Dostoevsky; an Essay in the Old Criticism* (New York, 1959). This is a brilliant "bad" book. It is bad only because of the ease of generalization by which great periods of Russian culture, of European literature, and the development of the novel are mixed together. But it is also a brilliant book because Steiner's insight is at times excellent. It is very readable.

*Stepanov, N. L., ed. *Tvorchestvo F. M. Dostoevskogo* (Moscow, 1959). An anthology of sixteen essays by Soviet scholars. Included are essays by Grossman, Evnin, and Nechaeva.

Trilling, Lionel. "Manners, Morals, and the Novel," *The Liberal Imagination* (New York, 1950).

Van der Eng, J. *Dostoievskij romancier; rapports entre sa vision du monde et ses procédés littéraires* (The Hague, 1957).

Vinogradov, V. "Neizvestny ocherk-fel'eton F. M. Dostoevskogo," *Voprosy literatury*, I (1961), 89–107.

Vinogradov, V. "Toproshayka: Un récit inconnu de Dostoevskij," *Revue des études slaves*, XXXVII (1960), 17–28.

Wasiolek, Edward. "*Aut Caesar, Aut Nihil:* A Study of Dostoevsky's Moral Dialectic," *PMLA*, LXXVIII (March, 1963), 89–97.

Wellek, René, ed. *Dostoevsky; A Collection of Critical Essays* (Englewood Cliffs, N.J., 1962).

INFLUENCES AND COMPARISONS

Astrov, Vladimir. "Dostoevsky on Edgar Allan Poe," *American Literature*, XIV (March, 1942), 70–74.

Astrov, Vladimir. "Hawthorne and Dostoevsky as Explorers of the Human Conscience," *New England Quarterly*, XV (June, 1942), 296–319.

Belchikov, N. F. "Dostoevsky i Pobedonostsev," *Krasny arkhiv*, II (1922), 240–255.

Belchikov, N. F. "Chernyshevsky i Dostoevsky," *Pechat' i revolyutsiya*, V (1928), 35–53.

Belchikov, N. F. "Turgenev i Dostoevsky," *Krasny arkhiv*, II (1927), 241–244.

Bennett, Arnold. "Tourgenieff and Dostoevsky," *Books and Persons* (New York, 1917), pp. 208–213.

Borshchevsky, Solomon Smaylovich. *Shchedrin i Dostoevsky; istoriya ikh ideynoy bor'by* (Moscow, 1956).

Byrnes, Robert F. "Dostoevsky and Pobedonostsev," *Jahrbucher für Geschichte Osteuropas*, IX (1961), 57–71.

Carr, Edward Hallett. "Turgenev and Dostoevsky," *Slavonic Review*, VIII (June, 1929), 156–163.

Coates, William Ames. "Dostoevsky and Gerhart Hauptmann," *American Slavic and East European Review*, IV (Dec., 1945), 107–127.

Futrell, Michael H. "Dostoevsky and Dickens," *English Miscellany*, VII (1956), 41–89.

Gissing, George. *Charles Dickens: a Critical Study* (London, 1898), pp. 221–223.

Gorky, Maxim. "O petrashevtsakh I. Turgeneve, F. Dostoevskom, L. Tolstom," *Literaturny kritik*, VI (1938), 41–81.

Gross, John J. "Melville, Dostoevsky and the People," *Pacific Spectator*, X (Spring, 1956), 160–170.

Halle, Thérèse. "Le phénomène du double chez Dostoïevsky et chez Maupassant," *Etudes slaves et Est-Européennes*, II (1957–1958).

Hoffman, Frederick J. "The Scene of Violence: Dostoevsky and Dreiser," *Modern Fiction Studies*, VI (1960), 91–105.

King, Henry Hall. *Dostoevsky and Andreev: Gazers Upon the Abyss* (New York, 1936).

Kirpotin, V. I. *Dostoevsky i Belinsky* (Moscow, 1960).

Knowlton, Edgar. "Russian Influence on Stevenson," *Modern Philology*, XIV (Dec., 1916), 449–454.

Lavrin, Janko. "Dostoevsky and Proust," *Studies in European Literature* (London, 1929), pp. 193–222.

Lloyd, J. A. T. "Dostoevsky and Flaubert," *Fortnightly Review*, CX (Dec., 1921), 1017–1027.

Neuschaffer, Walter. *Dostojewskijs Einfluss auf den englischen Roman* (Heidelberg, 1935).

Niemeyer, Carl. "Raskolnikov and Lafcadio," *Modern Fiction Studies*, IV (1958), 253–261.

Passage, Charles E. *Dostoevski the Adapter: a Study in Dostoevski's Use of the Tales of Hoffmann* (Chapel Hill, N.C., 1954).

Poggioli, Renato. "Kafka and Dostoevsky," *The Kafka Problem*, ed. Angel Flores (Norfolk, Conn., 1946), pp. 97–116.

Rammelmeyer, Alfred. "Dostojevskij und Voltaire," *Zeitschrift für slavische Philologie*, XXVI (1958), 252–278.

Schwartz, M. "Dostoevsky and Judaism," *Jewish Review*, IV (1933), 57–64.

Simmons, J. S. G. "F. M. Dostoevsky and A. K. Tolstoy: Two Letters," *Oxford Slavonic Papers*, IX (1960), 64–72.

Stammler, Heinrich. "Dostoevsky's Aesthetics and Schelling's Philosophy of Art," *Comparative Literature*, VII (Fall, 1955), 313–323.

Tseytlin, A. G. " 'Prestuplenie i nakazanie' i 'Les Misérables': Sotsiologicheskie paralleli," *Literatura i marksizm*, V (1928), 20–58.

Turrian, Marysia. *Dostojewskij und Franz Werfel; von ostlichen zum westlichen Denken* (Bern, 1950).

Vacquier, Tatiana. "Dostoevsky and Gide: A Comparison," *Sewanee Review*, XXXVII (Oct., 1929), 478–489.

Vinogradov, V. "Dostoevsky i Leskov (70-e gody, XIX veka)," *Russkaya literatura*, I and V (1961), 63–84 and 65–97.

Volynsky, A. A., ed. *Dostoevsky i Pushkin* (St. Petersburg, 1921).

Wasiolek, Edward. "Dostoevsky and *Sanctuary*," *Modern Language Notes*, LXXIV (Feb., 1959), 114–117.

Westbrook, Perry D. *The Greatness of Man; an Essay on Dostoevsky and Whitman* (New York, 1961).

PHILOSOPHY AND RELIGION

Baker, A. E. *Prophets for a Day of Judgment* (London, 1944), pp. 56–77.

*Berdiaev, Nikolai Aleksandrovich. *Dostoevsky*, trans. Donald Attwater (New York, 1957). Translation of *Mirosozertsanie Dostoevskogo* (Paris, 1923).

Bohatec, Josef. *Der Imperialismusgedanke und die Lebensphilosophie Dostojewskijs* (Graz, 1951).

Doerne, Martin. *Gott und Mensch in Dostojewskijs Werk* (Göttingen, 1957).

Fülop-Miller, René. *Fyodor Dostoevsky: Insight, Faith and Prophecy*, trans. Richard and Clara Winston (New York, 1950).

Glicksberg, Charles I. "Dostoevski and the Problem of Religion," *Bucknell Review*, VIII (1959), 202–217.

Gorodetzky, Hadejda. *Saint Tikhon Zadonsky, Inspirer of Dostoevsky* (London, 1951).

*Guardini, Romano. *Religiöse Gestalten in Dostojewskijs Werk* (Munich, 1947).

*Ivanov, Vyacheslav. *Freedom and the Tragic Life: A Study*

in Dostoevsky, trans. Norman Cameron (New York, 1957). The translation is weak, but the work is monumental.

Jarrett, James L. "Dostoevsky: Philosopher of Freedom, Love and Life," *Review of Religion*, XXI (Nov., 1956), 17–30.

Lossky, Nikolay O. *Dostoevsky i ego khristianskoe miroponimanie* (New York, 1953).

Masaryk, Tomas G. *The Spirit of Russia; Studies in History, Literature and Philosophy* (London, 1955).

Panichas, George A. "Fyodor Dostoevsky and Roman Catholicism," *The Greek Orthodox Theological Review* (Summer, 1959), 16–34.

Ramsey, Paul. "No Morality without Immortality: Dostoevsky and the Meaning of Atheism," *Journal of Religion*, XXXVI (April, 1956), 90–108.

Scott, Nathan. "Dostoevski–Tragedian of the Modern Excursion into Unbelief," *The Tragic Vision and Christian Faith*, ed. Nathan Scott Jr. (New York, 1957).

Shestov, Lev. *Dostoevsky i Nitshe, filosofiya tragedii* (Berlin, 1922).

Shestov, Lev. *Na vesakh Iova, Stranstvovaniya po dusham* (Paris, 1929).

*Shestov, Lev. *La philosophie de la tragédie; Dostoievsky et Nietzche*, trans. B. de Schloezer (Paris, 1926). This is a translation of *Dostoevsky i Nitshe*. The work is penetrating and provocative. It is a classic affirmation of Dostoevsky's nihilism and his rejection of humanistic and religious justification of life.

*Chestov, Leo. *Job's Balances*, trans. Camilla Coventry and C. A. McCartney (London, 1932).

Shestov, Leo. "The Gift of Prophecy," *Penultimate Words* (Boston, 1916), pp. 63–82.

Steinbuchel, Theodor, *F. M. Dostojewski; sein Bild vom Menschen und vom Christen* (Düsseldorf, 1947).

Strem, George C. "The Moral World of Dostoevsky," *Russian Review*, XVI (July, 1957).

Thorn, George W. "Dostoevsky as a Religious Teacher," *Contemporary Review*, CVIII (1915), 220–229.

Tsanoff, Radoslav Andrea. *The Problem of Life in the Russian Novel, Rice Institute Pamphlet*, Vol. IV, No. 2 (Houston, 1917).

Vatain, Laszlo. *Man and His Tragic Life* (New York, 1954).
Vysheslavtsev, B. "Dostoevsky o lyubvi i bessmertii," *Sovremenny zapiski*, L–LI (1932–1933), 288–304.
West, Rebecca. "Redemption and Dostoevsky," *New Republic*, II (June 5, 1915), 115–118.
Yarmolinsky, Avrahm. *Dostoevsky: A Study in His Ideology* (New York, 1921).
Zander, L. *Dostoevsky*, trans. Natalie Duddington (London, 1948).
Zander, L. *Tayna dobra; problema dobra v tvorchestve Dostoevskogo* (Frankfurt, 1960).
Zenkovsky, V. V. "F. M. Dostoevsky, V. Solovyov, and N. Berdyaev," *Russian Thinkers and Europe*, trans. Galia S. Bodde (New York, 1953), pp. 154–187.
Zenkovsky, V. V. *A History of Russian Philosophy*, trans. George L. Kline (New York, 1953), pp. 410–432.
Zernov, Nicolas. *Three Russian Prophets; Khomyakov, Dostoevsky, Soloviev* (London, 1944).
Zoppo, Franco. *Dostojevskij, il Dio russo e il Cristo russo* (Taranto, 1959).

PSYCHOLOGY
Adler, Alfred. *The Practice and Theory of Individual Psychology*, trans. P. Radin (London, 1924), pp. 280–290.
Beresford, J. D. "Psycho-analysis and the Novel," *The Freeman*, I (March 24, 1920), 35–39.
Burchell, S. C. "Dostoevsky and the Sense of Guilt," *Psychoanalytic Review*, XVII (April, 1930), 197–221.
Carp, Emile. *Rodion Raskolnikow, a Psychopathological Study*, trans. I. van den Bosch (Amsterdam, 1951).
Chamberlin, William Henry. "Dostoevsky, Prophet and Psychologist," *Russian Review*, VII (Spring, 1948), 34–40.
Dempf, Alois. *Die drei Laster; Dostojewskis Tiefenpsychologie* (Munich, 1946).
*Freud, Sigmund. *Dostoevsky and Parricide*, trans. D. F. Tait, in William Phillips, ed., *Art and Psychoanalysis* (New York, 1957), pp. 3–21.
Gibian, George. "C. G. Carus' *Psyche* and Dostoevsky," *American Slavic and East European Review*, XIV (1955), 371–382.
Kanzer, Mark. "Dostoevsky's Matricidal Impulses," *Psychoanalytic Review*, XXXV (April, 1948), 115–125.

Reik, Theodor. "The Study on Dostoevsky," *From Thirty Years with Freud,* trans. Richard Winston (New York, 1940), pp. 158–170.

Sachs, Wulf. *Psychoanalysis: Its Meaning and Practical Applications* (London, 1934), pp. 224–246.

Squires, P. C. "Dostoevsky's Doctrine of Criminal Responsibility," *Journal of Criminal Law,* XXVII (March, 1937), 817–827.

Squires, P. C. "Fyodor Dostoevsky: A Psychopathographical Sketch," *Psychoanalytic Review,* XXIV (Oct., 1937), 365–387.

Tymma, Ralph. *Doubles in Literary Psychology* (Cambridge, Mass., 1949), pp. 99–105.

POLITICS AND SOCIETY

Adams, Arthur E. "Pobedonostsev's Thought Control," *Russian Review,* XI (Oct., 1952), 241–246.

Berdyaev, Nicolas. *The Origin of Russian Communism* (New York, 1937), pp. 99–102 and *passim.*

Chulkov, Georgy. "Dostoevsky i utopichesky sotsializm," *Katorga i ssylka,* LI–LII (1929), 9–35 and 134–151.

Kohn, Hans. *Prophets and Peoples: Studies in Nineteenth Century Nationalism* (New York, 1946), pp. 131–160.

Kohn, Hans. "Dostoevsky and Danilevsky: National Messianism," *Continuity and Change in Russian and Soviet Thought,* ed. E. J. Simmons (Cambridge, Mass., 1955), pp. 500–515.

Kotsovsky, D. *Dostoevsky, Tolstoy i bolshevizm* (Munich, 1960).

Leshinsky, Tania. "Dostoevsky—Revolutionary or Reactionary?" *American Slavic and East European Review,* IV (Dec., 1945), 98–106.

*Moravia, Alberto. "The Marx-Dostoevsky Duel," *The Social History of Art,* Vol. 2 (New York, 1952).

*Moravia, Alberto. "The Marx-Dostoevsky Duel and Other Russian Notes," *Encounter,* VII (Nov., 1956), 3–12.

*Riasanovsky, Nicholas V. "Fourierism in Russia: An Estimate of the Petrashevcy," *American Slavic and East European Review,* XII (Oct., 1953), 289–302. Good English source for Dostoevsky's involvement in the Petrashevsky circle.

Sourine, G. *Le Fourierisme en Russie* (Paris, 1936).

Thorn, George D. "Sidelights on the Psychology of the Russian Revolution from Dostoevsky," *Contemporary Review*, CXIII (June, 1918), 695–700.

Warner, Rex. "Dostoevsky and the Collapse of Liberalism," *The Cult of Power* (Philadelphia, 1947), pp. 51–111.

Zeitlin, Jacob. "Dostoevsky the Reactionary," *New Republic*, II (March 20, 1915), 176–178.

VI. The Major Novels

Notes from the Underground

Beardsley, Monroe C. "Dostoevsky's Metaphor of the Underground," *Journal of History of Ideas*, III (June, 1942), 265–290.

*Frank, Joseph. *Dostoevsky and Russian Nihilism: A Context for "Notes from the Underground,"* unpublished dissertation, University of Chicago. Available on microfilm. An excellent introduction to social, political, and philosophical backgrounds of *Notes from the Underground*.

*Frank, Joseph. "Nihilism and Notes from the Underground," *Sewanee Review*, LXIX (1961), 1–33.

Jackson, Robert Louis. *Dostoevsky's Underground Man in Russian Literature* (The Hague, 1958). A history of Dostoevsky's influence on the use of the "underground" in Russian literature.

Matlaw, Ralph E. *Notes from the Underground and the Grand Inquisitor* (New York, 1960). Texts selected and translated by the editor, with relevant selections from works of Chernyshevsky and Shchedrin.

*Matlaw, Ralph E. "Structure and Integration in *Notes from the Underground*," *PMLA*, LXXIII (March, 1958), 101–109. Suggestive analysis of image patterns.

Traschen, I. "Dostoevsky's *Notes from Underground*," *Accent*, XVI (1956), 255–264.

Crime and Punishment

Beebe, Maurice. "The Three Motives of Raskolnikov: A Reinterpretation of *Crime and Punishment*," *College English*, XVII (1955), 151–158. Argument for consideration of Svidrigaylov as a "good" character, or at least for some qualification of the traditional view of him as an "evil" character.

Blackmur, R. P. *"Crime and Punishment: A Study of Dostoevsky,"* in *Essays in Modern Literary Criticism,* ed. Ray B. West (New York, 1952), pp. 472–489.

Florance, Edna C. "The Neurosis of Raskolnikov: A Study in Incest and Murder," *Archives of Criminal Psychodynamics,* I (1955), 344–396. A thoroughly unbelievable work of criticism, but fascinating application of Freudian commonplaces.

Gibian, George. "Traditional Symbolism in *Crime and Punishment,"* *PMLA,* LXX (Dec., 1955), 979–996.

Gissing, George. *Charles Dickens, A Critical Study* (London, 1903).

*Glivenko, I. "Glava 2, *Prestuplenie i nakazanie,"* *Krasny arkhiv,* VII (1924), 150–200.

*Glivenko, I. "Raskolnikov i Dostoevsky," *Pechat' i revolyutsiya,* IV (1926), 70–82.

Gwynn, Frederick L. "Faulkner's Raskolnikov," *Modern Fiction Studies,* IV (Summer, 1958), 169–172.

Hearn, Lafcadio, "A Terrible Novel," in *Essays in European and Oriental Literature,* ed. *Albert Mordell* (New York, 1923), pp. 189–194. Interesting early American reception.

Marx, Paul. "A Defense of the Epilogue to *Crime and Punishment,"* *Bucknell Review,* X (1961), 57–74.

Meijer, J. M. "Situation Rhyme in a Novel of Dostoevskij," *Dutch Contributions to the Fourth International Congress of Slavicists* (The Hague, 1958), pp. 115–128.

Pogozheva, L. "Kompozitsiya romana *Prestuplenie i nakazanie,"* *Literaturnaya ucheba,* VIII–IX (Aug.–Sept., 1939), 110–120.

*Rahv, Philip. "Dostoevsky in 'Crime and Punishment'," *Partisan Review,* XXVII (Summer, 1960), 393–425. Among many good points, an interesting comparison with Balzac's *Père Goriot.*

*Reeve, F. D. "In the Stinking City: Dostoevskij's *Crime and Punishment,"* *Slavic and East European Review,* IV (1960), 127–136.

*Snodgrass, W. D. "Crime for Punishment: The Tenor of Part One," *Hudson Review,* XIII (1960), 202–253. Perhaps the best article in English on *Crime and Punishment*. A very detailed analysis of Marmeladov's role in the novel and of the mare-beating scene. Psychological techniques sanely used.

Squires, P. C. "Dostoevsky's Raskolnikov: The Criminalistic Protest," *Journal of Criminal Law*, XXVIII (Nov., 1937), 478–494.

Wasiolek, Edward. "On the Structure of *Crime and Punishment*," *PMLA*, LXXIV (March, 1959), 131–136.

Wasiolek, Edward, ed. *Crime and Punishment and the Critics* (San Francisco, 1961).

The Idiot

Blackmur, R. P. "A Rage of Goodness: *The Idiot* of Dostoevsky," in *The Critical Performance*, ed. Stanley Edgar Hyman (New York, 1956), pp. 235–257.

Blanchard, Margaret. "Dostoevsky: The Idiot," *Explicator*, XXI (Jan., 1963), Item 41.

Guardini, Romano. "Dostoevsky's Idiot: A Symbol of Christ," trans. Francis X. Quinn, *Cross Currents*, VI (Fall, 1956), 359–382.

Lesser, Simon O. "Saint and Sinner—Dostoevsky's Idiot," *Modern Fiction Studies*, IV (Autumn, 1958), 211–224.

Malenko, Zinaida and James J. Gebhard. "The Artistic Uses of Portraits in Dostoevski's *The Idiot*," *Slavic and East European Journal*, V (1961), 243–254.

Manning, Clarence, "Alyosha Valkovsky and Prince Myshkin," *Modern Language Notes*, LVII (March, 1942), 182–185.

McCarthy, Desmond. "Drama and Dostoevsky," *Drama* (New York, 1940), pp. 91–94.

Michener, James, W. G. Rogers, and Lyman Bronson. "*The Idiot*," *Invitation to Learning*, IX (1953), 5–11.

Muir, Edwin. *The Structure of the Novel* (New York, 1929), pp. 73–80.

Sommavilla, Guido. "Il simbolismo de 'L'idiota' di F. Dostoevski," *Letture*, XIV (1959), 748–752.

Tate, Allen, "The Hovering Fly," *On the Limits of Poetry: Selected Essays, 1929–48* (New York, 1948), pp. 146–162.

Whitt, Joseph. "Dostoevsky's *The Idiot*," *Explicator*, XI (April, 1953), Item 45.

The Possessed

Blackmur, R. P. "In the Birdcage: Notes on *The Possessed* of Dostoevsky," *Hudson Review*, I (Spring, 1948), 7–28.
*Camus, Albert. "Absurd Creation," *Myth of Sisyphus and Other Essays* (New York, 1958), pp. 93–118.
Camus, Albert. *Les possédés; pièce en trois parties adaptée du roman de Dostoïevski* (Paris, 1959).
Dolinin, A. "Ispoved' Stavrogina," *Literaturnaya mysl'*, I (1922), 139–162.
*Grossman, Leonid. "Dostoevsky v rabote nad Bakuninym," *Katorga i ssylka*, XVI (1925), 74–91.
Grossman, Leonid. "Speshnev i Stavrogin," *Katorga i ssylka*, IV (1924), 130–136.
*Howe, Irving. "Dostoevsky: the Politics of Salvation," *Politics and the Novel* (New York, 1957).
*Ivanov, Vyacheslav, "Osnovnoy mif v romane 'Besy'," *Russkaya mysl'*, III–IV (April, 1914), 111–117.
Katkov, G. "Steerforth and Stavrogin on the Sources of *The Possessed*," *Slavonic and East European Review* (May, 1949), pp. 468–488.
McDowall, Arthur. "*The Possessed* and Bolshevism," *London Mercury*, XVII (Nov., 1921), 53–61.
*Rahv, Philip. "Dostoevski in 'The Possessed,'" *Image and Idea: Fourteen Essays on Literary Themes* (Norwalk, Conn., 1949), pp. 86–110.
Stenbock-Fermor, Elizabeth. "Lermontov and Dostoevskij's Novel *The Devils*," *Slavic and East European Journal*, XVII (1959), 215–230.
Volynsky, A. L. *Kniga velikogo gneva. Kriticheskie stat'i o 'Besakh'* (St. Petersburg, 1904), pp. 3–127.
Woolf, Virginia. *Granite and Rainbow* (London, 1958), pp. 126–130.

The Adolescent and *The Dream of the Ridiculous Man*

*Dolinin, A. S. *V tvorcheskoy laboratorii Dostoevskogo* (Moscow, 1947).
Komarovich, V. L. "Genezis romana 'Podrostok'," *Literaturnaya mysl'*, IV (1925), 366–386.
Rosen, Nathan. "Breaking Out of the Underground: The 'Failure' of 'A Raw Youth'," *Modern Fiction Studies*, IV (1958), 225–239.

Trahan, Elizabeth W. "The Golden Age—Dream of a Ridiculous Man?" *Slavic and East European Journal*, XVII (1959), 349–371.

The Brothers Karamazov

Amend, Victor E. "Theme and Form in 'The Brothers Karamazov'," *Modern Fiction Studies*, IV (1958), 240–252.

Bertenson, Sergei. " 'The Brothers Karamazov' at the Moscow Art Theater," *American Slavic and East European Review*, XVI (1957), 74–78.

Blackmur, R. P. "Between the Numan and the Moha: Notes Toward a Theory of Literature," *The Lion and the Honeycomb* (New York, 1955), pp. 307–308.

Brewster, Dorothy, and Angus Burrell, *Modern Fiction* (New York, 1937), pp. 40–64.

*Camus, Albert. *The Rebel*, trans. Anthony Bower (New York, 1954), pp. 50–56.

*Cizevsky, Dmitri, "Schiller und die 'Brüder Karamazov'," *Zeitschrift für slavische Philologie* (1926), pp. 1–42.

*Gorky, Maxim. "O karamazovshchine," *Russkoe slovo* (Sept. 22, 1913) in *Sobranie sochinenii v tridtsati tomakh*, Vol. 24 (Moscow, 1953).

*Guardini, Romano. "The Legend of the Grand Inquisitor," trans. Sally Cunneen, *Cross Currents*, III (Fall, 1952), 58–86.

Hacker, Andrew. "Dostoevsky's Disciples: Man and Sheep in Political Theory," *Journal of Politics*, XVII (Nov., 1955), 590–613.

Kanzer, Mark. "The Vision of Father Zossima," *American Imago*, VIII (Dec., 1951), 329–335. A Freudian interpretation of Alyosha's fall and redemption.

Komarovich, V. L. *Die Urgestalt der Brüder Karamasoff: Dostojewskis Quellen, Entwurfe und Fragmente*, ed. René L. Fülop-Miller and Friedrich Eckstein (Munich, 1928).

*Lawrence, D. H. "The Grand Inquisitor," *Selected Literary Criticism*, ed. Anthony Beal (London, 1955), pp. 233–241. Lawrence defends the truth of the Grand Inquisitor against the "falseness" of Christ.

Maceina, Antanas. *Der Grossinquisitor; geschichtes philosophische Deutung der Legende Dostojewskijs* (Heidelberg, 1952).

Manning, Clarence A., "The Grand Inquisitor," *American Theological Review*, XV (Jan., 1933), 16–26.

Matlaw, Ralph E. *The Brothers Karamazov; Novelistic Technique* (The Hague, 1957).

Maynard, John. *Russian Influx* (London, 1939), pp. 292–307.

*Rahv, Philip. "The Legend of the Grand Inquisitor," *Partisan Review*, XXI (May–June, 1954), 249–271. Examination of sources for "The Grand Inquisitor" and generally helpful insights.

Ramsey, Paul. "God's Grace and Man's Guilt," *Journal of Religion*, XXXI (Jan., 1951), 21–37. Comparisons with existentialist philosophy.

Ramsey, Paul. "No Morality without Immortality: Dostoevski and the Meaning of Atheism," *Journal of Religion*, XXXVI (April, 1956), 90–108.

*Rozanov, V. "Posleslovie k kommentariyu 'Legendy o velikom inkvizitore,'" *Zolotoe runo*, XI–XII (Nov.–Dec., 1906), 97–101. Important addition to his basic work on the Legend.

Sewall, Richard B. "The Tragic World of the Karamazovs," *Tragic Themes in Western Literature*, ed. Cleanth Brooks (New York, 1955), pp. 107–127.

Slochower, Harry. "Incest in *The Brothers Karamazov*," *American Imago*, XVI (1959), 127–145.

Stocker, Arnold. *Ame puisse; réalisme psychologique des frères Karamazov* (Geneva, 1945).

Strem, George. "The Moral World of Dostoevsky," *Russian Review*, XVI (1957), 15–26.

Vivas, Eliseo. "The Two Dimensions of Reality in *The Brothers Karamazov*," *Sewanee Review*, LIX (Winter, 1951), 23–49.

Wasiolek, Edward. "Dostoevsky's *The Brothers Karamazov*," *Explicator*, XVI (1957), Item 7.

Weinrich, M. I. "Ideological Antecedents of *The Brothers Karamazov*," *Modern Language Notes*, LXIV (June, 1949), 400–406.

Index

Index

251

INDEX